The Peter and Paul Altarpiece and Friedrich Pacher

The Peter and Paul Altarpiece and Friedrich Pacher

Avraham Ronen

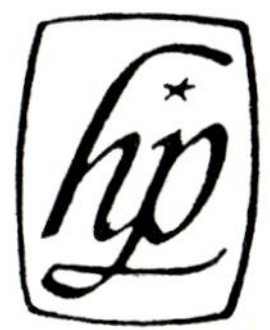

HUMANITIES PRESS
New York 1974

HUMANITIES PRESS
New York   1974

First published in 1974 in the United States of America by Humanities Press.

Copyright © 1974 by Avraham Ronen

Designed by Alex Berlyne

ISBN 0 391 00356-9

Composed and bound by Keter Press, Jerusalem;
printed by Japhet Press, Tel Aviv, 1973

Contents

Acknowledgements

Every research work is the fruit of complex collaboration that involves not only institutions, which help cover its expenses, but many individuals, from humble church custodians to museum directors and university professors who offer their help to the author in many ways. Among the many persons and institutions without whose generous help this book could not have been written and published, I am particularly indebted to the following:

The research in Europe was financed by grants of the Deutsche Akademische Austauschdienst, the Italian Foreign Office and the Fritz Thyssen Foundation. Two special grants given by Tel Aviv University covered the expenses of typing the manuscript, the preparation of most of the photographs and the greater part of the expenses of the printing. My thanks are due to Dr W. Treue of the Deutsche Forschungsgemeinschaft. I also thank Dr Niemoler, former Cultural Councillor of the German Embassy in Tel Aviv; Dr E. Gerlini, former Director of the Italian Institute in Tel Aviv, and the present Director, Dr Marco Miele; Mr I. Levanon; Professor W. Grab and particularly Professor M. Lazar of Tel Aviv University, for their generous aid in obtaining the above-mentioned grants.

Of the many scholars who helped me gather the documentary and photographic material in Europe, I wish to mention Professor V. Oberhammer of the University of Vienna; Dr E. Egg, Director, and Dr O. Kostenzer, Librarian, of the Ferdinandeum, Innsbruck; Professor W. Sauerländer, Director of the Zentralinstitut für Kunstgeschichte; and Dr G. Goldberg and G. Scheffler of the Bayerische Staatsgemäldessammlungen, Munich; Dr K. Wolfsgruber, Director of the Diozesan Museum, Brixen; Reverend M. Beitner, Librarian of Neustift; and Professor N. Rasmo, Superintendent of the Galleries of the Trentino Alto Adige and Director of the Museums of Trento and Bolzano.

The kind hospitality of the directors and staff of the Bibliotheca Hertziana in Rome and of the Kuntshistorisches Institut in Florence turned much of my research work in Italy into a most rewarding experience.

Professor B. Bagatti, Director of the Studium Biblicum Franciscanum, and P. A. Mertens, its Librarian, not only granted permission to take the photographs of the seven Jerusalem panels but offered their generous help to me and to my faithful photographer, Mr A. Hai.

Introduction

Whereas Italian art has always attracted the attention of students and scholars the world over, German art has essentially remained the exclusive province of Austrian and German art historians. This is particularly true of fifteenth-century German painting. The fact that the only book ever to have appeared in English on Michael Pacher – one of the greatest exponents of German art – is a translation, and that it was published only in 1971, is symptomatic.

This book presents a single work, the *Peter and Paul Altarpiece*, painted by Friedrich Pacher, who was a member of Michael Pacher's circle. The greater part of the paintings that originally belonged to this altarpiece – seven scenes from the lives of its titular saints – were donated to a tiny church in Tiberias more than 110 years ago and were later transferred to Jerusalem. The donor was fully aware of the fact that his gift deprived German art historians of the opportunity to study the original paintings. In fact, fifty years elapsed before photographs made in Tiberias in 1911, brought the seven panels to the attention of European scholars for the first time. The immediate result was the publication of two articles on the *Peter and Paul Altarpiece*, both of which appeared in the following year. Only one of these articles, by Philip Maria Halm, contained the complete set of reproductions of the altarpiece, including those of the seven Tiberias panels. These same seven photographs were reproduced for the second and last time by Johann von Allesch in his monograph on Michael Pacher (1931).

Since the middle of the nineteenth century, scholars have shown a steadily growing interest in the, until then, little-known German masters of the fifteenth century. Regional schools were studied by specialized experts, often spurred by local patriotism. At the beginning of the twentieth century, the great artistic heritage of the Tyrol region was beginning to occupy its true place of importance in the panorama of German Art History. Thanks to the pioneer work of scholars like E. Förster, Karl Schnaase (1862, 1879), G. Dahlke (1885), Hans Semper (1887–1911), Robert Stiassny (1903, 1919) and Walter Mannowsky (1910), the figure of Michael Pacher gradually emerged from obscurity.

These scholars were also responsible for the first serious studies on Michael Pacher's artistic *milieu*, including the painter Friedrich Pacher. Documents published by D. Schönherr (1878–93) and Stiassny (1900), Semper's book on Michael and Friedrich Pacher (1911) and O. Döring's on Michael Pacher and his circle were the first of a considerable number of publications which gradually brought Friedrich Pacher and his *oeuvre* out of obscurity. The remarkable number of works that are attributed to Friedrich Pacher is the accumulated result of a number of studies, some of which are still in progress.

However, Friedrich Pacher's artistic career has remained an unsolved enigma. The greatest gap in the knowledge of this master's *oeuvre* was his largest – and perhaps finest – extant work, the *Peter and Paul Altarpiece* from Sterzing.

As early as the beginning of the twentieth century, Stiassny and Semper proved that the seven Jerusalem panels originally belonged to the same altarpiece, the central panel and predella of which were discovered in the Enzenberg Collection in Tratzberg Castle. Halm's 1912 article summed up all that was known about this work and considerably contributed to the understanding of Friedrich Pacher's style and artistic creation. However, Halm and, to a greater extent, later authors were handicapped in their research by the impossibility of studying the paintings of the shutters of the *Peter and Paul Altarpiece* in the original. Actually, no further research on this work has been attempted since 1912. The disappearance of the original photographs of the seven Jerusalem panels after 1931 caused complete scholarly neglect of this part of the altarpiece for another forty years.

The main purpose of this book, therefore, is to revive the interest of students and art lovers in this forgotten work, while its chief merit for the uninitiated is the visual information offered by means of the reproductions, all made from recent photographs. The catalogue contains a detailed discussion of the iconography and style of each of the pictorial units of the altarpiece. It should be noted that German painting in the latter half of the fifteenth century developed a particular iconographic vocabulary which was frequently inspired not only by the usual literary sources but by popular tradition. The *Peter and Paul Altarpiece* is a treasury of motifs inspired by this interesting and rather short-lived chapter of German iconographic tradition, which did not last very much longer than the beginning of the sixteenth century. The text figures illustrate the stylistic relation between the *Peter and Paul Altarpiece* and other works by Friedrich Pacher and his circle.

The Peter and Paul Altarpiece and Friedrich Pacher

The history of the *Peter and Paul Altarpiece* begins in Sterzing (the Italian Vipiteno), a small town in the South Tyrol region, near the Brenner Pass. In the artistic history of the region, this town is chiefly remembered for the altarpiece carved and painted by the great Hans Multscher and members of his workshop (1456–8) for the local parish church.

Around the year 1400 Hans Jöchl, a prosperous citizen from Stegen (near Bruneck [Brunico]) in the Puster Valley, established himself in Sterzing. Shortly afterwards he built the family's estate in the north-western outskirts of the town (Fig. 1). It is still known as the Jöchlsthurn (*Thurn* being the Tyrol dialectical variant of *Turm* [tower]). A stone dated 1474 inscribed with the name of his elder son, Lienhard, appears on the vault of the Chapel of Sts Peter and Paul attached to the Jöchlsthurn. (Fig. 2). The construction of the chapel was apparently completed in the same year or the following one. It was consecrated in 1476, and two years later a chaplaincy was instituted in it. According to local tradition, the chapel was built by Lienhard Jöchl and his younger brother Hans 11. It was for this chapel that the Jöchl brothers commissioned the *Altarpiece of Sts Peter and Paul*, which forms the subject of this study.[1]

In 1643 the Jöchlsthurn was inherited by the Enzenberg zum Freyenthurn family. The altarpiece remained *in situ*, apparently in its original form, until 1744, when it was refashioned in the late Baroque style, then particularly in vogue in southern Germany and Austria. The rectangular central panel was, either then or shortly afterwards, mutilated in order to fit it into a new elaborate Rococo frame. It was probably during this period that the wings of the altarpiece were separated from the central panel and the painted scenes from the lives of the Apostles were sawn off from the wings. However, their exact location at that period remains unknown. Around 1850 the central panel and predella (Pl. 1) were transferred to the residence of the Enzenberg family in Tratzberg Castle (near Schwaz in the Inn Valley, Austria), where they remained until they were acquired by the Tiroler Landesmuseum Ferdinandeum in 1957.[2] The surviving seven panels of the shutters were sold 'where and when, nobody knows', to Johann Nepomuk Sepp, a professor of Christian History at Munich University.[3] Sepp, an ardent patriot, devout Catholic and active member of the Bavarian Parliament, made two voyages to the Holy Land. When he returned from his first visit in 1846, he induced King Ludwig 1[4] to try to strengthen the weak position of the German Catholics in the Holy Land by helping to establish a Bavarian missionary station in Palestine.

In 1848 the Tyrolese priest Barnabas Rufinatcho, who served in Nazareth as a Guardian, founded the station in the convent of St Peter in Tiberias. It was for the church of this convent that Sepp sent the seven panels with a certain Brother Felix as his personal gift in 1861. He had a stone tablet fixed to the wall of the church bearing the following inscription:

ICONES SEPTEM AD ALTARIS ET TEMPLI ORNATUM
PIA ELARGITIONE DABAT
MONACHENSIS PROFESSOR DR. J. NEPOM. SEPP
OPERIS DE VITA JESU AUCTOR ET TERRAE SANCTAE
DESCRIPTOR
IN PIAM PEREGRINATIONIS MEMORIAM
ANNO 1861.[5]

The Bavarian missionary station had only a short-lived existence. The Franciscan brothers soon took hold of the convent, and in 1888 dispirited Sepp could only bitterly remark that as far as the study of German Art History was concerned, the seven pictures could be considered as lost.[6] This pessimistic prophecy proved to hold quite true for more than half a century and still applies, though to a lesser extent, to this day. The paintings were stored for a long period in the loft of the convent. Later they adorned the walls of the refectory of the Franciscan Hospice, where the Munich sculptor Sebastian Osterrieder found them, still hanging, in 1911. The photographs made by Osterrieder on the occasion of his visit to Tiberias remained the only visual reference for all subsequent German scholars who dealt with this subject.[7]

Only the masterly execution of the painting and the superb quality of the pigments and the ground saved the pictures from utter ruin during their long exposure to the baking heat of Tiberias, one of the hottest places in Israel. But the inevitable appearance of cracks in the panels seems to have induced the Franciscan authorities to transfer the paintings to Jerusalem, where they now hang in the Aula Magna of the Studium Biblicum Franciscanum in the Convent of the Flagellation.[8]

As with other works by Friedrich Pacher (except for the *Baptism*), no documentary evidence for the attribution of the *Peter and Paul Altarpiece* has been found. Sepp thought that the seven panels donated by him were the work of Michael Pacher. However, subsequent research, carried out mostly at the beginning of the twentieth century, has proven that the central panel of the *Peter and Paul Altarpiece* (now in Innsbruck) and the seven Jerusalem paintings originally belonged to the same altarpiece, which should be attributed on stylistic grounds to Friedrich (and not Michael) Pacher.[9] This attribution is the currently accepted one.

Michael and Friedrich Pacher were once considered to be brothers, or at least relatives, but this traditional belief has not yet been proven. Although documentary evidence is still lacking, it is fairly certain that the artistic careers of these two painters crossed more than once and that Friedrich was deeply influenced by this great master. The study of Michael Pacher's work, therefore, is particularly important for the understanding of Friedrich's *oeuvre* and its attribution and dating.

Michael Pacher was the greatest artist active in the Tyrol in the second half of the fifteenth century. Although he is invariably documented as a *maler* (painter), he was also one of the best sculptors of his age. However, it is in his best authentic paintings that Pacher really towers above his contemporaries in the Tyrol region.

The place and date of his birth are still uncertain, but he is recorded from 1467 in Bruneck, where he had his own workshop. On the other hand, there existed a *Pacherhof* ('Pacher Yard', i.e., estate or farm) in Neustift (Novacella), a village near the famous Benedictine monastery in the Eisack (Isarco) Valley, 3 miles north of Brixen. According to recently discovered documents, it is there that Friedrich Pacher must have been born.[10] To make the problem of the Pachers and their origin still more complicated, there was also a Leonard Pacher, who was provost of the monastery of Neustift in 1467–83. He apparently ordered paintings from both Michael and Friedrich, and it was probably he who ordered Michael Pacher's pictorial masterpiece the *Altarpiece of the Fathers of the Church* (Alte Pinakothek, Munich [Fig. 9]) for the remodelled basilica of the monastery. Recently, new attempts have been made to relate all three Pachers to the same family, but the proposed genealogies are still open to serious doubts.[11]

Though much of Michael Pacher's treatment of space (and more than is usually admitted by students of his art) is derived ·from Flemish precedents (particularly Rogier Van der Weyden), he was undoubtedly the first German artist to have derived from North Italian painting its peculiar treatment of linear perspective as an active element in composition. Within the context of German Art History, Michael Pacher can be considered as a revolutionary artist.[12] Pacher's paintings, like those of Mantegna, are characterized by an extremely low vanishing point and the frequent application of violent foreshortening. However, Michael Pacher, like all his German contemporaries, remained immune to the influence of Italian Classicism, of which Mantegna, who inspired Pacher in many ways, was the greatest exponent in North Italy.

In 1471 Michael Pacher was commissioned to create an altarpiece for the parish church of St Wolfgang on the Abersee (east of Salzburg). The huge polyptych (completed in 1481), his largest extant work, included both sculpture and paintings. It is in this work, justly considered as a landmark in the history of German painting, that the artistic careers of Michael and Friedrich Pacher clearly cross.

Michael Pacher's pictorial *oeuvre* does not represent a homogeneous unity. While some of the stylistic differences between his various works may be explained by their belonging to different periods in his artistic development, differences between parts of the same work can only be explained by the collaboration of workshop assistants. Unfortunately, none of Michael's assistants are mentioned in any of the few surviving documents which refer to his works, and the identification of their names and their respective share in the execution of Pacher's works has remained a matter of pure conjecture.

The collaboration of workshop assistants is particularly evident in Pacher's *magnum opus* in St Wolfgang, in which there is hardly a scene that does not betray, at least in the execution of some details, the hand of one or several assistants. Of the eight scenes painted on the inner pair of shutters of the *St Wolfgang Altarpiece* (four scenes from the life of the Virgin and four scenes from the life of Christ) only the four scenes from the life of the Virgin were apparently painted completely or mostly by his hand. In the eight scenes painted on the outer pair of shutters (four scenes from the life of Christ and four scenes from the life of St Wolfgang [Figs 4, 51]) the deviations from Michael's style are much more marked and have distinctive common characteristics which have been attributed, since the beginning of this century, to a supposed chief assistant. This assistant has been identified by most writers as none other than Friedrich Pacher, whose altarpiece from Sterzing forms the main subject of this study.[13]

Very little is known about Friedrich Pacher's life and artistic career. Even his date of birth has not been verified.[14] According to recently discovered documents, he seems to have been a native of Neustift, but he is later (1474) documented as a citizen of Bruneck, where he owned a house. It is not impossible that he was first attracted to Bruneck by the opportunity of working in Michael Pacher's workshop, but he must have established a workshop of his own there no later than the middle of the 1470s. In his own time, Friedrich Pacher enjoyed more than local fame, and after Michael's death in 1498, he was apparently considered the best painter in the region. The Emperor Maximilian invited him to his court at Innsbruck for a professional visit in 1501 and three years later entrusted him with the task of examining the famous medieval frescos in Runkelstein Castle (Castel Roncolo) near Bozen. In 1489–92 he served as the parochial church *Pfleger* (caretaker), and in his later life (1503–4, 1507–8) he held the office of a judge in his adopted town. He probably died shortly after 1508.

Friedrich Pacher's only signed and dated work is the *Baptism*, painted in 1483 for the church of St John in the Hospital of the Holy Ghost in Brixen (now in the Lady's Church, Munich [Fig. 5]).[15] Although damaged and partly overpainted, this work has remained the only legitimate point of departure for the identification of Friedrich's *oeuvre*, including his supposed activity as an assistant and collaborator of Michael Pacher, for none of his other works is either documented or signed. It should, therefore, be kept in mind that the considerable corpus of works which has been gathered under Friedrich Pacher's name, through the accumulated results of studies by various scholars during the last eighty years, has been attributed to him exclusively on the basis of stylistic considerations.[16]

Let us examine some of the essential characteristics of Friedrich's style as revealed in the *Baptism*. This work appears to be somewhat primitive and archaic when confronted with Michael's authentic work. This is particularly evident in the treatment of the figures, in which Michael Pacher's three-dimensional and plastic sense of form is supplanted by a much drier and linear style. There is a tendency to flatten the figures and to simplify and stylize their details. The proportions and postures of the figures are less natural, and their expressions less restrained and refined. The so-called 'kiss-lips'[17] are characteristic of this tendency.

Whereas Michael Pacher is deeply concerned with a rational rendering of space and volume and tends to develop these structural elements of the composition in his landscape background as well, Friedrich is primarily concerned with the two-dimensional and decorative aspects of the composition. The two principal figures, the angels and their draperies, the cloud, the script-roll and the dove are arranged without any clear differentiation of their positions in space. They all appear to belong to a single plane and form a two-dimensional screen, through the gaps of which only small patches of distant landscape are seen. Since these distant views are deprived of their spatial context (the passages from foreground to middle and background), they, too, have a two-dimensional effect.

Their principal function seems to be to fill the spaces between the figures, rather than to create a real feeling of depth. This compositional feature recurs constantly, though with many variations, in most of the works attributed to Friedrich Pacher, the Jerusalem panels included.[18] Not only the stylistic and compositional characteristics of the *Baptism*, but also much of its typological and pictorial vocabulary recur in other works by Friedrich Pacher.

The view of a fortified city which appears in the background of the *Baptism* recurs in many other landscape backgrounds of Friedrich's works. It is always rendered with the painstaking precision of a miniaturist. Friedrich Pacher seems to have devoted equally detailed attention to small naturalistic details – birds, flowers and plants – which appear in two of the St Wolfgang scenes and in the Jerusalem panels as well.[19]

The Gothic script-roll which presents the words of the Lord (curiously represented as a blank nimbus emerging from the cloud) is an archaistic motif which is characteristic of Friedrich's conservative temperament.[20] Significantly, script-rolls rarely appear in Michael Pacher's works, which were generally conceived in a more 'modern' spirit. They are, however, a persistent feature in Friedrich's works and always have a particular design, of which the neat triangular folds (absent in the *Baptism*) are the hallmarks.[21]

The architectural structure which frames the scene is a curious combination of a rectangular 'window' and a double arch formed by the two Gothic pinnacles which bend inwards, one from each side. This architectural paradox, in which ornamental elements are transformed into structural ones, is a variant of the Gothic portal which had already appeared in Rogier Van der Weyden's works and later in those of his Flemish followers, who, in their turn, inspired German painters in the second half of the fifteenth century. Friedrich seems to have derived this particular motif from a print by the Master E.S. (Fig. 4), who inspired him in many other ways.[22]

In employing this traditional decorative element, Friedrich exhibits remarkable versatility and inventiveness. For example, in the numerous complex architectural fantasies which enframe the figures and scenes which he painted on the vaults and walls of the Dominicans' Cloister in Bozen in and around 1496 (Figs 17, 19), none of the formal schemes is repeated.[23] A double arch, which included bent pinnacles like those in the *Baptism*, once enclosed the composition of the central panel of the *Peter and Paul Altarpiece* (Col. Pl. 1) from above. It has almost completely disappeared as a result of the mutilation of the panel, but the bent pinnacles are still visible.

The marble window with the statically arranged fruit and birds on its sill is a rare instance in which Friedrich appears to have been directly inspired by North Italian antecedents.[24] This motif never recurs again in the master's *oeuvre*.

Friedrich's apparently archaic style has sometimes given rise to the opinion (no longer accepted) that he was the elder of the two Pachers and that his early activity preceded that of Michael Pacher. But the fact that many of his figures and compositions seem to have been inspired by works of Michael Pacher has convinced recent students that he was probably a follower of Michael, rather than his precursor.[25]

The same problem concerning the attribution of Michael Pacher's authentic work exists in regard to the works ascribed to Friedrich, i.e., that of distinguishing between the master and members of his circle or his followers. There are two main theories concerning this problem. According to the first theory, the works attributed to Friedrich Pacher should be divided among several artists of his circle, each of whom was responsible for the creation of a distinct group of works.[26] Other scholars, including the present one, maintain that although Friedrich Pacher was undoubtedly assisted by several members of his workshop, and that consequently the stylistic divergences between various works attributed to him are frequently remarkable, none of these works has revealed any artistic personality which is consistently and clearly independent of Friedrich's, and which could create without his direct inspiration or instruction.

In the present state of our knowledge of Friedrich Pacher's life and work, the second theory, which ascribes to Friedrich Pacher and his workshop' the considerably large body of works which bear the general characteristics of his style, appears to be more acceptable. This unitarian theory can be corroborated by the fact that Friedrich Pacher seems to have repeatedly used certain pictorial motifs which recur with little variation in various works produced in his workshop. Thus, works which appear to be remarkably different from each other in the general aspect of execution and which were sometimes even assigned to different members of his circle might nevertheless include details which are analogous in typology or even in style (Col. Pl. VI, Fig. 41).

Once these recurring details – which range from entire figures to a set of folds on a sleeve (Pl. 19, Fig. 39) – were invented and designed by Friedrich, they continued to serve as a ready-made, formal vocabulary for the master and his workshop assistants. It is not impossible that Friedrich sooner or later established a division of work in his studio, according to which each assistant became responsible for, and specialized in, the execution of specific motifs. Many of these details were probably copied from works that were still in the workshop.

A painting by Friedrich Pacher was thus a product of the combined efforts of the artist and his workshop assistants. It was rarely – or never – produced by a single hand, either Friedrich's or any of his assistants' although occasionally his own hand or that of one of his assistants might predominate in the execution of a painting. Most of the stylistic differences between some of the works attributed to Friedrich Pacher should, therefore, be explained as resulting from differences in the proportion of the individual share of the master and any of his various assistants in the execution. But despite their apparently individual 'touch', none of these assistants seems to have developed into an independent creator.

Friedrich Pacher's distinctive workshop practice is also reflected in the *Peter and Paul Altarpiece*.

Many details which recur in different panels of the altarpiece also appear in other works attributed to the master.

Nevertheless, these analogies do not constitute sufficient evidence for establishing the work's chronology. The stylistic differences between works painted in Friedrich's workshop have frequently been explained as a reflection of the various phases of the master's artistic development. However, the fact that either the stylistic analogies or divergencies between the works attributed to Friedrich Pacher may be interpreted as resulting from his workshop practice, on the one hand, and the scarcity of dated works, on the other, make it extremely difficult to arrange the corpus of works attributed to Friedrich Pacher in a convincing chronological order on the basis of stylistic analysis.[27]

This is why the chronology of the *Peter and Paul Altarpiece* is still disputed. Although Sepp claimed that one of the Jerusalem panels was dated 1475, no date has been found on any of the panels. Sepp's dating, which was probably founded upon the year in which the Peter and Paul chapel in Sterzing was completed, has been held in doubt by several scholars, who accepted 1474 only as a *terminus a quo* for the altarpiece. Some of them dated it much later, even as far as towards the end of the century. However, such a late dating is less convincing than Sepp's.[28]

The *Peter and Paul Altarpiece* seems to follow the structural and iconographical scheme common in South German altarpieces with revolving shutters (or wings) known as *flügelaltäre*. The scheme frequently adopted in South Tyrol altarpieces was a painted or carved central piece – with the image of the saint or a representation of a principal scene from his life – and two wings painted with a cycle of scenic representations of episodes from his life. (Figs 29–33). When two saints formed the main subject, the respective narrative cycles of their lives would be symmetrically divided between the two wings of the altarpiece. The scenes on the shutters were normally arranged in two tiers. Usually the scenic representations appeared only on the inside of the shutters, while outside might be depicted figures of saints or, more often, an unrelated subject of a more general character, e.g., a Christological scene, an Annunciation, etc.[29]

As the altarpiece was usually opened on feast days, it was customary to lavish the more costly materials, such as gold ground, on the central panel and the inner sides of the shutters (which were seen when the altarpiece was open), while the outer sides of the shutters (seen during the weekdays, when the altarpiece was closed) were painted throughout with 'natural colours'.

The front of the central panel of the *Peter and Paul Altarpiece* (Pl. 1) displays the images of its two titular saints, and eight scenic representations of episodes from their lives were originally painted on the wings.

In Friedrich Pacher's surviving *oeuvre*, the *Peter and Paul Altarpiece* is exceptional in its having a central piece painted on the back as well as on the front. The back of the central panel of a Tyrolese altarpiece was usually painted with a decorative design (as in Michael's *Coronation of the Virgin* [Munich]) or an independent set of images that generally had no thematic relation to the main subject of the altarpiece (as in Michael Pacher's altarpiece in St Wolfgang). 'The Last Judgement', painted on the back of the Peter and Paul panel, is a typical example (Fig. 20).

Unlike the Italian predella, that of the German altarpiece was seldom dependent upon the iconographical programme of the main panels. In the *Peter and Paul Altarpiece*, the predella depicts kneeling figures of the two donors – the Jöchl brothers – flanking that of St Veronica with her veil (Pls 1, 5–8). This motif might, however, bear some relation to the iconography of the central panel, as we shall see later on. The reverse is painted with a decorative foliage pattern (Fig. 20).

Like the upper part of a Tyrol altarpiece, the predella, too, was sometimes fitted with revolving shutters. This, however, is not the case in the predella of the *Peter and Paul Altarpiece*.

Unlike the shutters of other altarpieces painted by Friedrich Pacher, those of the *Peter and Paul*

Altarpiece were originally painted on both sides with eight (and not four) scenic representations of episodes from the lives of its titular saints. Of these, only seven have survived.

The fact that the paintings in Jerusalem and Innsbruck originally belonged to a now-dismembered and dispersed altarpiece raises the problem of its reconstruction, which, obviously, also involves a consideration of its iconographical programme. The problem of distinguishing the panels which had originally belonged to the exterior of the shutters from those which had belonged to their inner sides was solved by Döring and Halm.

It has been observed that three of the seven surviving scenes are painted with natural-sky background, while the four remaining ones have the usual gold-brocade background. Consequently, the first group (of which one panel is evidently missing) originally belonged to the external sides of the shutters, while the second group obviously adorned the inner sides.

In the original state of the altarpiece, the eight scenes were no doubt evenly distributed between the two apostles, as well as between the two shutters, so that a single shutter – painted on the outside with two scenes with 'natural' sky and on the inside with two scenes with gold ground – was dedicated to each of the apostles. The location of the scenes on the shutters was logically determined by the position of the saints in the central panel. Thus, the four scenes from the life of St Peter were painted on the left shutter (of these, one which originally belonged to the external side is now missing), while the right shutter was painted with four scenes from the life of St Paul.

The scenes on the exterior of the shutters belonged to the earlier lives of the Apostles and were derived from the New Testament, while the four scenes on the inner sides of the shutters were derived from apocryphal legends related to the last days of the two Apostles, ending on the lower part of each shutter with the martyrdom of the saints. Most of these legends are retold in the *Legenda Aurea*, which probably served as the principal literary source for these scenes.[30] The episodes from the lives of the two saints thus proceed in parallel chronological order, beginning with the upper scenes on the exterior of the shutters and ending with the lower scenes on the inner sides.

We have already mentioned the fact that the shutters of the *Peter and Paul Altarpiece* were originally composed of panels painted on both sides. There were four panels in all, two for each shutter. In the eighteenth century the paintings on the back of each panel were separated from those on the front by splitting the panels. Thus, eight thinner panels were created, each with a scene painted on one of its sides.

Recently taken photographs of the reverse sides of the seven Jerusalem panels have shown that the wood grain on the back of three of the four scenes with gold-brocade ground match exactly with the mirror image of the wood grain on the back of the three surviving scenes with natural-sky background. The three pairs of scenes formed in this manner constitute three of the four original panels.

Of the fourth panel only one scene, the 'Liberation of St Peter' (Pl. 20) – which was originally the first scene from his later life – painted with a gold-brocade ground, has survived. The scene (with a natural-sky background) which was originally painted on its reverse is still missing; it was the first one from the early life of St Peter.

Taking into account the above considerations, the reconstruction of the original arrangement of the scenes on the shutters of the *Peter and Paul Altarpiece* will be as follows (Figs 7,8):[31]

Left Shutter:
Scenes from the Life of St Peter

Outer side (Fig. 7): Early life
1a Missing
2a St Peter Walking on the Water

Inner side (Fig. 8): Last Days
1b The Liberation of St Peter
2b The Martyrdom of St Peter

Right Shutter:
Scenes from the Life of St Paul

Outer side (Fig. 7): Early Life
3a The Conversion of Saul
4a Ananias Healing Saul

Inner side (Fig. 8): Last Days
3b The Parting of the Apostles
4b The Martyrdom of St Paul

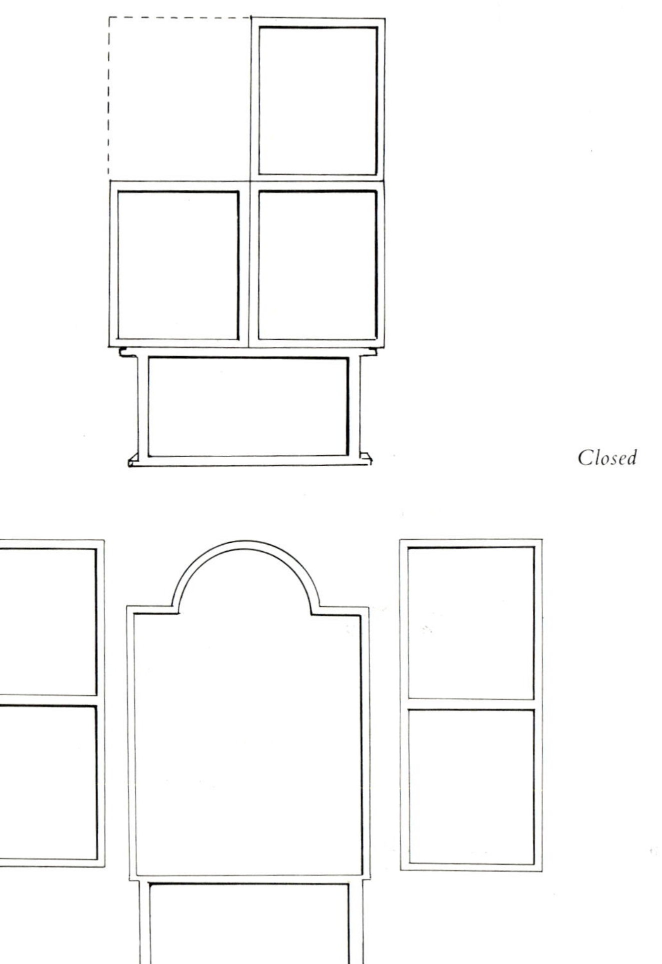

Closed

Open

Catalogue

Central Panel

Front: Sts Peter and Paul.

Oil and tempera on wood, gold-brocade ground. H. 256 cms, w. 169 cms (Col. Pl. 1, Pl. 1).[32] Tiroler Landesmuseum, Ferdinandeum, Innsbruck. Formerly coll. Sighard Graff Enzenberg, Schloss Tratzberg (Schwaz).

Peter and Paul, the Princes of the Apostles, appear together frequently in works of art (Figs 11, 12, 25, 40). Their parallel historical significance, the suffering of their martyrdoms contemporaneously and their shared feast day made them common titular saints for churches and a frequent subject for altarpieces.[33]

Peter is on the left and Paul is on the right. The two Apostles stand barefooted on a multi-coloured tiled floor. They are sheltered by twin flamboyant baldachins. The physical features of the saints conform to the German variants of a centuries-old pictorial tradition which has its roots in Paleo-Christian art. Peter is a strongly built, broad-faced, elderly man with curled white hair and a short, square beard. Paul is a middle-aged, dark-haired man with a beard longer than that of Peter. He looks somewhat balder than his companion (although, like Peter, he has a tuft of hair on his forehead).[34]

The saints appear with their traditional attributes: St Peter, the first Vicar of Christ, wears the triple papal tiara and a magnificent purple robe over a white pallium. In his left hand, he holds the key of the Kingdom of Heaven, (Matthew 16: 16–19, 18:18) which, according to popular tradition, also opens the Gates of Paradise for the Blessed. St Paul wears a green gown over a red-brocade dress. The sword, his usual attribute – the symbol of his martyrdom and of the Church Militant (of which he is the embodiment), is precariously balanced on its tip on his right.

St Paul holds an open book of his Epistle to the Romans and points to its opening verses: 'PAULUS SERVUS JHU [JHESU] XPI [CHRISTI]' (*Romans* 1:1). His head (Pl. 3) is shown in a somewhat clumsily foreshortened three-quarter view, and his eager look is turned upwards towards the angel who leans forward from between the roofs of the two canopies, extending a script-roll towards each of the Apostles (Fig. 13). The two inscriptions are derived from verses in the Gospels and the Acts of the Apostles, which refer to Sts Peter and Paul as the chosen leaders of the Christian community.

Paul's roll reads: 'TU ES VAS EL'CIONIS [ELECTIONIS] SANCTE PAULE.' This refers to the passage in which Christ appears to Ananias and orders him to cure Paul's blindness: '*Vade, quoniam vas electionis est mihi iste*' ('Go, since he is a chosen vessel unto me' [Acts 9:15]).

"

Peter's script roll reads: 'TU ES PASTOR OVIU[M] SCE [SANCTE] PETRE.' This refers to the passage in the Gospel where Christ designates Peter as the shepherd of His sheep: '*Pasce agnos meos . . . pasce oves meas*' ('Feed my lambs . . . feed my sheep' [John 21:15, 17]).

The plaited basket with fruit, in the niche on the base of the central pier, is perhaps an allusion to the story of St Paul's flight from Damascus (Acts 9:25). The object in the other niche is not clearly identifiable.[35]

The central pier of the double Gothic baldachin is decorated with the figures of Sts Stephen and Sebastian painted in yellowish-golden monochrome in imitation of stone sculpture (Pl. 4). The two saints appear at the moment of their martyrdom. St Sebastian, bound to the *aedicula*, is pierced by arrows, while St Stephen's head is struck by a heavy stone. Both figures are executed with a freshness and immediacy which the more rigid major figures seem to lack. There is a rather fascinating contrast between the simulated hard material of which they appear to be made and the pictorially rendered softness of their flesh.[36]

The background is of the usual gold-brocade type. The decorative design stamped on the gesso ground is based on an acanthus motif which was frequently used by both Michael and Friedrich Pacher.[37]

Stylistic Considerations

Not only the composition of the Peter and Paul panel, but also most of its principal components and several of its smaller details are closely related to, and probably directly inspired by, Michael Pacher's masterpiece the *Altarpiece of the Fathers of the Church* (Alte Pinakothek, Munich [Fig. 9]). The general idea of the twin Gothic baldachins, their sculptural decoration (it is now difficult to guess how the side buttresses, which are now missing, appeared originally and whether or not they also were decorated with sculpture), the central perspective of the floor (which creates a unified space

system for the two elements of the composition), the geometric design of the floor and even its colour scheme all find their analogies in Michael Pacher's work. Even Michael's peculiar manner of letting the light always fall from the right is applied in the same fashion in the Peter and Paul panel.

Many smaller details in Friedrich's work also seem to have been derived directly from the *Altarpiece of the Fathers of the Church*. Two details in the figure of St Peter are analogous to those in Michael's *St Gregory*: the papal tiara, with its beautiful decorative foliage motif; and the huge golden fibula in the form of a Gothic quadrilobe, with the figure of Christ, as the Man of Sorrows, rising from his sarcophagus.[38]

Another typological analogy is the green cover of Peter's book, with its boldly projecting golden knobs. A very similar design appears in the *missal* held by the devil in a scene from the life of St Wolfgang painted on one of the shutters of the *Altarpiece of the Fathers of the Church* (Fig. 45).[39]

Despite the foregoing, the question of whether the Peter and Paul panel is an adaptation of the central panel of the *Altarpiece of the Fathers of the Church* or *vice versa* can be regarded as a legitimate one, even if Michael's priority in age is granted, since the chronology of the *Altarpiece of the Fathers of the Church* (which is neither documented nor dated) is still disputed.[40]

It is precisely in those details which Friedrich seems to have borrowed from Michael that the stylistic differences between the two artists are most strikingly revealed. While Michael's work has a characteristic architectonic and spatial conception, Friedrich's attitude is essentially non-architectonic, and he has little interest in spatial implications. The perspective system of the floor in the Peter and Paul panel is less consistent, and the horizon is three times higher than the extremely low one which is used in Michael's work.[41] Friedrich's canopies, with their characteristic swelling contours are – unlike Michael's rectilinear canopies – not clearly related to the perspective system of the floor. Whereas Michael's *Fathers of the Church* are seated within rectangular walled cells surmounted by compact volumetric canopies, and the whole structure is enclosed within massive rectangular niches, Friedrich's Apostles are sheltered by open baldachins in which the flamboyant decoration on the walls of Michael's canopies is transformed into skeletal structures.

However, what Friedrich's work loses in architectonic feeling and spatial coherence, it gains in organic feeling and the brilliant development of Late Gothic decorative motifs. The beautiful flamboyant canopies, with their gracefully entwined twigs and branches (which are particularly free and imaginative in the minor canopies), can rival Michael's best creations (*cf.* Fig. 18).[42]

Although less than half of the elaborate decorative composition of the upper part of the panel has survived, enough is left to enable a conjectural reconstruction of its original design by means of a comparison with other works by Friedrich Pacher. The most striking analogies can be found in the frescos of the Dominicans' Cloister at Bozen and in the *Baptism*.

In the upper part of the so-called *Hortus Conclusus* fresco (*The Annunciation symbolized by the Hunter approaching the Lady and the Unicorn*, Bozen, Dominicans' Cloister), there is a Gothic canopy which is similar to what those in the Innsbruck panel must have looked like in their original state (Fig. 17). It is accompanied by bent pinnacles which recall those in the Peter and Paul panel.

It has already been noted that before the mutilation of the Innsbruck panel, the two hollow pinnacles which rise and bend sideways from the central pier formed twin arches that must have looked very similar to those in the Munich *Baptism* (Fig. 5). Of the two 'real' arches which once enclosed the whole composition from above, only the lower parts stemming from the central pier have survived.

In the frescos at Bozen, Friedrich frequently resorted to the same device of enclosing the scenes within twin arches. In the remains of a fresco, of which only the ruined *Last Supper* has survived, twin arches springing from a central pier (again accompanied by bent pinnacles) form

a design similar to that which must have existed in the Peter and Paul panel before its mutilation (Fig. 19).

Another detail in the Peter and Paul panel which might be related to Michael Pacher's style is the violently foreshortened face of the angel above (Fig. 13). An analogous motif is found in one of the angels in Michael's 'Death of the Virgin' from the *St Wolfgang Altarpiece*. This characteristic *tour de force* of figure-perspective was probably inspired by the North Italian masters of the 'Hard Style'.[43] Friedrich seems to have developed his own variant of this motif, which is characterized in his work, as usual, by a more linear style than that of Michael. Similar angels recur in several other works by him, including 'The Martyrdom of St Katherine' in the Neustift Gallery (Fig. 33) and 'The Warning for the Flight into Egypt' (from the *Altarpiece of the Virgin*, Ferdinandeum, Innsbruck, [Fig. 14]). A similar angel also appears in a painting by Friedrich Pacher's follower – Marx Reichlich's *Adoration of the Magi* (Ferdinandeum, Innsbruck), dated 1498, which depends heavily on Friedrich Pacher.

The Peter and Paul panel includes several other features and details which are peculiar to Friedrich Pacher's personal style. Haloes with a radial ornamental design resembling a cut orange, or its simpler linear variants, frequently appear in Friedrich Pacher's paintings, particularly in his frescos at Bozen and Neustift (Figs 19, 28, 33, 34). In the Peter and Paul panel, this design is stamped on a thick gesso ground, while a variant is drawn directly on the gold-leaf in the scene of 'St Peter Walking on the Water' (Jerusalem [Pl. 10]). Such radial ornamental design is completely absent in Michael Pacher's work, in which the concentric ornamental design is prevalent.[44] On the other hand, the strongly foreshortened halo of St Paul is probably inspired by Michael Pacher or by his usual source of inspiration – the North Italian painters.

In the Peter and Paul panel, the corrugated skin of the saints is rendered by long, hook-shaped strokes which create a two-dimensional pattern characteristic of Friedrich's non-plastic style. This device recurs in other works of his, particularly in the 'Martyrdom of St Katherine' (the figure of the Emperor [Fig. 33]).

The script-rolls, with their peculiar triangular folds, are identical in style and calligraphy to those in other works by Friedrich Pacher (Fig. 16) and recur in the Jerusalem panels.

DERIVATIONS

Closely related to the Peter and Paul panel are the figures of the two Princes of the Apostles flanking a statue of St Korbinian in an altarpiece dedicated to this saint (the Church of St Korbinian, near Assling [Fig. 11]). They were certainly painted by Friedrich Pacher, but the date of the altarpiece is unknown.

The most important derivation from the composition of the Peter and Paul panel is the magnificent central piece of the *Sts James and Stephen Altarpiece*, painted in 1506 for the Church of Neustift by Marx Reichlich (Alte Pinakothek, Munich [Fig. 10]). As in the Innsbruck painting, the two life-sized figures are symmetrically arranged on a receding floor plane, and the architectural frame includes the same twin arches in the upper part. Unfortunately, Reichlich's work was cut in the upper part and probably also at the bottom. However, in its original state it must have been even closer in form to the Peter and Paul panel than it is at present.

The figural decoration of the jambs in the *Sts James and Stephen Altarpiece* might support a hypothesis that the Innsbruck panel was similarly decorated on its sides before it was mutilated. The canopies above the sculptures are diminutive variants of those above the figures of Sts Stephen and Sebastian. Reichlich's work is thus an important point of reference for the reconstruction of the Peter and Paul panel.[45]

Another certain derivation is a bust of St Peter (Municipal Museum, Bozen [Fig. 15]) painted on a small panel, probably a shutter of a lost predella. It is generally (and justifiably) attributed to one of Friedrich Pacher's workshop assistants.[46] A woodcut by Jörg Breu representing Sts Peter and Paul is rather reminiscent, in its composition, of the Innsbruck panel, while the architectural background is inspired by classical Renaissance ideas (Fig. 12). The standing figures of saints which appear on the shutters of the altarpieces by André Haller, a native of Sterzing and an epigone of the Brixen school of painting, seem to be the last echo of the Peter and Paul panel.[47]

PHYSICAL STATE

In its original state, the panel was rectangular and measured approximately 256 × 222 cms. In the eighteenth century it was cut in the upper part, central longitudinal section and sides. In 1886 Robert Vischer could still see the painting exhibited in Tratzberg Castle as two separate 'wing paintings'.[48] Strips approximately 3 cms wide were cut from the inner sides of the bisected halves before they were rejoined together. Much wider strips, about 23–24 cms, were cut from each of the outer sides.[49]

As a result of the mutilation of the panel, many details of the paintings on both sides were partly or totally lost. The principal losses to the baldachins and the architectural frame have already been mentioned. In addition, the loss of the middle longitudinal section has narrowed the central pier and the corbel on which the two sculptures stand and damaged the figures themselves. The loss of the central section can also be observed in the distortion of the geometric design of the floor and its perspective system. The remains of the arches above now intersect, whereas originally they should only have been tangent to each other. The angel's left shoulder and Paul's script-roll are damaged too. On the right a part of Paul's left foot and the hilt of his sword were cut away.

LITERATURE

Robert Vischer, *Studien für Kunstgeschichte* (Stuttgart, 1886), p. 458; H.G. Semper, *Offizielle Bericht über die Verhandlungen des VII internationalen Kunsthistorischen Kongresses in Innsbruck* (Berlin, 1902), pp. 58, 65; *idem., Alttirolische Kunstwerke des XV und XVI Jah.* (Innsbruck, 1902), Plate Volume, Pl. V; R. Stiassny, 'Die Pacher Schule', *Repertorium für Kuntswissenschaft*, Vol. XXVI, 1903, p. 26; Mannowsky, p. 84; Semper, 1911, pp. 102 ff., 243–4, 391, Fig. 101; Döring, 1912, pp. 301, 302; 1913, pp. 140–1, 147, 148, Pl. 76; Halm, pp. 573–4, 587–9, 594 –6, Pl. 8; Allesch, 1931, pp. 200–4, Pl. 72; Thieme-Becker, p. 121; Oberhammer, 1950, p. 46, n. 46, Pl. 54 (detail); Stange, pp. 184–5, Pl. 288; Pächt, p. 78, Pl. 66; E. Egg, *Tiroler Landesmuseum Ferdinandeum*, (Innsbruck, *s.d., c.* 1964), p. 15; *Gotische Tafelbilder aus dem Tiroler Landesmuseum* (*s.d., c.* 1965), detail of St Peter (colour); Böck, 1972, p. 183.

Reverse: 'The Last Judgement.'

Oil and tempera (Fig. 20).

Above, surrounded by a mandorla, Christ is sitting on one rainbow with his feet resting on another. His pose is the traditional combination of the *ostentatio vulneris* and that of the World Judge. His open robe reveals the wound of the lance in his right rib. His raised right hand, showing the wound of the nail, blesses the righteous, while his lowered hand, holding a sword, condemns the sinners. This twofold aspect of the Last Judgement – salvation and damnation – is repeated in the symbolic lily branch and the sword issuing from Christ's mouth. The redundancy of the motif of the symbolic sword is rather rare.

Kneeling on the clouds on both sides of the Redeemer, Mary and St John form the traditional *deesis* that intercedes for the resurrected souls, who rise from their open graves below. The landscape is plain and barren; only a few trees and some rocky hills disturb its monotony. Paradise is not represented, but the three figures rising from their graves invoking Christ with their dramatic gestures clearly represent the Blessed (Pl. 9), while on the right a devil hooks a sinner to the gaping mouth of Hell, from which his victim tries in vain to save his falling friend.

The traditional iconography of this abridged representation of the Last Judgement could have been inspired by a contemporary print (Figs 22, 23).[50]

STYLISTIC CONSIDERATIONS

The Italianate frontal perspective of the graves and the typical violent foreshortening of the figure of one of the resurrected souls (Pl. 9), which was justly compared to the fallen executioners in the 'Martyrdom of St Katherine' (Fig. 33),[51] betray the style of Friedrich Pacher. Landscape details of oval bushes and feathery trees with long, thin stems, similar to those in the 'Last Judgement' and not unlike those in contemporary Umbrian paintings, recur in others of his works.[52]

The sketchy execution with 'dry', thinly laid paint, the lack of glazes and the dull colour scheme have induced some of the very few authors who have cared to refer to this painting to attribute it to a workshop assistant (*Geselle*) of Friedrich Pacher. However, some vigorously drawn details might indicate the active participation of the master in their execution, while the poor quality of the three heavenly figures might be attributed, at least in part, to the painting's poor state of preservation (see below). The facial features of Mary recall those of the queen in the Conversion scene in the *Altarpiece of St Katherine* (Neustift [Fig. 32]).[53]

DERIVATIONS

A variant of the heavenly scene appears in a fresco painted by Friedrich Pacher on the half-dome of the apse of the little chapel in Taufers Castle (above Sand in Taufers (Campo Tures), north of Bruneck [Fig. 21]).[54]

For the mutilation of the panel, see the description of the front side of the panel, above. The painting is in rather poor condition and has been restored throughout more than once. Only a few details in the lower section have maintained their original aspect.

Considerable parts of the figures of Mary and St John were cut away with the sides of the panel.

The gaps in the middle section of the panel, particularly in Christ's torso and head, in the rainbows and in one of the resurrected souls, have been clumsily restored. Christ's waist looks strangely slim as a result of the faulty restoration.

Literature

Döring, 1913, p. 147; Halm, pp. 588, 589, 603, Pl. 9; Thieme-Becker, p. 121.

Predella

Front: St Veronica with her veil and the two Jöchl brothers.

Oil and tempera, gold-brocade ground. H. 75 cms, w. 150 cms (Pl. 5). Tiroler Landesmuseum, Ferdinandeum, Innsbruck.

In the centre, St Veronica is sitting on a low stone parapet or bench, displaying her veil with the image of Christ's head. Veronica's veil (or *sudarium*) frequently appears in fifteenth-century German predella paintings, as well as in engravings. Since this motif is iconographically related to Sts Peter and Paul, they often appear holding it (Fig. 25). This was probably the reason for the inclusion of the motif in the predella of the *Peter and Paul Altarpiece*.[55] St Veronica is flanked below by the kneeling figures of the donators, Lienhard – presumably on the left (Pl. 7) – and Hans II Jöchl – on the right (Pl. 8).[56] They are kneeling on simple blocks of wood with their hands joined in prayer. The script-rolls seem to echo their prayers and might also bear some reference to the scene on the back of the central panel, since their text seems to allude to the Last Judgement.

The script-roll on 'Lienhard's' side reads: 'o

onipotes et mieicos deo / misere mei sc/d' [?] magn' [o omnipotens et misericors deus miserere mei secundum magnam (misericordiam tuam) (a variant of Psalm 50:2)].

The inscription on 'Hans'' side quotes the last words of Christ: 'in manus tuas domine comento [commendo] spiritum meu[m]' (Psalm 30:6; Luke 23:46).

At least in one other case, this text is clearly related to the iconography of the Last Judgement.[57]

On the ground are two coats of arms of the Jöchl family, together with the forepart of a leaping white steer. The one on the right is similar to the coat of arms which was installed in the carved ceiling of Jöchlsthurn by Mathias Jöchl in 1469 and is still *in situ* (Fig. 3).

Stylistic Considerations

The two patrons are portrayed in the three-quarter view inherited from Flemish painting. They are dressed in heavy red gowns with fur collars and wear caps. The characterization is well individualized and apparently realistic.[58] From their appearance, the brothers could be between thirty and fifty years old.

The figure of St Veronica (Pl. 6) is very similar

to the stiff, pious women who appear in the 'Sermon of St Wolfgang' and in the 'Raising of Lazarus' from the *St Wolfgang Altarpiece* and in some of Reichlich's works. Like them, she wears the compact traditional South German head-dress. Her blue dress falls in hard, angular folds.

The refined execution and solemn, tragic expression of Christ's head, which dominates this heraldic composition, have aroused the enthusiasm of several earlier writers. It has been observed that the treatment of Christ's hair, as well as that of the Jöchl brothers, is much softer and more naturalistic than the harder, regular curls of the Princes of the Apostles and of most figures in the other parts of the altarpiece, excepting Paul's soft hair in the 'Ananias Healing Saul' (Pl. 19).[59]

PHYSICAL STATE

The original frame is missing, and the painting is retouched in many places.

LITERATURE

See central panel, and particularly: Döring, 1913, pp. 140, 145, 146, Pl. 78; Halm, pp. 589, 590, 605, 609–10, Pl. 10, 24, 25; Allesch, p. 204, Pl. 73.

Reverse: Acanthus and vine ornament.

Grey monochrome on blue ground (Fig. 20).

The acanthus leaf motif is of the same kind that appears in the gold-brocade ground in the Peter and Paul panel. Such leaf motifs were quite common in Late Gothic art (Fig. 26) and were particularly favoured by Michael Pacher and his school.[60]

Seven Scenes from the Lives of Sts Peter and Paul. Jerusalem, Convent of the Flagellation.

'St Peter Walking on the Water'.

Oil and tempera. H. 124.8 cms, w. 105 cms (Pl. 10).

This was the second of the two scenes painted on the exterior of the left shutter. (The first scene has not survived.) The subject is derived from Matthew 14:22–31. After the miracle of the multiplication of the loaves and the fishes, Jesus sent his disciples on a boat over the Sea of Gennesaret. Suddenly there arose a great storm, 'and in the fourth watch of the night Jesus went unto them walking on the sea ... Jesus spake unto them, saying, Be of good cheer, it is I ... and Peter answered him and said, Lord, if it be thou, bid me come unto thee on the water. And he said, Come. And when Peter was come down out of the ship, he walked on the water, to go to Jesus. But when he saw the wind boisterous, he was afraid; and beginning to sink, he cried, saying, *Lord save me* [in the script-roll: DOMINE SALVU(M) ME FAC]. And immediately Jesus stretched forth his hand and caught him, and said unto him, *O thou of little faith, wherefore didst thou doubt?* [in the script-roll: MODICE FIDEI QUARE DUBITASTI]'.

As is usual in Friedrich Pacher's works, the *dramatis personae* appear in the foreground. On the left, the powerfully foreshortened boat appears to approach the spectator, with its sail wound and its oars idle.[61] A white-bearded apostle on board seems to address Christ with his left hand. He wears what appears to be a fisherman's dress, a simple white tunic whose hard and angular folds give the impression of a leathery texture. The sinking Peter is trying to swim towards Christ. His pug-nosed profile will recur in the other scenes from his life which belong to the same altarpiece (Pls 21, 25).[62]

On the right, the magnificent figure of Christ (Col. Pl. II) wearing a plain purple gown with heavy sculptural folds stoops to save the sinking Peter, grasping Peter's extended hand and blessing or soothing him with his own free hand. There is a somewhat ingenuous realism in the rendering of the strained muscles of Peter's right hand and in the way his wet garment, similar to that of the Apostle in the boat, clings to his half-sunken body.

The evident similarity between the sinking Peter and the Apostle in the boat (Pl. 11) and the rhetoric gesture of the latter has led Halm to the opinion that the Apostle in the boat should be identified as Peter. According to this interpretation, Peter appears twice in the painting, once while he is still in the boat, challenging Jesus; and the second time when he is in the water (Pl. 14). Such an interpretation poses two iconographical problems. First, if the scene is a continuous representation of two different episodes, why does the figure of Christ not appear twice? And why does Peter not have a script-roll, if he is really speaking from the boat? Secondly, according to this interpretation Peter was the only man on board during the night voyage on the stormy Sea of Gennesaret, while the biblical text speaks clearly of the *Apostles* and not of a single Apostle. Actually, most pictorial representations of this scene include several Apostles in the boat.[63]

The high vanishing point of the perspective offers a panoramic view over the sea and a flat landscape interrupted by the steep craggy hill, which is inspired by North Italian paintings, especially those by Mantegna in his late period.

Contrary to the narrative in the Gospel, the scene is flooded with a cool morning light, and the surface of the calm sea is broken only by gentle ripples. The shore on the left is dotted with bays and river estuaries, the nearest of which serves as a natural moat to the town of Gennesaret, represented as a medieval fortified city (Col. Pl. III, Pl. 12). It is surrounded by a turreted wall with covered ramparts and a gatehouse leading to the wooden jetty. The site and the buildings seem to have been inspired by contemporary South German urban architecture, but the scene also includes some fantastic details, such as the enormous octagonal tower (to the right of the mast) and the round belfry (on the left) which resembles a Moslem minaret.

STYLISTIC CONSIDERATIONS

The foreshortening of Christ's left hand is a feat of virtuosity which appears to be a characteristic expression of Friedrich's absorption of North Italian ideas. A clumsier variant appears in his *Triptych of the Trinity* (Österreichische Galerie, Vienna [Fig. 28]).[64] The gesture is rather reminiscent of the analogous gestures of Leonardo's *Madonna of the Rocks* (Fig. 35) and of Christ in Michelangelo's *Last Judgement*[65] (painted much later, of course).

Variants and details of the beautiful landscape which serves as a setting for this scene recur in others of the Jerusalem panels (see below) and in several other works by Friedrich Pacher,[66] but it is here that Friedrich's landscape style reaches its highest stage of development. Trees with long, slender stems and thick foliage, very much resembling those in this scene, also appear in Michael Pacher's 'Flight into Egypt' in the *St Wolfgang Altarpiece*, but they recur much more consistently in Friedrich Pacher's works, including 'The Conversion of Saul' and 'The Martyrdom of St Paul' from the *Peter and Paul Altarpiece* (Pls 15, 29) and two scenes from the *Altar of the Virgin* in Innsbruck: 'The Visitation' and the (mutilated) 'Flight into Egypt' (Fig. 34). The feathery trees in 'The Last Judgement' (Fig. 20) are a lighter variant of this type. The tiny figures in the background, particularly the shepherd and his cows on the left (Pl. 13) recur in other works by Friedrich Pacher ('The Warning for the Flight into Egypt', Ferdinandeum, Innsbruck).

Even in these minute details, Friedrich remains faithful to his favourite show of virtuosity in figure foreshortening. Here, too, he seems to have followed Michael Pacher, in whose works animals generally appear in violently foreshortened postures.[67]

Physical State

The panel is relatively well preserved, though it became somewhat convex owing to great fluctuations in the temperature of the place in which it was stored for years. There are traces of superficial cleaning, but the colours are still darkened by an old, yellowish varnish.

Literature

Döring, 1912, pp. 302, Fig. on p. 303; Döring, 1913, p. 140, Fig. 77; Halm, pp. 576–7, Fig. 1; Allesch, *passim*, Fig. 74; Bagatti, p. 144, Fig. on p. 143; Picirillo, Figs on pp. 198, 199–200.

'The Conversion of Saul'.

Oil and tempera on wood. H. 124.7 cms, w. 105 cms (Pl. 15).

This scene, the first from the life of St Paul, originally decorated the upper half of the outside of the right shutter. This central episode in the early life of the saint, generally interpreted as his *vocation*, frequently appears in religious art. The subject is derived from Acts 9:1ff: 'And . . . he [Saul] came near Damascus [in order to persecute the disciples of Jesus]: and suddenly there shined round about him a light from heaven: and he fell to the earth and heard a voice saying unto him, *Saul, Saul, why persecutest thou me?* [in the script-roll: SAULE, SAULE QUID ME PE(R)SEQUERIS]. And the Lord said. . . *it is hard for thee to kick against the pricks* [in the script-roll: DURU(M) EST TIBI CONTRA STIMUL(OS) CALCIT(RARE)]. And he trembling and astonished said, *Lord, what wilt thou have me to do?* [in the script-roll: DOMINE QUID ME VIS FACERE].'

On the upper left, the bust of Christ is emerging from a cloud (Pl. 17). He is dressed in the same purple gown as in the preceding scene. His right hand is lifted in blessing, while his left, stretched forward in a rhetorical gesture, generates golden rays, some of them rather like shafts, which reach Saul in the lower-right corner of the panel and topple him from his white horse. The violently foreshortened beast falls forward on its knees and stretches its nose towards the right, thus completing the dynamic diagonal which begins with Christ.

Saul falls to the right with outstretched limbs. Astounded and dismayed, he tries desperately to lean on his left hand, which is partly hidden by his helmet. His right hand is raised to protect his eyes from the glaring light. He wears a short leather tunic over his armour, olive-green hose and red boots, and a red mantle is fastened around his neck.

The painter seems to have attempted to reach a certain degree of similarity between the representation of the Apostle here and his image in the central panel, although here Saul looks much younger. The dramatic character of the scene is expressed not only by the diagonal movement in the main action (which will recur in 'The Martyrdom of St Paul' [Pl. 29]), but also by the dynamic grouping of the secondary figures and the variety of their reaction to the miraculous event taking place before them.

The small escort platoon is split into two groups

by Saul and his horse. The five horsemen riding in the van continue their way to the right, heading for Damascus and apparently unaware of their fallen commander (Col. Pl. iv). Only the last of them (exactly in the centre of the picture), a coarse-faced standard-bearer, seems to have taken notice of the miraculous accident at the last moment. He casts a hasty, frightened glance over his shoulder, without stopping his galloping horse. The resulting *contraposto* of the glance and the movement is a masterpiece of dramatic description (Pl. 16).

The first two soldiers in the rear guard on the left (Pl. 18) are apparently fully aware of the extraordinary event taking place before their eyes. The first of them has stopped his horse, which rears on its legs, while his surprised comrade raises his hand to his head. Again, the beast is rendered in a strongly foreshortened pose.[68] The vivid realism of the soldiers and their gestures is admirable. They look like German mercenaries, rather than Roman soldiers, and their dresses, armour, and weapons are rendered with the understanding of an expert.

The landscape background is very similar to that in the preceding panel. It resembles even more closely the background in the 'Martyrdom of St Katherine', (Neustift) which, incidentally, also includes fleeing horsemen analogous to those on the right of the Jerusalem painting (Fig. 33).

DERIVATIONS

'The Conversion of Saul' (Neustift Gallery), which originally belonged to the inner side of a wing of the now-dismembered *Altarpiece of St Paul*, appears to be a reduced version of the same scene in the *Peter and Paul Altarpiece* (Fig. 36).[69]

PHYSICAL STATE

The painting is, on the whole, well preserved. It was superficially cleaned at an unknown date. There are some minor cracks and small scratches on the panel.

LITERATURE

Halm, p. 582, Pl. 4; Döring, 1912, pp. 303, 304, Pl. on p. 303; 1913, p. 142; Allesch, pp. 210–11, Pl. 78; Bagatti, p. 142; Picirillo, p. 202, Fig. on p. 201.

'Ananias Healing Saul'.

Oil and tempera on wood. H. 124.5 cms, w. 96.4 cms (Col. Pl. 5).

The second scene from the life of St Paul originally decorated the lower half of the outside of the right shutter. The scene is one which is rarely represented in art; the subject is derived from Acts 9:12, 17, 18.

Saul, shocked and blinded after his conversion, took lodging at Judas' home in Damascus. Ananias, fulfilling the Lord's order, 'entered into the house; and putting his hands on him said, 'Brother Saul, *the Lord, even Jesus*, that appeared unto thee in the way as thou camest *hath sent me that thou mightest receive thy sight, and be filled with the Holy Ghost* [in the script-roll: SAULE FRATER DNS (DOMINUS) IHS (JHESUS) MISIT ME UT VIDEAS (ET) IMPLEARIS SPU (SPIRITU) SCTO (SANCTO)]. And immediately . . . he received sight forthwith, and arose and was baptized.'

The scene takes place in a vaulted vestibule, or loggia, which is open to the right. It has six columns of variegated marble, each of a different colour and texture. The vestibule leads to a timber-roofed room built on a slightly higher level, which is preceded by a double Gothic arch. The action takes place, as usual, in the foreground. Saul is dressed exactly as he was in the preceding scene, although here his armour and tunic are almost completely covered by the red gown which could hardly be seen in the 'Conversion'.

He is leaning hesitantly on a blind man's stick with a pointed metal tip. As in the preceding scene, Saul, who is yet only a saint-to-be, has no halo above his head.

Ananias, a magnificent middle-aged Northern type (Pl. 19), is the very opposite of Saul. He is the embodiment of resolute action. Both his powerful profile and his healing gesture radiate energy and determination. Even his rigid white curls constitute a contrast to Saul's soft brown hair.

The man clad in red and wearing a large biretta standing behind Saul and a little to the left, has been identified as Judas, Saul's host.[70] Four soldiers, probably members of Saul's escort, are rather excitedly witnessing the miracle.

STYLISTIC CONSIDERATIONS

At first sight, the round arch which partly encloses the scene looks as if it is a part of the façade of the vestibule. But rather than belonging to the building, it is actually the surviving part of a symmetrical architectural frame of a type which was quite common in fifteenth-century paintings. The mutilation of the right side of the panel has deprived it of the right part of the arch and its supporting member and has marred its original formal meaning.

The original symmetrical form and pictorial function of the arch which frames the scene of 'Ananias Healing Saul' can be understood if we compare it with the better preserved 'Circumcision' from the *Altarpiece of the Virgin* (Ferdinandeum, Innsbruck), which is framed by an arch exactly analogous in form and function to that in the Jerusalem panel (Fig. 38). Friedrich Pacher adopted here a simpler and much earlier type of architectural frame than that used in the elaborate sculptured portal of his signed *Baptism* or in Michael's 'Death of the Virgin' (*St Wolfgang Altarpiece*) which is inspired by Rogier Van der Weiden's *Miraflores Altarpiece*. While the architectural frame of 'Ananias Healing Saul' might likewise have ultimately been derived from a work by Rogier,

the direct source is probably the Master E.S.[71]

The architectural setting of 'Ananias Healing Saul' is the only representation of an interior to appear in the *Peter and Paul Altarpiece* and is the grandest of its kind in Friedrich's *oeuvre*. It is the only convincingly realistic vaulted space painted by him, where not only the perspective system but also the lighting is conceived in such a way as to create an illusion of real space.[72] The perspective of the building is conceived as a single focus system in which all the orthogonals should (but do not exactly) meet at one point – a little to the left of Judas' head.

The representation of a miracle taking place in a vaulted interior with onlookers peeping at the scene from between the pillars and the pictorial conception of the architecture may be considered as a homage to Michael Pacher, with whose Gothic interiors in the *St Wolfgang Altarpiece* Friedrich must have been well acqainted.[73] However, Judas' house looks rather modest in size and in architectural design in comparison with the elaborate structures of Michael Pacher's imposing interiors, and thus comes closer to some of the more modest Flemish prototypes. The difference between the spatial conception of the two artists is again particularly evident in the treatment of perspective. In Michael Pacher's works, figures and architecture belong to the same perspective system and diminish in size in direct proportion to their distance from the beholder, while Friedrich's figures have no clear relation to the perspective system of the architecture. Consequently, their position in space remains rather ambiguous and their distance from the beholder is difficult to determine.

Colourful architectural details frequently appear in Michael Pacher's works and might well have inspired Friedrich Pacher, though here, too, the latter tends to concentrate on the decorative and ornamental details rather than on the overall colour scheme. This is particularly evident in the treatment of the marble columns and the arches. The same decorative-ornamental devices and colour combinations which appear in the architectural members of Judas' house recur in 'St Katherine

Refuses to Adore the Idols' (Neustift [Fig. 29]), in which, incidentally, the same type of columns that appear in Judas' house also recur. These columns, with their characteristic 'ring' ornament, are one of the most consistent elements in Friedrich Pacher's *oeuvre*.[74]

Some of the human types appearing among the bystanders in this scene seem to be part of Friedrich Pacher's fixed typological vocabulary. The bulbous face of Judas and the childlike profile of the soldier leaning against a column appear again in the following scene from the life of St Peter, and also recur in the *Altarpiece of St Katherine* (Neustift Gallery [Figs 29, 30]).[75]

The angular folds of Ananias' sleeve find their exact analogy in the angel of the 'Annunciation' on the outside of the left shutter of the *Altarpiece of St Katherine* (Fig. 39) and also closely resemble those in Friedrich's other 'Annunciation' at Innsbruck (Fig. 42). The deep folds of his heavy green gown are evidently inspired by fifteenth-century German wood sculpture.

PHYSICAL STATE

A piece about 10 cms wide has been sawn off from the right side of the panel. This is proven by the difference between its width and that of the other Jerusalem panels and by the above stylistic analysis of the original composition.

There is a vertical split on the left side of the panel. The two parts have been left wide apart after a recent clumsy restoration. The surface of the panel has become convex as a result of long exposure to heat, and the paint has fallen off in a few spots. There are traces of a relatively recent cleaning, but the new varnish has already begun to darken.

LITERATURE

Döring, 1912, pp. 304, 309, Pl. on p. 305; 1913, pp. 142, 144, 145; Halm, pp. 583–4, 599, 602, 603, Pl. 5; Hempel, 1931, pp. 21, 22, Fig. 28; Allesch, pp. 207–8, Pl. 79; Bagatti, p. 142; Picirillo, p. 202, Fig. on p. 201.

'The Liberation of St Peter'.

Oil and tempera on wood, gold-brocade ground. H. 124.6 cms, w. 105.6 cms (Pl. 20).

This is the first of the four panels originally belonging to the inner sides of the shutters. 'The Liberation of St Peter' was the upper scene on the left shutter of the altarpiece. It includes two episodes: Peter's liberation and flight from the Mamertine Prison in Rome, and his meeting with Christ outside the southern gate of Rome (Pl. 21), better known as the *Quo Vadis* episode. The story is derived from a passage in the *Legenda Aurea*, which quotes the earlier sources (Linus, Leo). Jacopo probably also made use of the so-called Apocryphal *Acts of St Peter* and of the Apocryphal *Passions of Sts Peter and Paul*.

The first episode is rather rarely represented in art and should not be confused with the much more common subject of the liberation of St Peter from the Jerusalem Prison – an earlier episode from the life of the saint (Acts 12:13 ff.), in which Peter was liberated by an angel.

After the fall of Simon Magus, 'Nero . . . committed [the two Apostles] to a high official named Paulinus, who cast them into [the Mamertine] prison, under the guard of two soldiers, Processus and Martinianus. But they were converted by Peter, and opened the prison, setting the two apostles free.'

On the left Peter is led by one of his two liberators out of the door of the prison towards the open gate of the city wall. All that can be seen of the second guard is a part of his turbaned head and a leg. In the left foreground, two soldiers – a young groom and a fully armed halberdier, who is sitting on a block of masonry with his back to the spectator – look impassively on the scene.

The second episode follows on the right, outside the city wall, and is narrated in the *Legenda Aurea*: 'But Peter, yielding at last to the entreaties of the brethren, decided to quit Rome. But when he came to one of the city gates, at the place where the Church of Saint Mary ad Passus stands today, as Leo and Linus tell us, he came face to face with Christ Himself; and he said to Him: "*Lord, whither goest Thou?*" And our Lord responded: "*I go to Rome, to be crucified anew!*" [in the script-rolls: DOMINE QUO VADIS? VENE (VENIO) ROMAM UTRUM (ITERUM) CRUCIFIGI] . . . And Peter said: "Then, Lord, I too return to Rome, to be crucified with thee!"'[76]

Peter walks on a winding path strewn with pebbles, which might represent the Via Appia, and encounters Christ, who is standing on an oval stone, carrying his cross (characteristically foreshortened) on his shoulder.[77]

The colour scheme of this painting, like that of the three following ones, is rather limited. Except for the green patches in the glimpse of landscape, various tints of red and blue are used for the garments, and pale browns, yellows, ochres and pinks for the architecture.

STYLISTIC CONSIDERATIONS

The perspective view of the street is probably inspired by Michael Pacher, and could have again been derived from the *Altarpiece of the Fathers of the Church* ('St Wolfgang and the Devil' [Fig. 45]). But unlike Michael Pacher, Friedrich bars the view of the street by the densely grouped and unproportionally large figures in the foreground, thus spoiling the effect of depth (which is the watermark of Michael's perspective views). As in the Ananias scene, the arrangement of the figures lacks coherent spatial conception, and they are not related to the perspective system of the architecture. The same phenomenon recurs in the two street scenes on the right wing of the *Altarpiece of St Katherine* (Neustift [Figs 30, 32]). In one of these scenes – 'The Conversion of the Queen' (Fig. 32) – the same compositional device

of the *repoussoire* figure of a seated halberdier is used.[78]

The architectural details seem to have been inspired by actual buildings of the period. The steeple and the gable of a church (?) in the background are typical Tyrol style and recur in other works by Michael and Friedrich Pacher.

In the '*Quo Vadis*' scene, the same principle already applied in the first scene from the life of St Peter is repeated: the profile pose which denotes action and movement is reserved for the Apostle, while the immobile apparition of Christ is represented in a frontal view.

Nearly all the human types, and even details of the figures represented in this scene, recur in others of the Jerusalem panels and in other works by Friedrich Pacher. The pug-nosed profile of Peter in the '*Quo Vadis*' scene recurs in two other panels in Jerusalem – 'St Peter Walking on the Water' and the 'Parting of the Apostles (Pls 10, 25). The figure of Christ, which has essentially the same features as in the two preceding panels, is rather reminiscent of other representations of him in works by Michael Pacher (*cf.* 'The Death of the Virgin' from the *St Wolfgang Altarpiece*, and the same subject from the *St Lawrence Altarpiece*, Alte Pinakothek, Munich) and by the Master of Uttenheim ('The Death of the Virgin', Alte Pinakothek, Munich; *The Agony in the Garden*, Kunsthistorisches Museum, Vienna). It recurs in 'The Death of the Virgin' from the *Altarpiece of the Virgin* (Innsbruck) by Friedrich Pacher.

Processus and Martinianus, Peter's liberators, are respectively similar to Judas and the turbaned soldier in 'Ananias Healing Saul'. Peter himself (and even the design of his blue gown) is strikingly similar to Joseph in the *Adoration of the Magi* in Mitterolang (Fig. 41). His groping right hand also seems to belong to Friedrich Pacher's fixed typological vocabulary. Exact analogies can be found in the hands of the Old King in the *Adoration of the Magi*, in that of St Katherine in 'St Katherine Refuses to Adore the Idol'[79] and in that of the *Prophet* above the *Expulsion of Heliodoros* (Bozen, Dominican Cloister) (Figs 41, 29, 16).

The haloes above the heads of Peter and Christ are represented, as in many works by Michael and Friedrich Pacher, as three-dimensional objects, subject to visual foreshortening. Peter's halo in the liberation scene on the left looks as if an attempt had been made to represent it as reflecting the saint's head.[80]

PHYSICAL STATE

Two wide cracks run through the panel. The figure of Christ has lost the paint in several places. A yellow varnish tones down the colour.

LITERATURE

Döring, 1912, p. 304; 1913, p. 142; Halm, pp. 578–82, 592, Pl. 2; Allesch, pp. 208–9, 211–12, Fig. 76; Bagatti, p. 144; Picirillo, pp. 200–1, Fig. on p. 199.

'The Martyrdom of St Peter'.

Oil and tempera on wood, gold-brocade ground. H. 124 cms, w. 105.4 cms (Pl. 22).

The literary source is again a passage from the *Legenda Aurea* which is based on several earlier apocryphal legends, of which only the writings of Marcellus and Leo are cited. According to these sources, Peter expressed his wish to be crucified with his head downwards. He explained this extraordinary request by saying: '*My Master came down from heaven to earth,* and so was lifted up on the cross, *but I, whom He has deigned to call from earth to heaven* [in the script-roll: DNS (DOMINUS) MEUS DE CELO AD TRA (TERRA) (D)ESCE (N)DIT. ME AUT(EM) DE TRA (DE TERRA) AD CE (COELUM) REVO(CARE) DIGAT (DIGNATUR)] wish to be crucified with my head towards the earth and my feet pointing towards heaven.'[81]

STYLISTIC CONSIDERATIONS

On the left Peter is bound to the cross, unlike Italian iconographic tradition (*cf.* Fig. 44), but not yet nailed to it.[82] The painter apparently did his best to render faithfully the effects of the binding ropes on Peter's red gown and those of gravity on his body in its peculiar upside-down position. As in the '*Quo Vadis*' scene, the cross is foreshortened, though here the rendering of the perspective is less successful.

Two fully armed soldiers occupy the centre of the composition. Their figures overlap each other in such a way as to make it rather difficult to distinguish between their respective limbs. Both appear to be directly involved in the execution. One of them, with legs spread strangely wide, scrutinizes the martyr attentively, shading his eyes with his left hand and supporting his enormous halberd with the same arm.

The other soldier seems to be reporting to his superiors about the execution. He is touching the left arm of the cross and pointing to it with his left hand. The commander of the execution platoon (Agrippa?) is a dark-bearded, weird, ugly creature with a long aquiline nose and contorted, rather oriental-looking features (Col. Pl. VII). He appears to be highly excited by the scene. His left hand is placed on the hilt of his great oriental scimitar.[83]

Like other villains in Friedrich Pacher's *oeuvre*, he wears a fantastic turban, which, in this case, strangely resembles an Indonesian *stupa*. The red flag he holds is inscribed with the Roman S.P.Q.R. A civilian dignitary, who also has a long, aquiline nose, is calmly observing the scene of the martyrdom, laying his hand on the shoulder of the contorted villain. His decorous dress – a red gown lined with fur, with golden clasps and a red helmet (a fantastic variant of the Phrigian cap) – might indicate that he is the supreme authority in the scene (Nero?).[84]

The dense grouping of the figures on a single plane is characteristic of Friedrich Pacher's treatment of pictorial space. The soldiers and their victim form a continuous frieze in the foreground.

Here Friedrich Pacher again proves his expert knowledge of medieval arms and armour. Whereas the turbaned halberdier in the centre wears the same type of armour already seen in the preceding panels, his two comrades wear characteristic knobbed armour, a variant of which appears in Michael Pacher's early work – the 'Departure of Pope Sixtus' from the *St Lawrence Altarpiece* (Österreichische Galerie, Vienna). Peter's facial features recur in those of St Joseph in 'The Circumcision of Christ' from the *Altarpiece of the Virgin* by Friedrich Pacher (Fig. 38). The right hand of the halberdier recalls that of the fallen Saul in the 'Conversion' scene, in which the landscape background is a variant of that in the 'Martyrdom of St Peter' (Col. Pl. IV).[85]

PHYSICAL STATE

There are three longitudinal cracks on the right side of the panel and the paint has fallen off in several places. The varnish has darkened, but some traces of an early drastic cleaning can still be observed.

LITERATURE

Döring, 1912, pp. 304–5, 1913, p. 142; Halm, pp. 582, 600, Pl. 3; Allesch, Pl. 77, p. 210; Bagatti, p. 144; Picirillo, Fig. on pp. 200, 202.

'The Parting of the Apostles'.

Oil and tempera on wood, gold-brocade ground. H. 124.6 cms, w. 105.4 cms (Pl. 25).

Although the two Princes of the Apostles appear together in this scene, it can obviously only have belonged to the right shutter. It is the first of the last two scenes from St Paul's life, derived from apocryphal legends related to the saint's Passion and Martyrdom. The subject is derived from the *Legenda Aurea*, which quotes a letter by Dionisius Areopagita to Timothy concerning the martyrdom of Sts Peter and Paul.[86]

This scene should not be confused with either of the other two episodes from the lives of the two Apostles – their meeting and their imprisonment.[87] The *Legenda Aurea* relates that 'when the moment of their separation came, Paul said to Peter: "*Peace be with thee, cornerstone of the Church, shepherd of the lambs* of Christ" [in the script-roll: PAX TECU(M) FU(N)DAME(N)TU(M) ECCL(ES)IAR(UM) PASTOR OVIUM (ET) AGNOR(UM)]. And Peter said to Paul: "*Go in peace, preacher of truth and good mediator of salvation to the just!*" [in the script-roll: VADE I(N) PACE P(RE)DICATOR BON(O)RUM MEDIA-(TOR) (ET) DUX SALUTI IUSTORUM].'[88]

The dual aspect of the subject seems to have suggested the bilateral symmetry of the composition. The two Apostles, each followed by a group of soldiers, face each other on both sides of the central axis of the composition, which is marked by a bearded soldier who is trying to separate them. The other soldiers, in accordance with the description in the *Legenda Aurea*, are doing their best to make the parting of the Apostles as unpleasant as possible. The two saints join their bound hands while their left hands struggle desperately. The four suffering hands form the geometric as well as the spiritual focus of the composition. The contrast between the physical appearance of the two Apostles enlivens the rigidity of the symmetrical composition. Peter's choleric temperament is well expressed in his striding posture, which recalls the '*Quo Vadis*' scene. His characteristic profile also recurs in the 'St Peter Walking on the Water' scene. His red gown is the same as that in the scene of his Martyrdom.

Paul's heavy, phlegmatic features are the very opposite of Peter's (Pl. 26). He is represented with his traditional physical attributes: middle-aged, tall, bald with a long dark beard. His figure is rather reminiscent of the priest in the 'Presentation to the Temple' from the *Altarpiece of the Virgin* (Innsbruck). His rather oriental features and his beautiful, sad eyes are particularly expressive. Paul, too, wears the same dark-green gown which will be worn by him in the following scene, that of his Martyrdom.

The violent enmity which surrounds the Apostles is broken by one of the soldiers who seems to be trying to dissuade his comrade from tugging at Peter's robe and from pulling his gown (Pl. 27).[89] The pennant decorated with the figure of a scorpion is a traditional emblem of the forces of evil (i.e., the Roman soldiers and the Jews) in fifteenth-century pictorial representations of the Passion of Christ, and particularly of the Crucifixion.[90] The characteristic triangular folds of the script-rolls also recur here. The landscape is restricted to a narrow stretch in the foreground, which is covered with particularly naturalistic and beautiful flowers (Pl. 28).

PHYSICAL STATE

There are two longitudinal cracks on the left side of the panel. The varnish has become dirty and opaque, but earlier damage to the original paint can still be seen underneath, particularly on Paul's gown. The ugly design of Paul's halo is probably the result of the work of a restorer who misinterpreted the reflection of the Apostle's head on the halo (see Pl. 21) as part of a cross (which is out of place here in any case).

LITERATURE

Halm, p. 584, Pl. 6; Döring, 1912, p. 304; 1913, pp. 142–4; Allesch, Pl. on p. 207; Bagatti, p. 144; Picirillo, pp. 203–4, Fig. on p. 200.

'The Martyrdom of St Paul'.

Oil and tempera on wood, gold-brocade ground. H. 124 cms, w. 106 cms (Pl. 29).

The iconography is chiefly derived from the *Legenda Aurea*.[91] There are no dialogues and, consequently, no script-rolls are used. The martyr is still kneeling on the left with hands joined in prayer. Blood spouts forth from his open veins. A red gown covers his green dress, and its angular folds recall those in 'The Martyrdom of St Katherine' (Fig. 33).

The tremendous blow of the executioner's great sword had just sent Paul's head to the ground, where it bounced three times. Each time the head touched the ground, says the legend, a spring gushed forth. The three miraculous fountains can be seen in the foreground.[92] The head, rendered in a characteristic Mantegnesque foreshortening, rests on the third fountain in the lower right corner of the panel.

As in 'The Conversion of Saul', the composition is dominated by a diagonal movement, beginning at the executioner's shoulder and running along the sword downwards to the severed head in the bottom right-hand corner. The strange, striding posture of the executioner, which repeats the contour of his victim, recurs in other martyrdom scenes by Friedrich Pacher.[93]

As far as physical feasibility is concerned, the representation of the decapitation is hardly acceptable. A pirouette like that performed by the executioner with his heavy sword would certainly have sent him straight to the ground, and his sword, which is partly overlapped by a soldier's leg, could not have reached that point without cutting through this leg as well as through the martyr's raised hands. However, the spectator will hardly notice such minor incongruities. He

will, rather, be impressed by the pictorial realism
of the scene and by the powerful image of the executioner (Pl. 30), perhaps the most vigorous and expressive in a long series of picturesque hangmen
and torturers that appear in Friedrich Pacher's
altarpieces.

The two curious hats which appear on the red
flag (the standard of which constitute the central
vertical axis of the painting) recall both medieval
Jews' hats and soldiers' helmets. They have no
doubt the same emblematic meaning as the scorpion in the preceding scene. This motif frequently
appears in fifteenth-century German representations of the Passion of Christ (Fig. 48).[94]

On the right a dense group of soldiers forms
a massive menacing block from which clubs,
spearheads, halberds, pointed helmets and feathers
protrude and pierce the skyline.[95] The two-
dimensional conception of the group is characteristic of Friedrich's archaistic style. The facial features
of the standard-bearer (Fig. 49) are reminiscent of
those of the hangman, but he looks more humane
and even seems to sympathize with the martyred
saint. His expressive features recall a prophet in
the frescos of Bozen (Fig. 50).[96]

Another soldier seems to be drawing the attention of a bearded man on the right to the head of
the saint and to the miraculous fountain. This
man is the ubiquitous villain who appears in every
scene of martyrdom painted by Friedrich Pacher.
Here he might represent either Nero or Agrippa

(Pl. 31).[97] The three figures in the middle distance
recur in the backgrounds of several scenes in
the *St Wolfgang Altarpiece* and in other works
by Michael and Friedrich Pacher.[98]

The foreground is studded with the usual naturalistic flowers. The round porch in the wall is identical with that found in 'The Parting of the Apostles'.
This painting is related particularly to two other
scenes of martyrdom painted by Friedrich (Figs
33, 47).[99] The two trees on the left are analogous
in form and style to those in the two paintings
of 'The Flight into Egypt' by Michael Pacher
(St Wolfgang) and Friedrich (Innsbruck [Fig. 34]).

PHYSICAL STATE

There are two longitudinal cracks in the panel.
The left one was further enlarged by a recent
restoration of the frame. The colour has come
off in several parts, particularly from the saint's
gown. The varnish has become yellow and opaque,
but the original paint underneath is generally
well preserved.

LITERATURE

Halm, pp. 584–6, Pl. 7; Döring, 1912, pp. 305–6;
1913, p. 144; Allesch, Pl. on p. 215; Bagatti, p. 144;
Picirillo, pp. 202–3, Figs on p. 203.

List of Text Figures

Text Figures

I 2

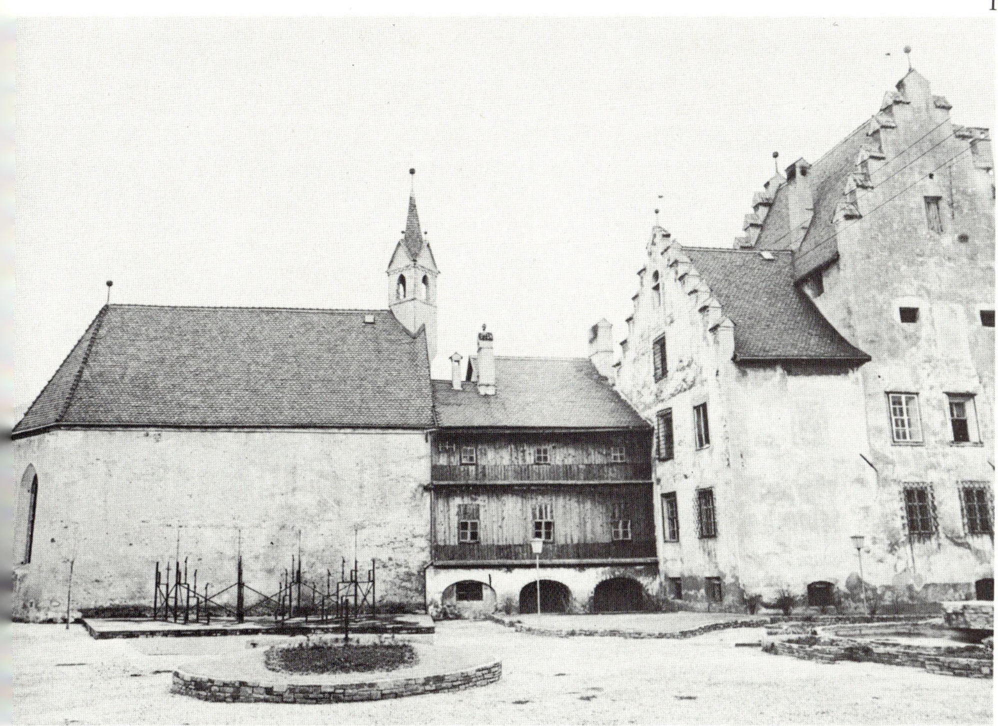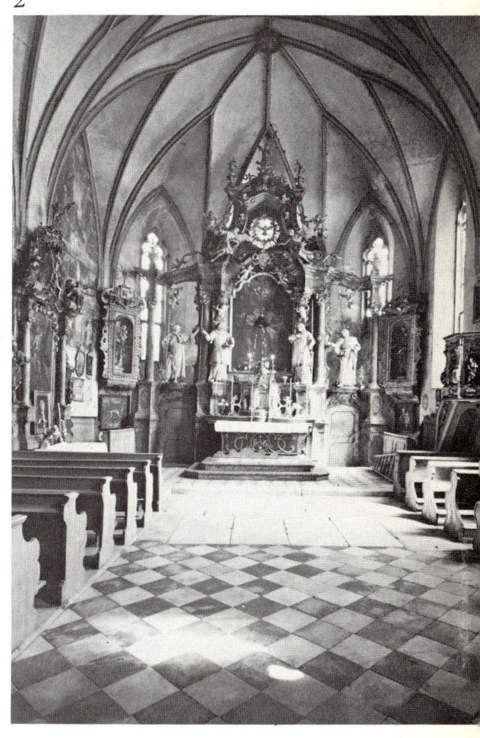

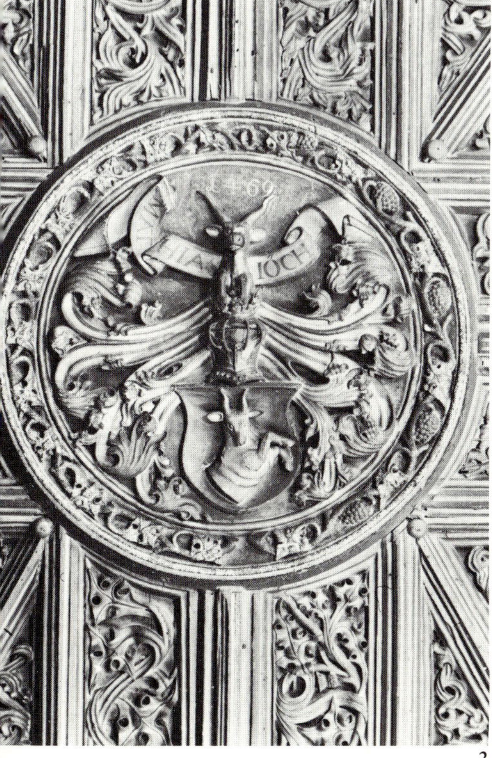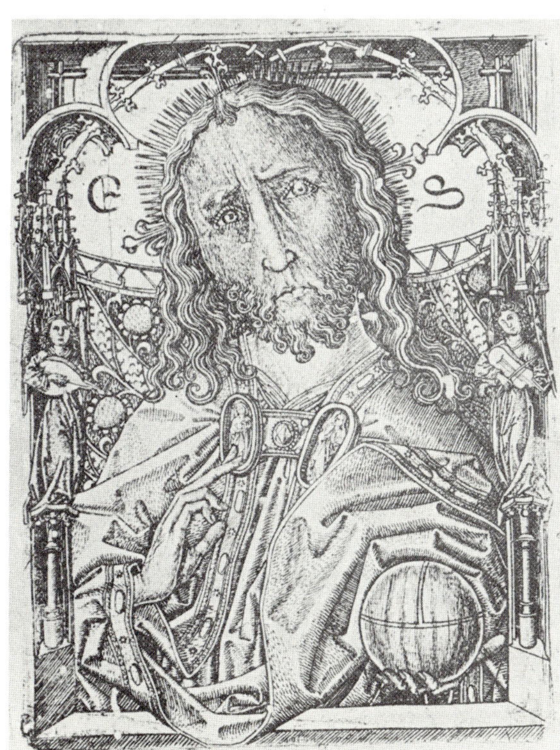

3 4

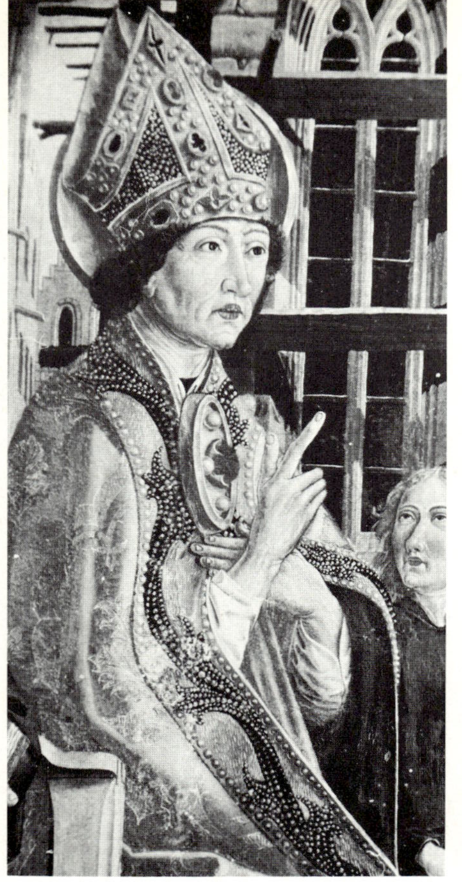

6

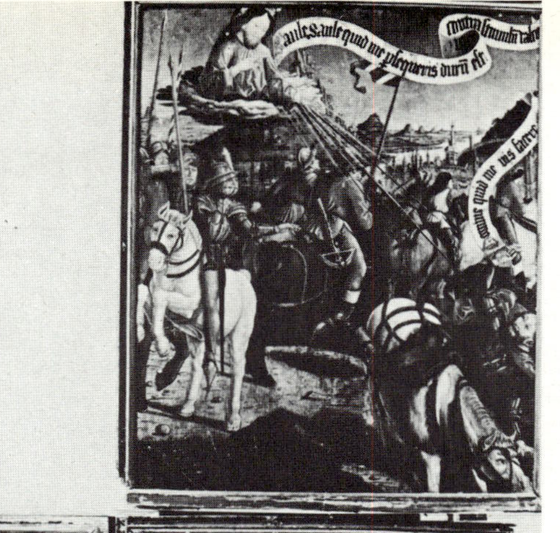

MISSING

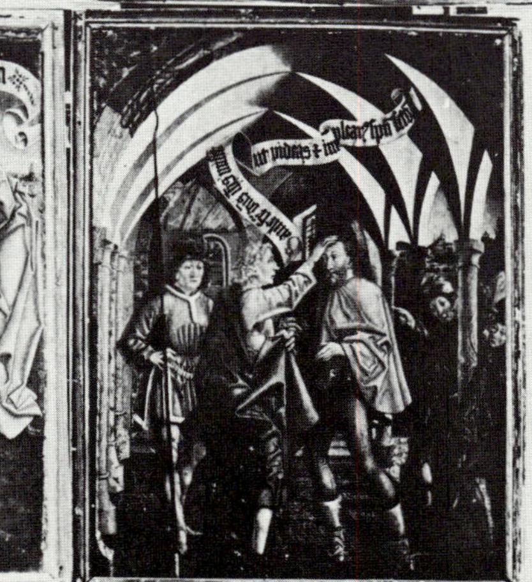

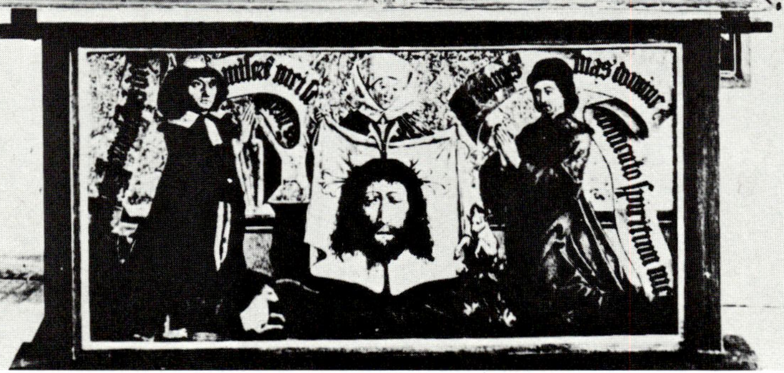

7

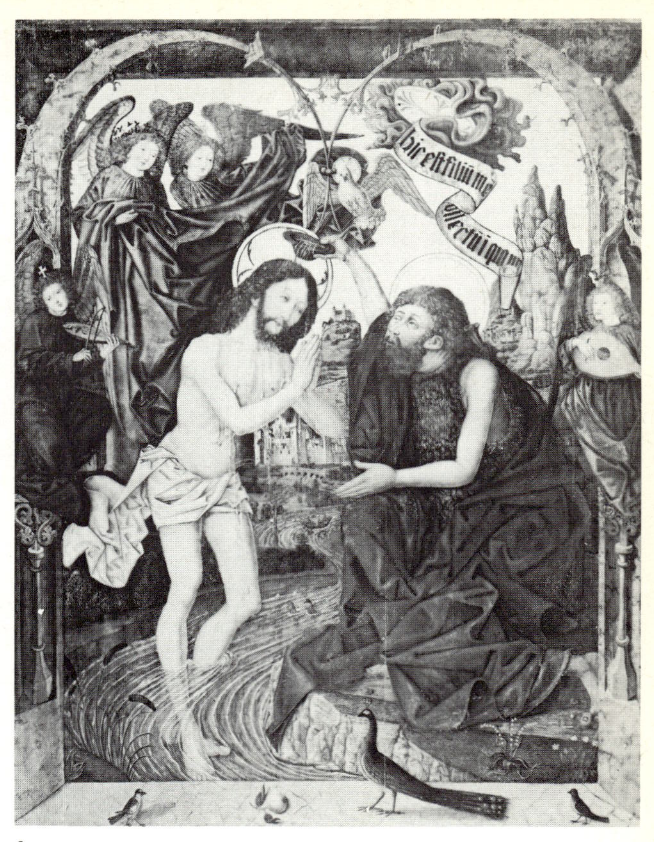

5

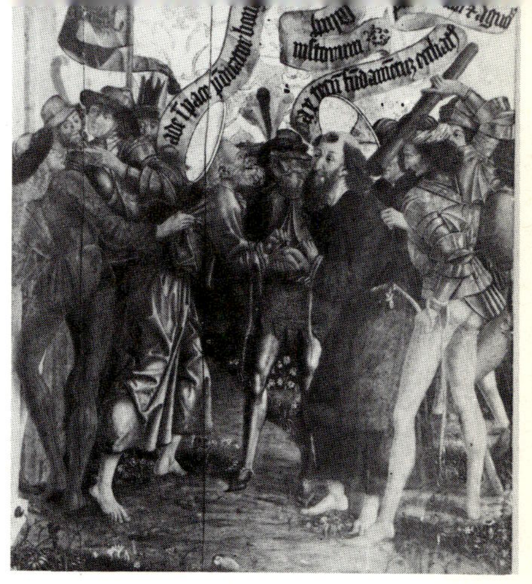
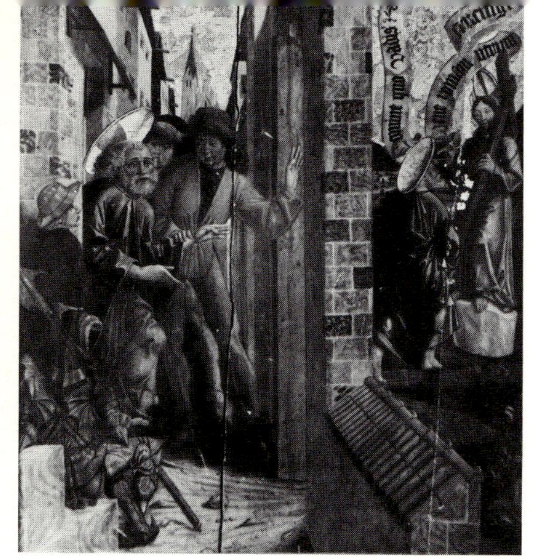
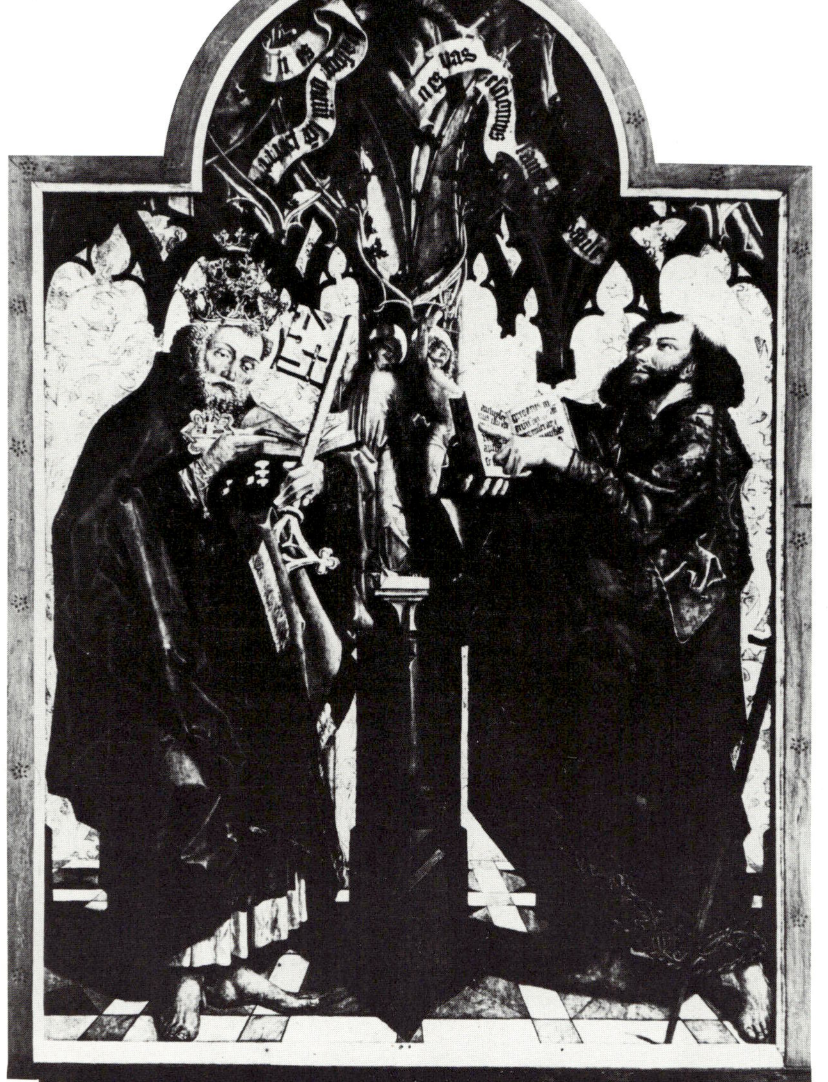
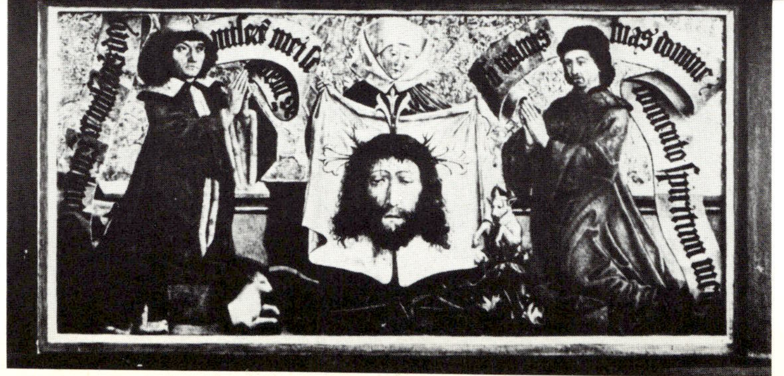
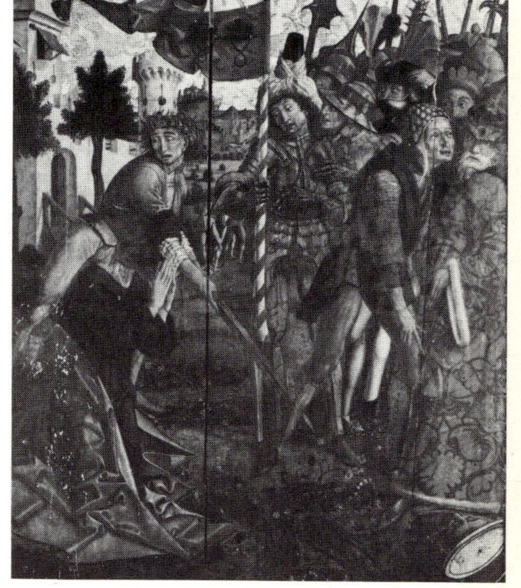
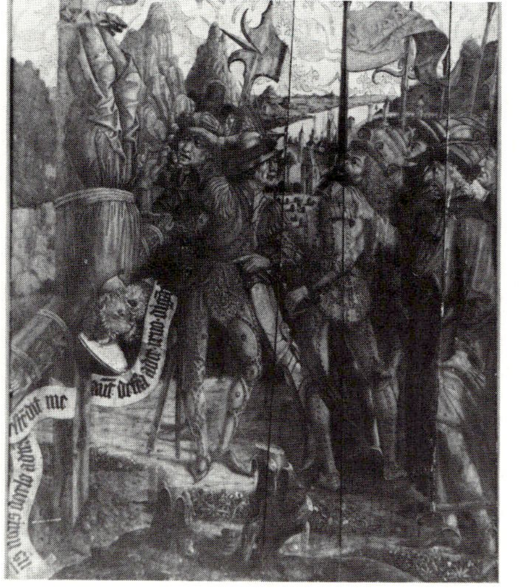

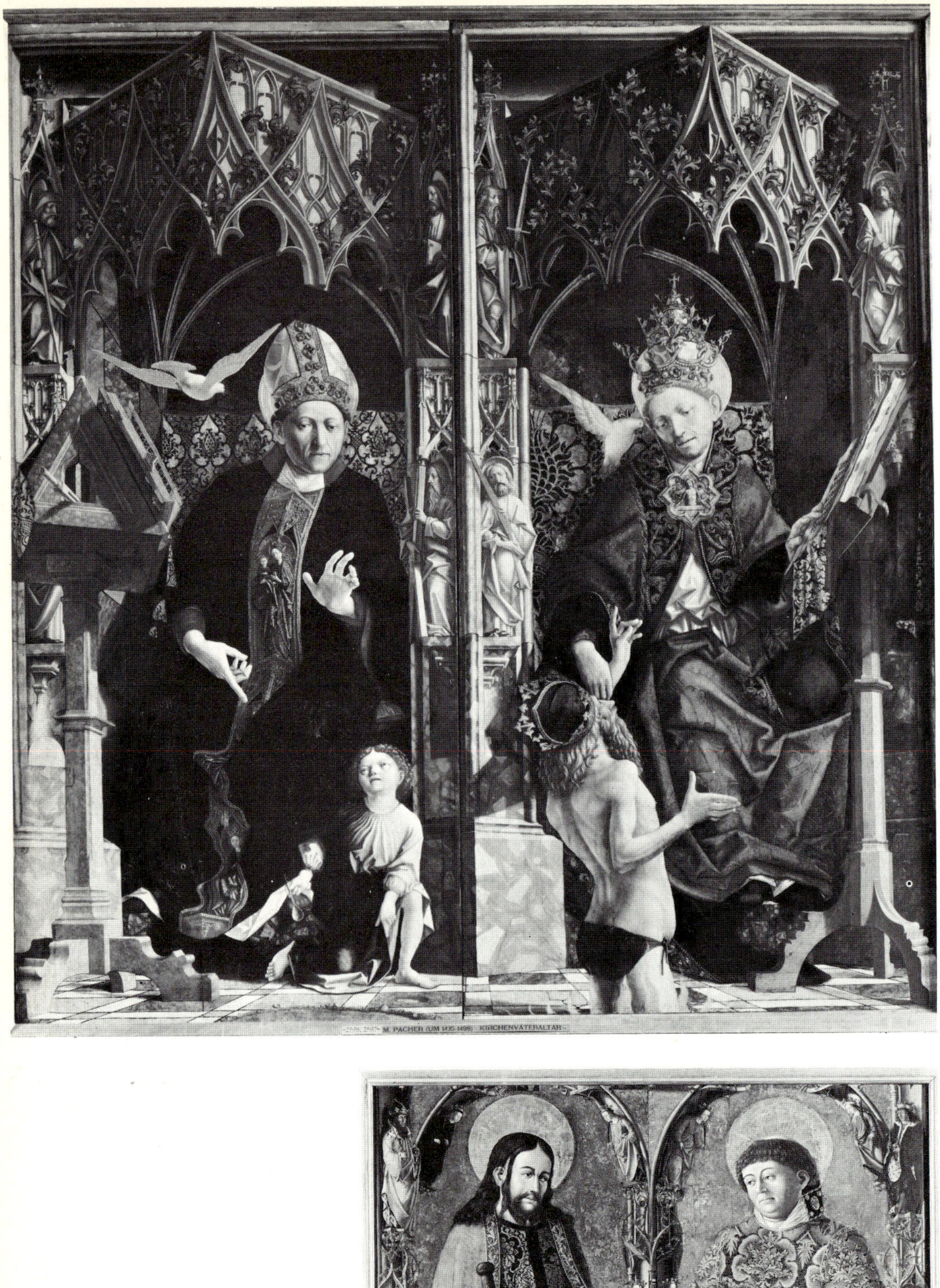

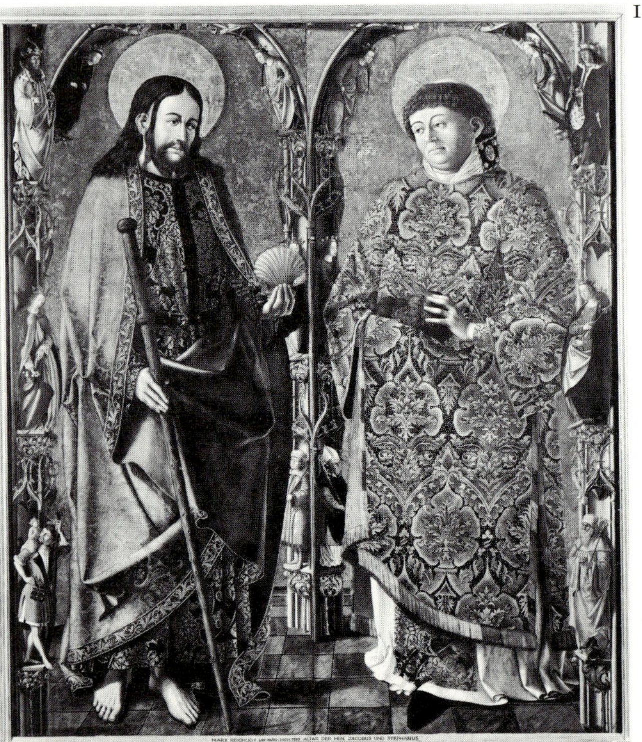

M. PACHER (UM 1435-1498) KIRCHENVÄTERALTAR

9

10

MARX REICHLICH (UM 1460-NACH 1520) ALTAR DER HHL. JACOBUS UND STEPHANUS

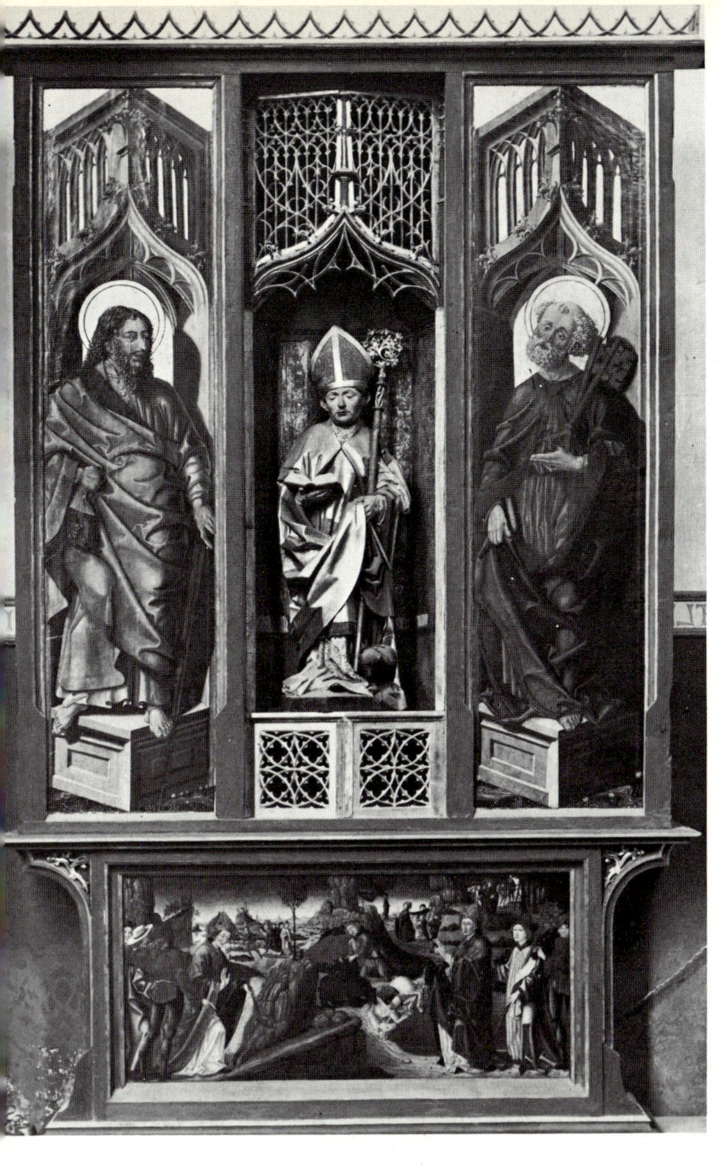

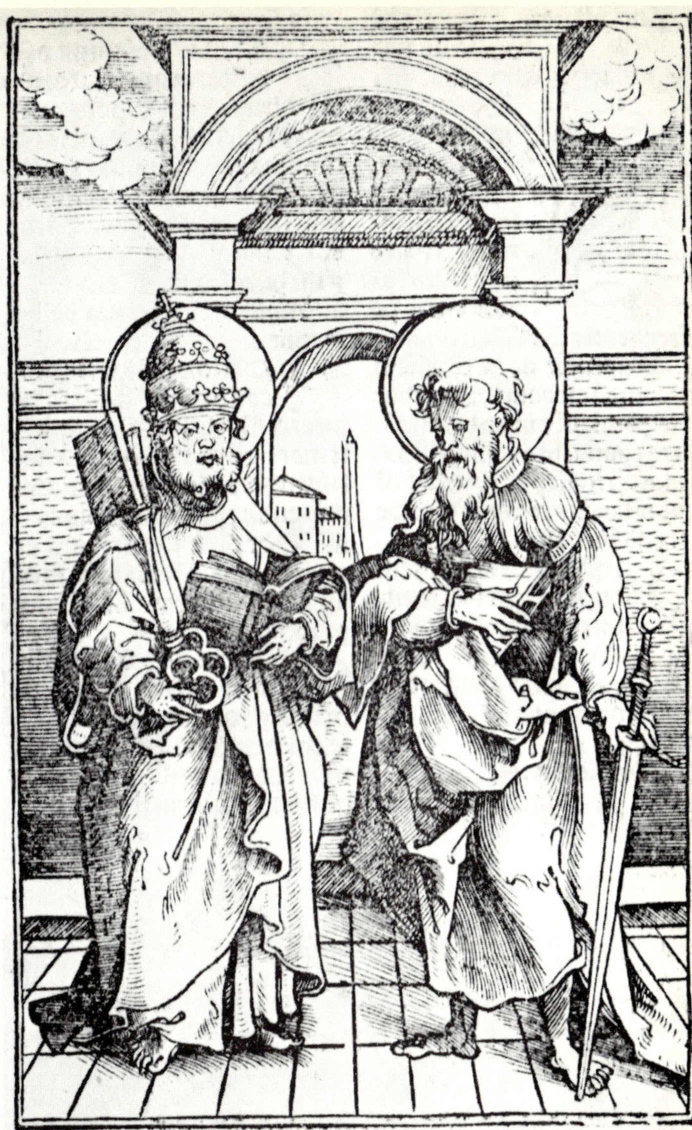

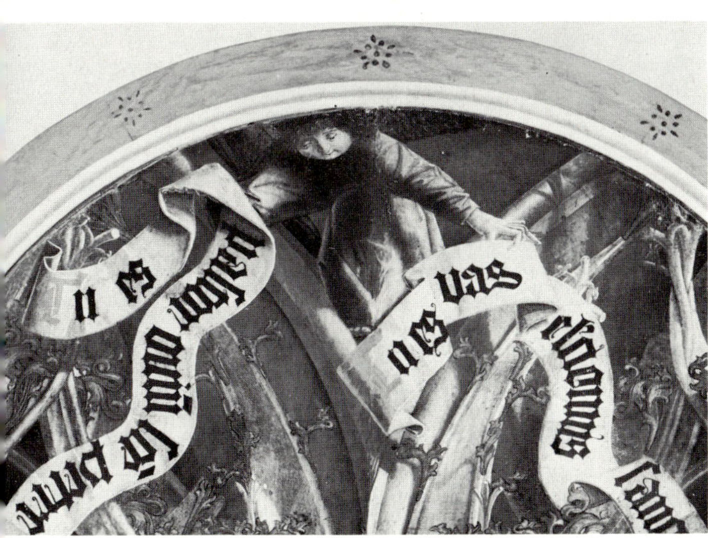

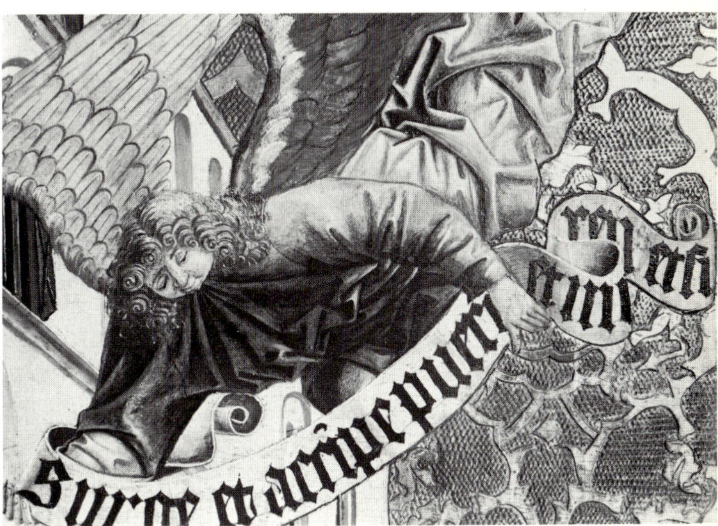

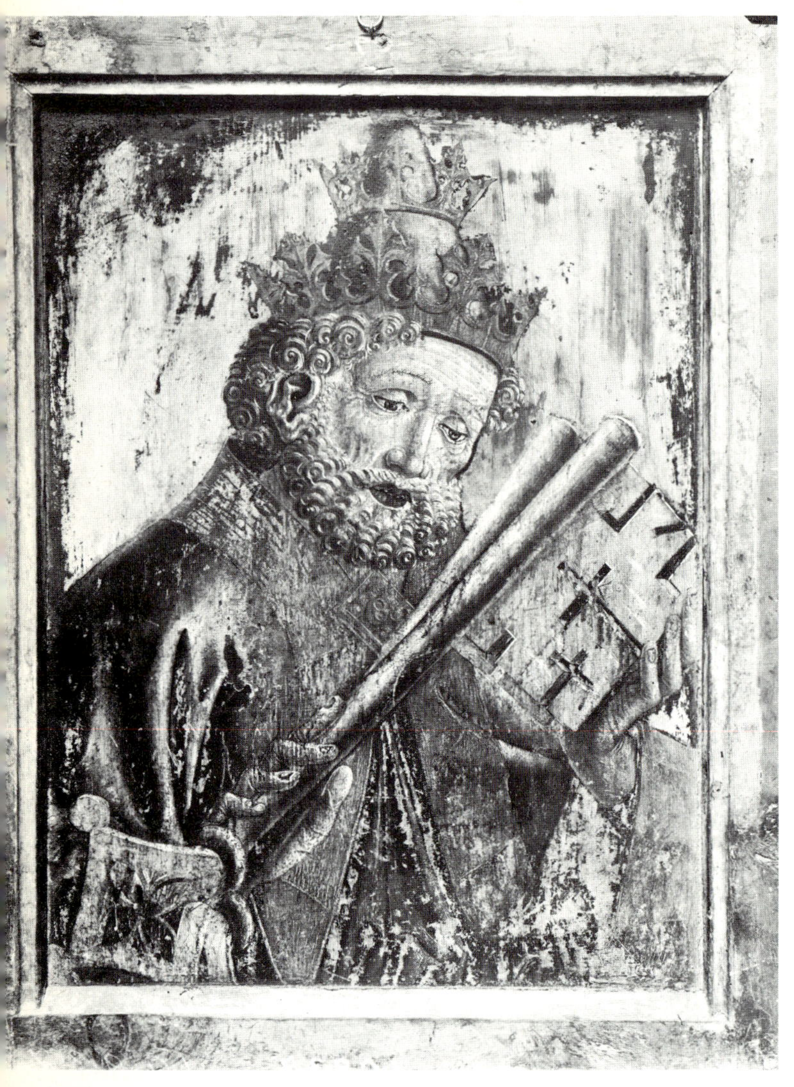

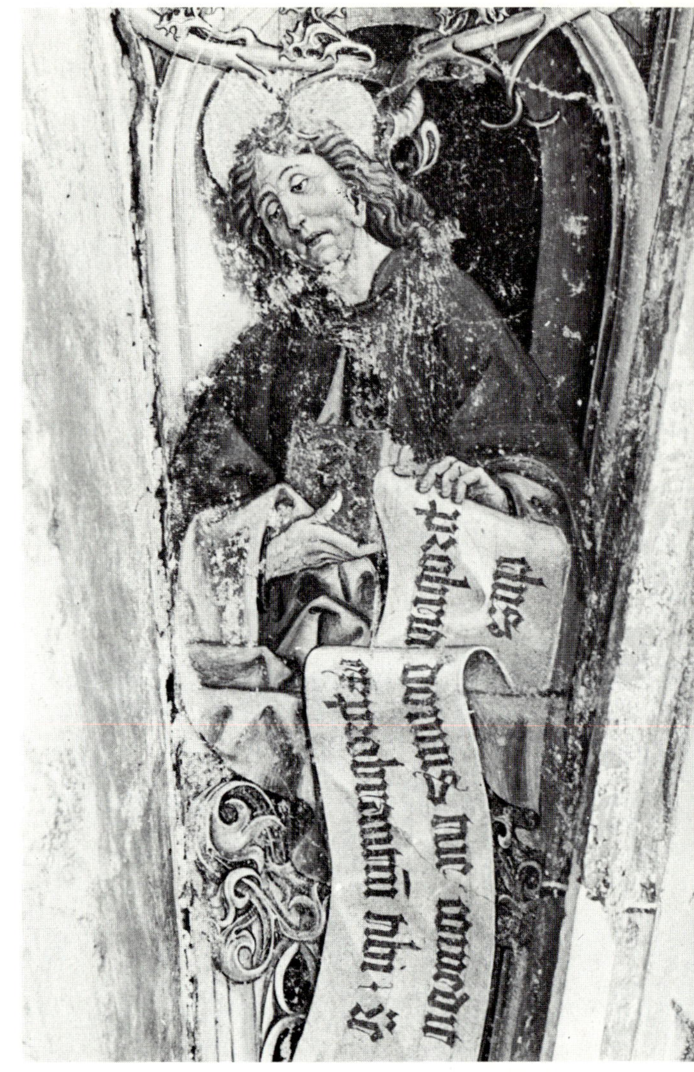

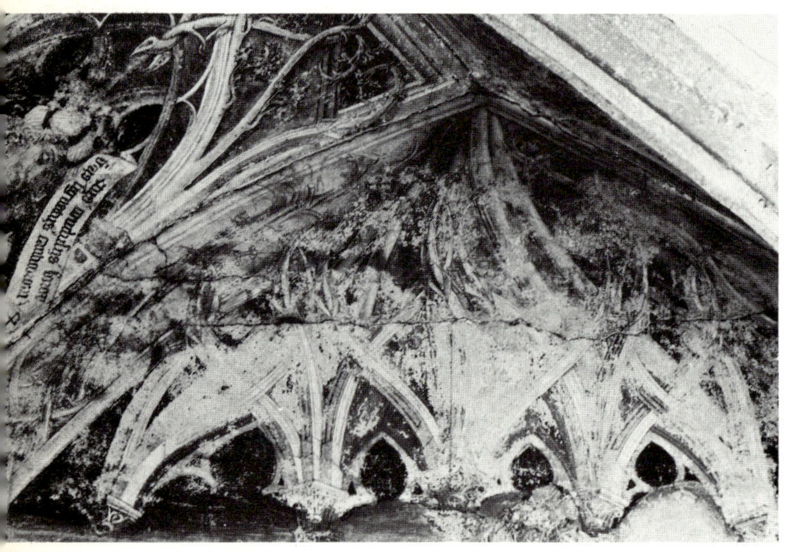

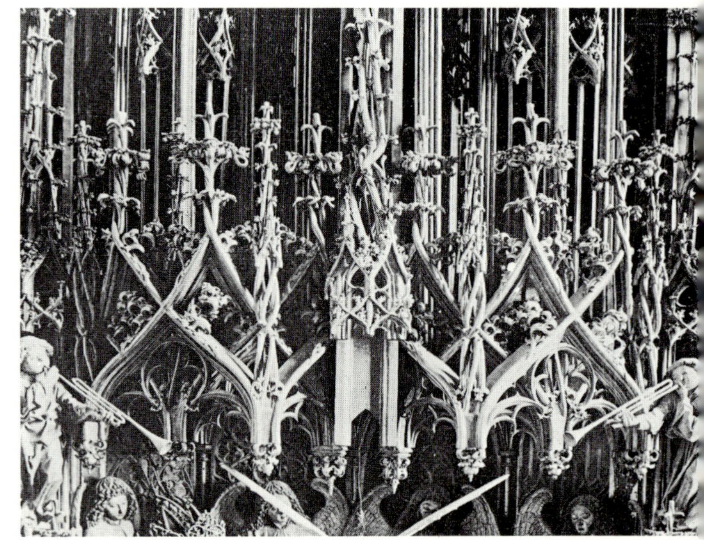

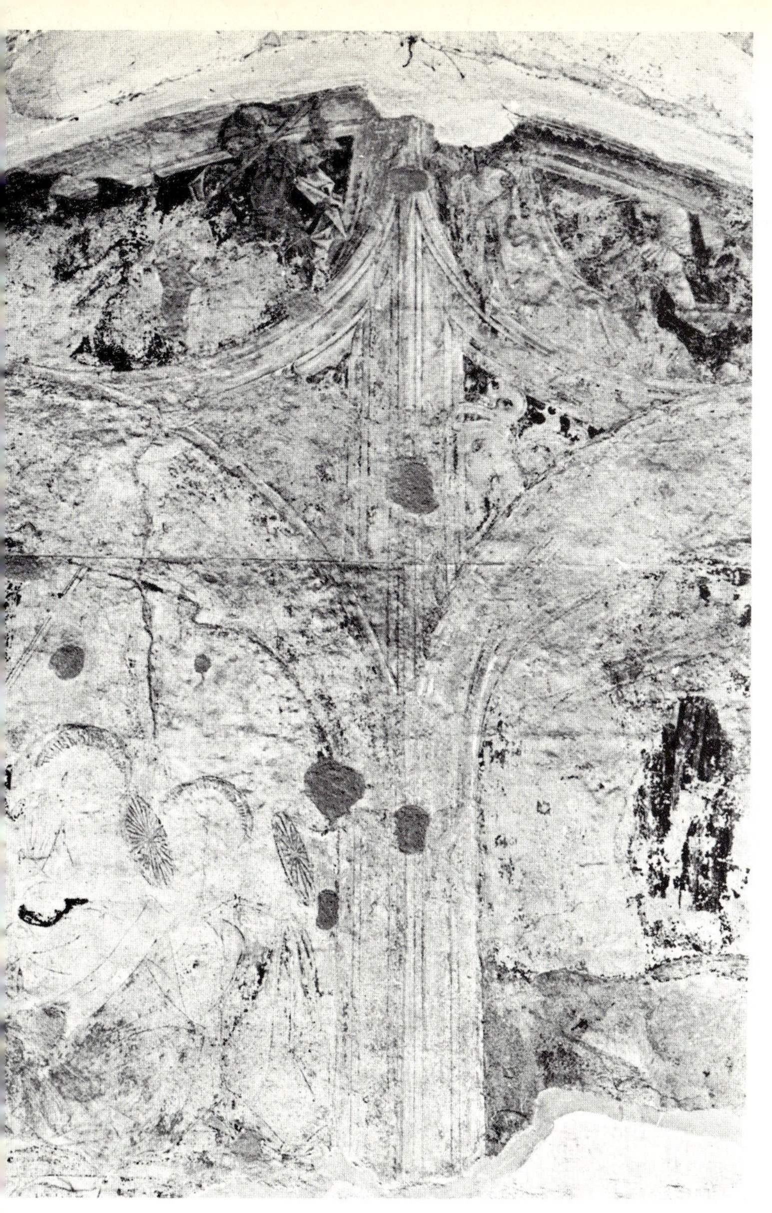
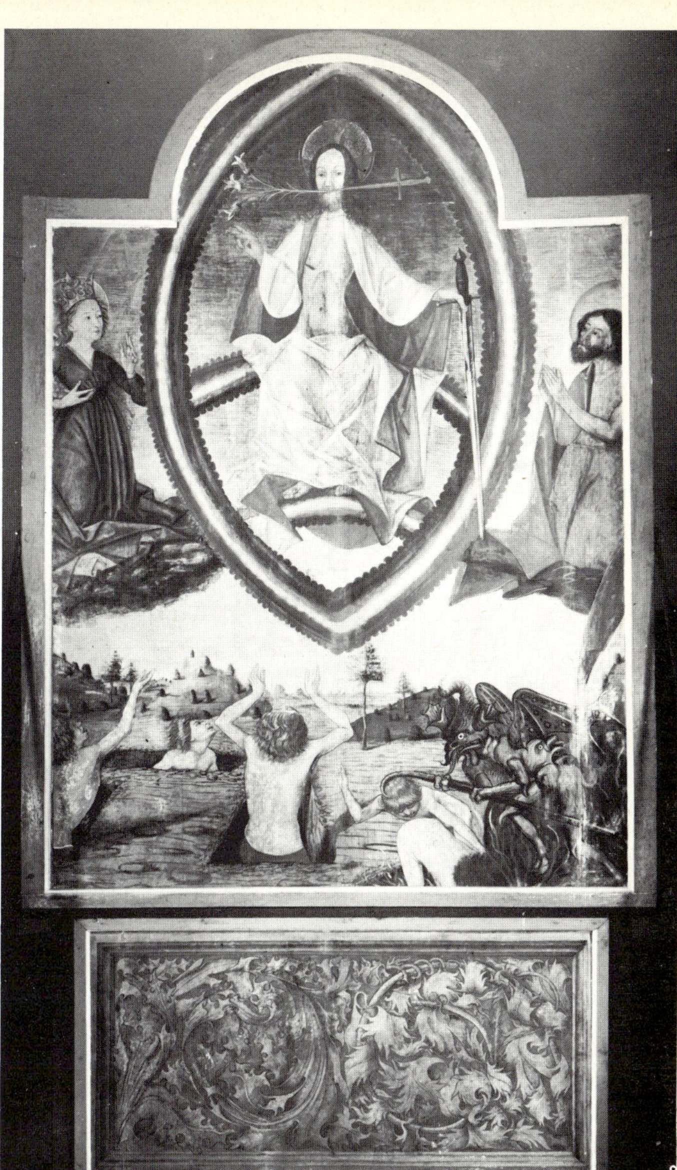

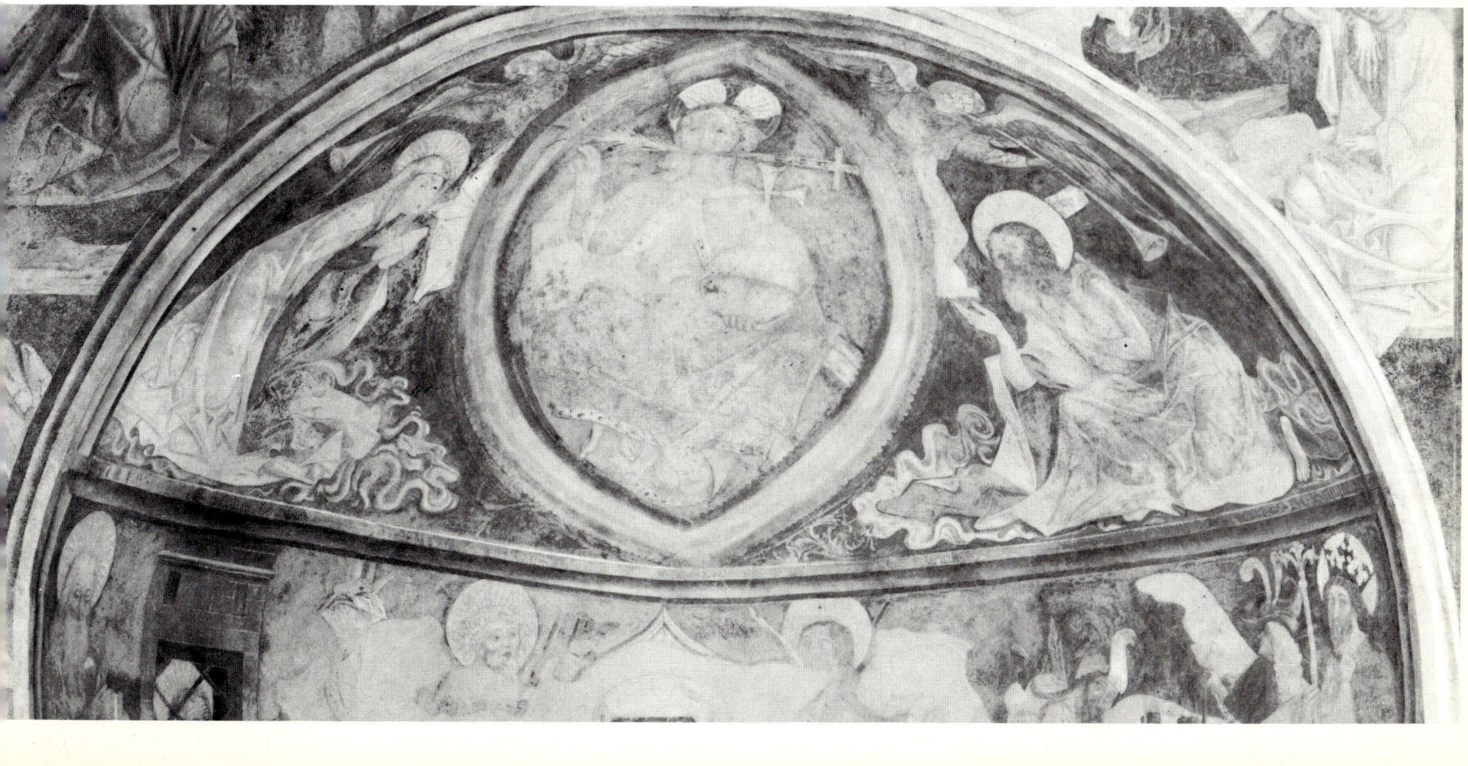

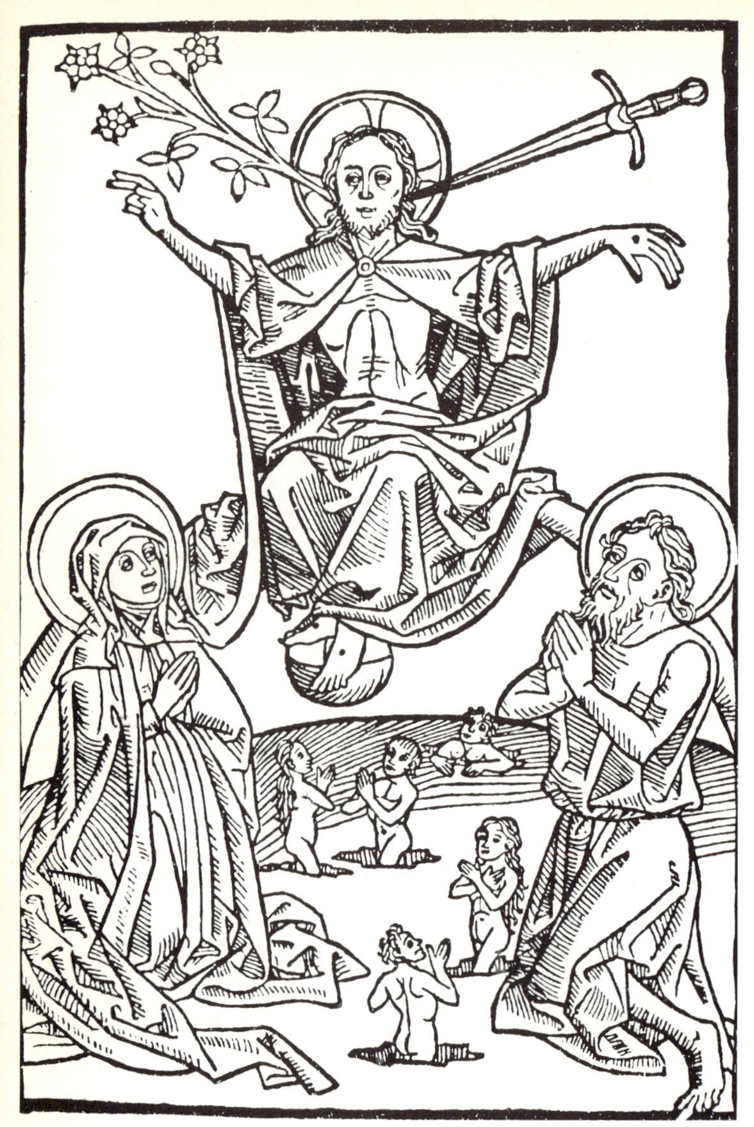

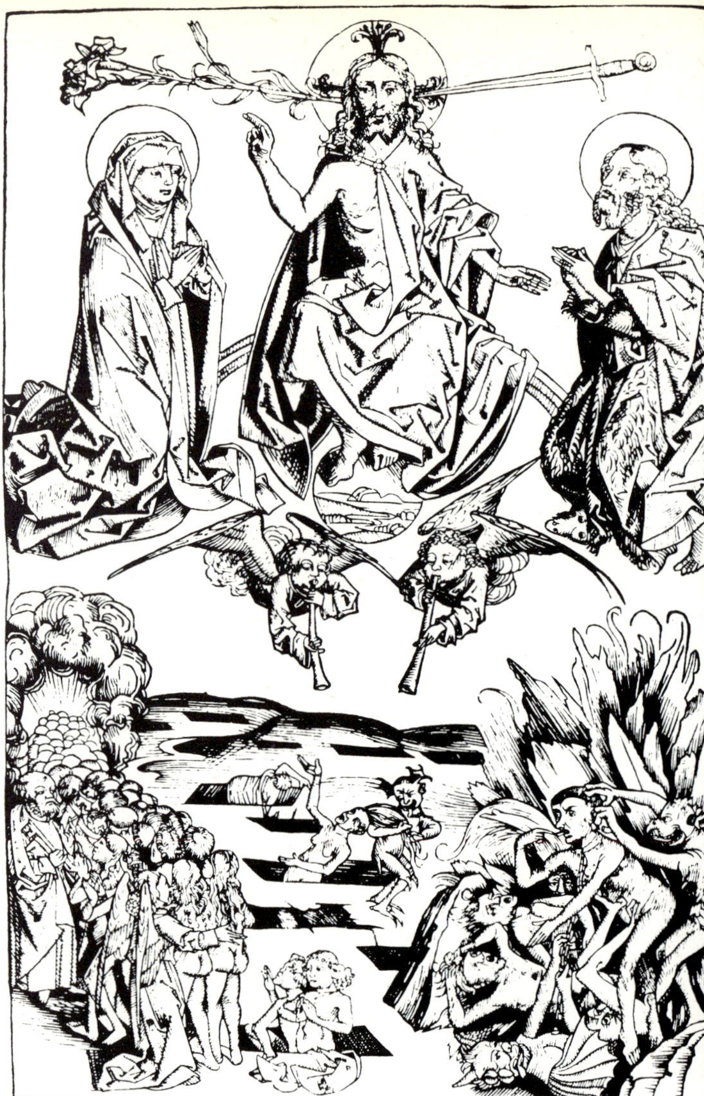

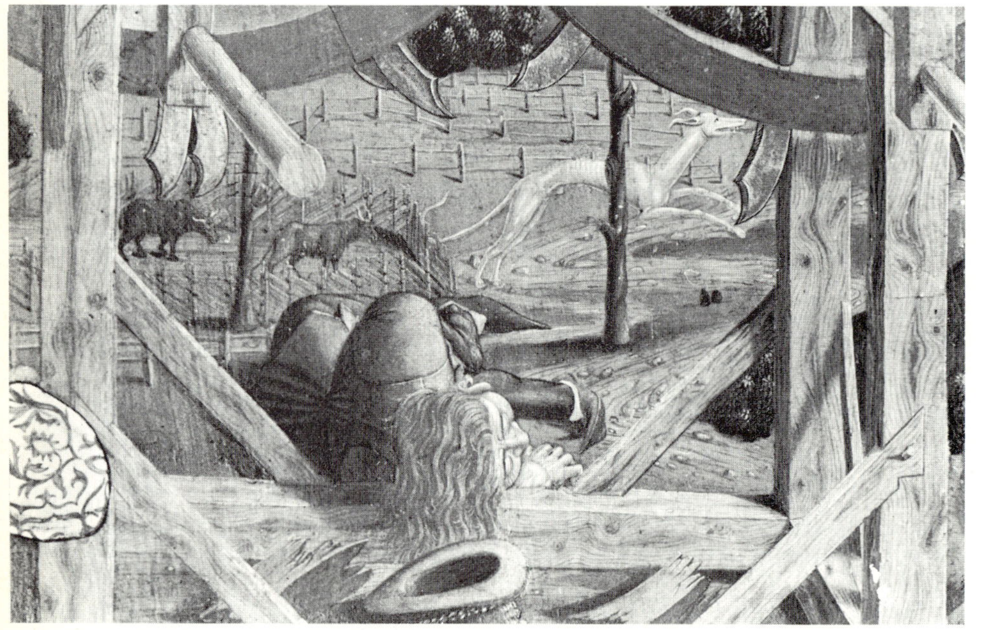

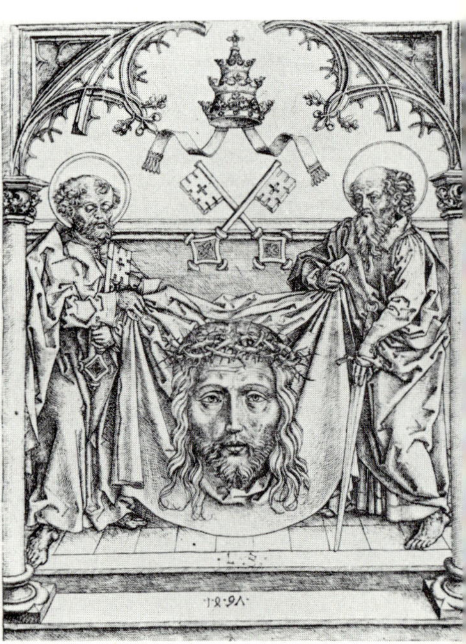

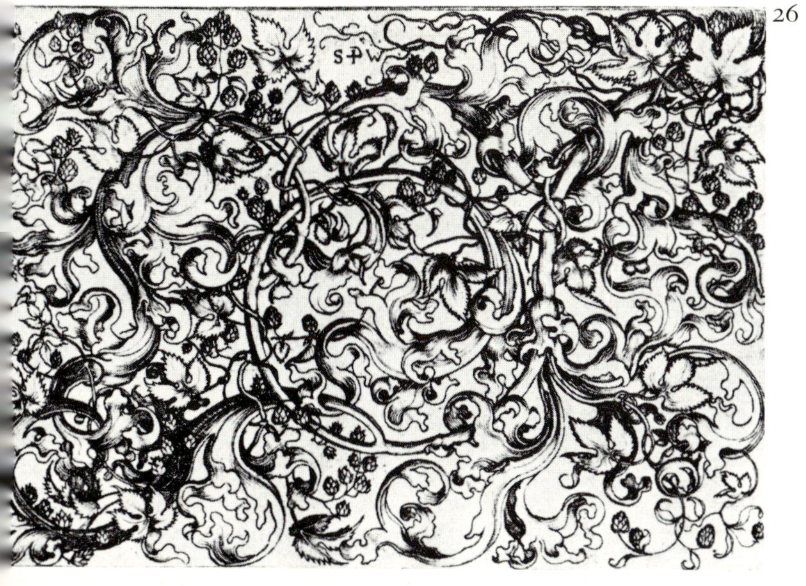

26

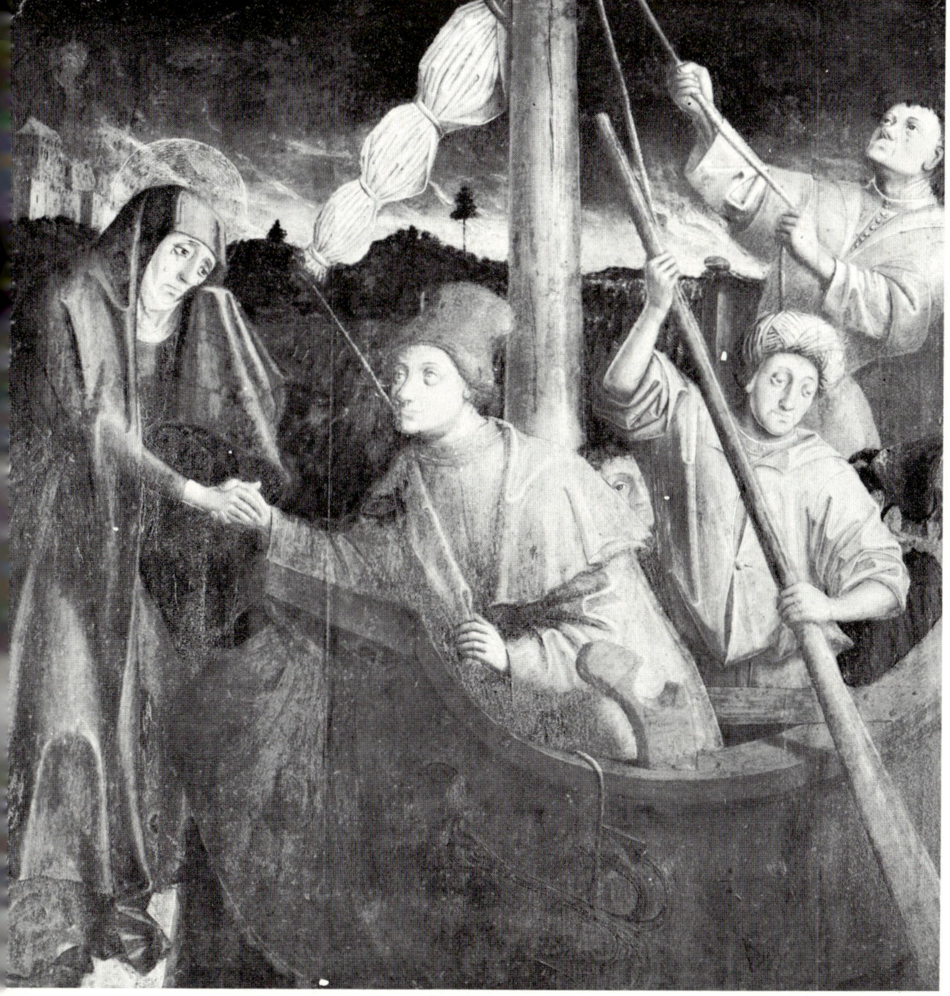

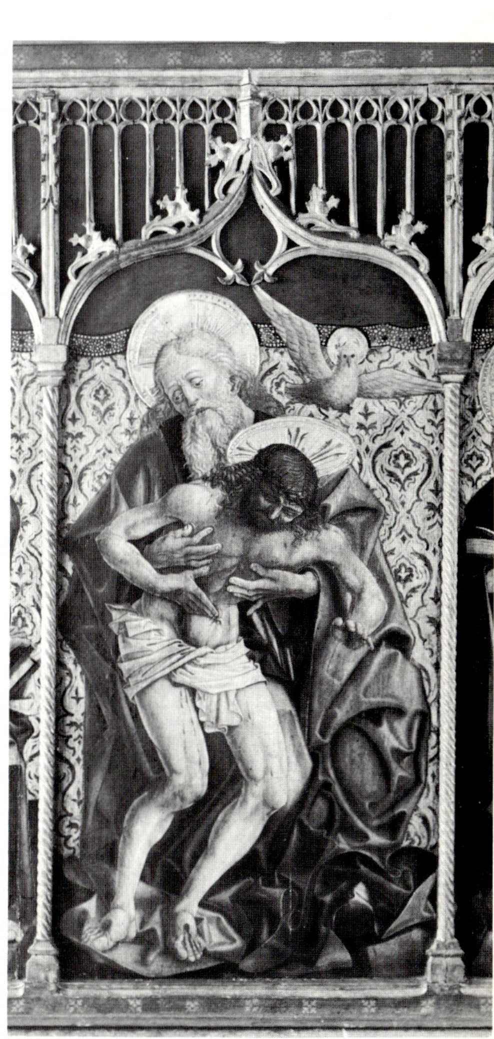

27   28

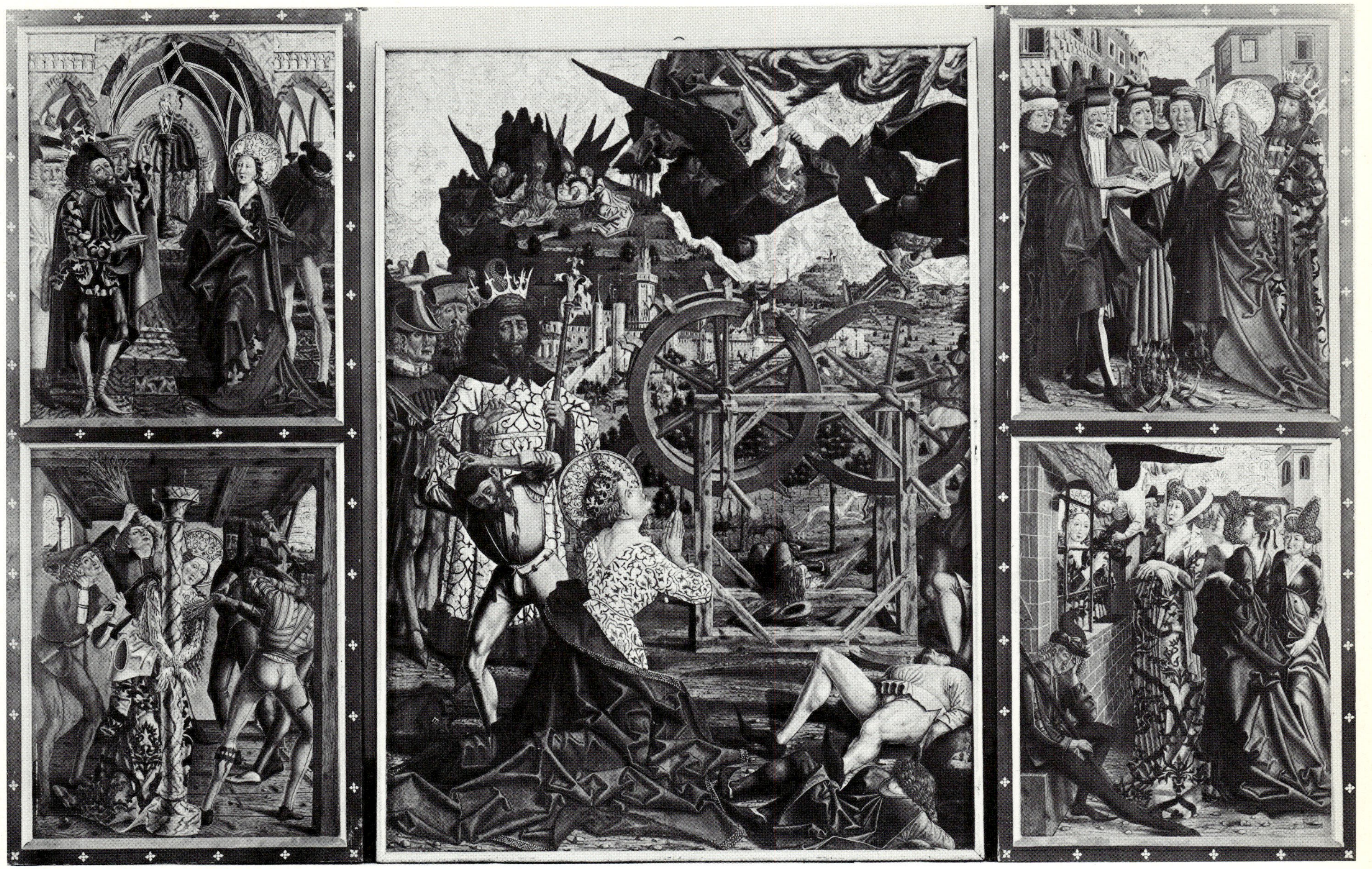

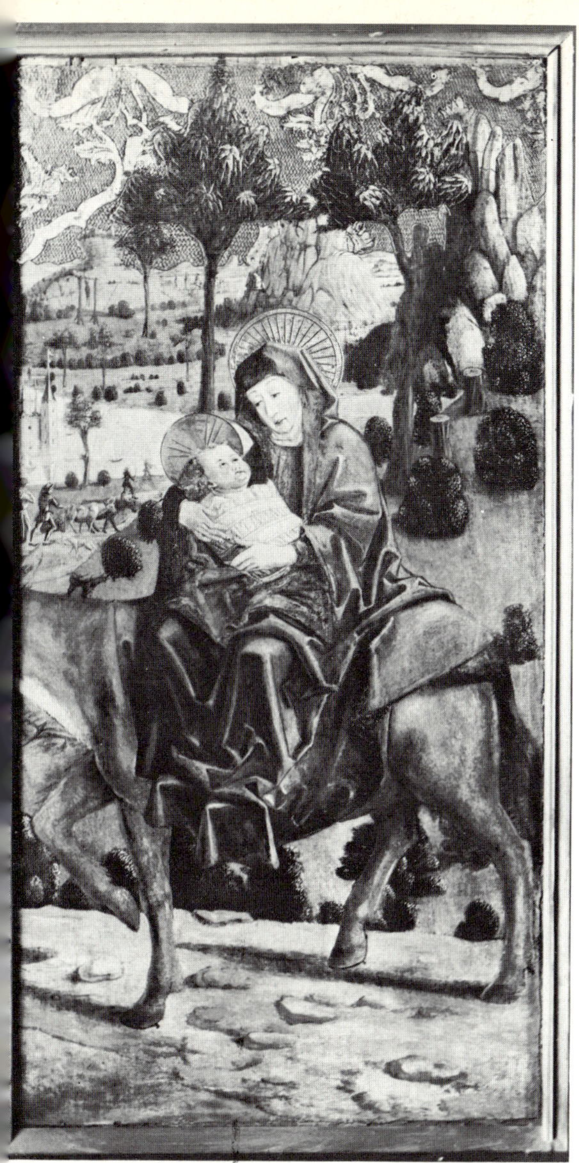

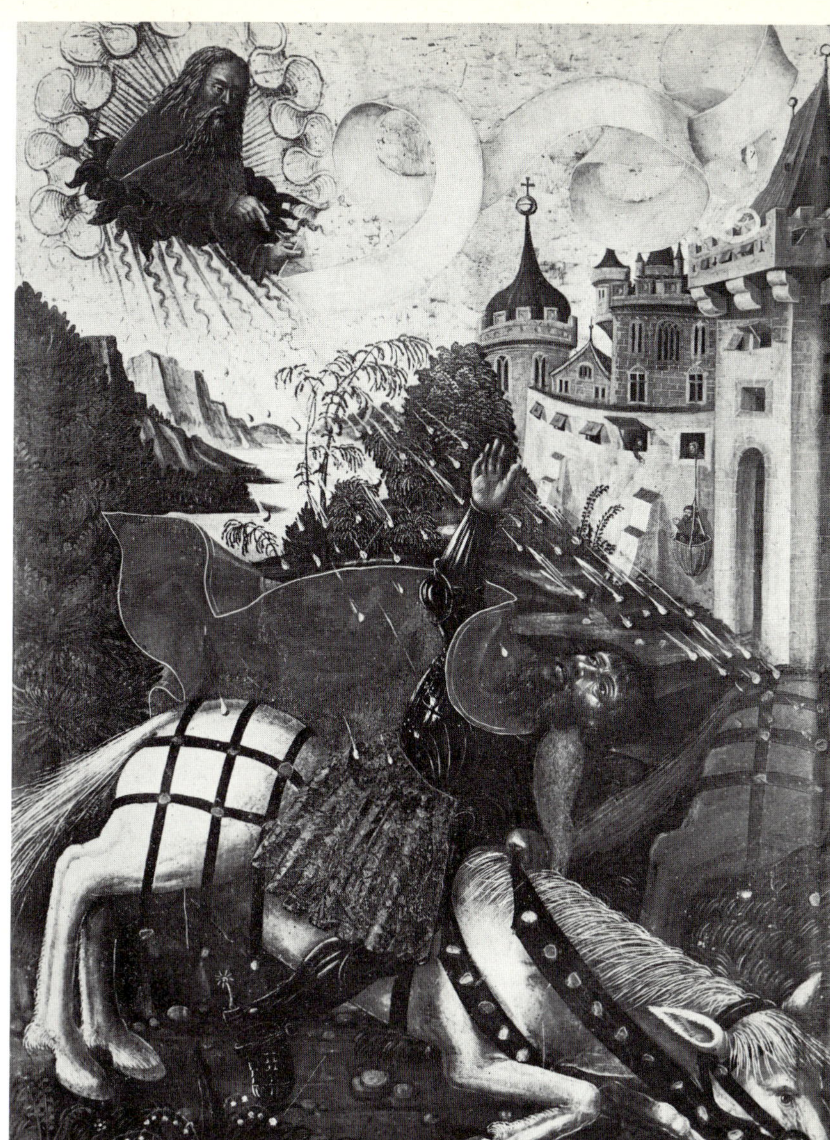

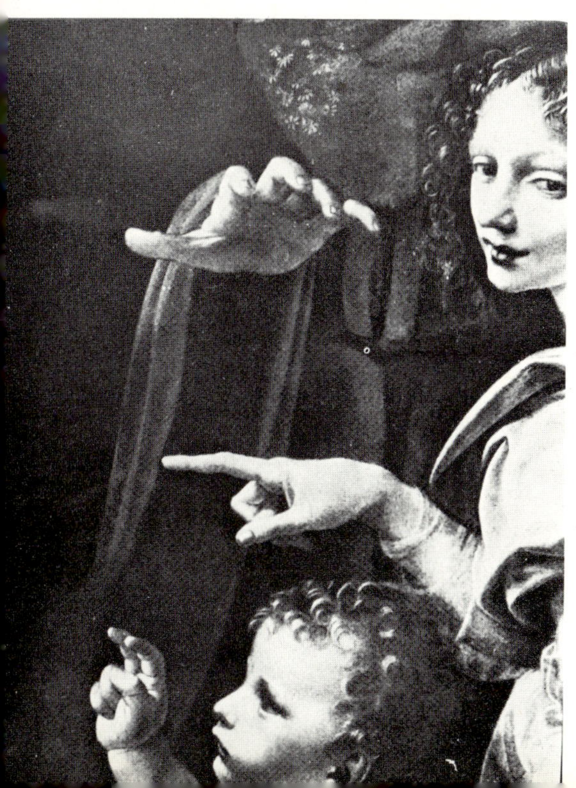

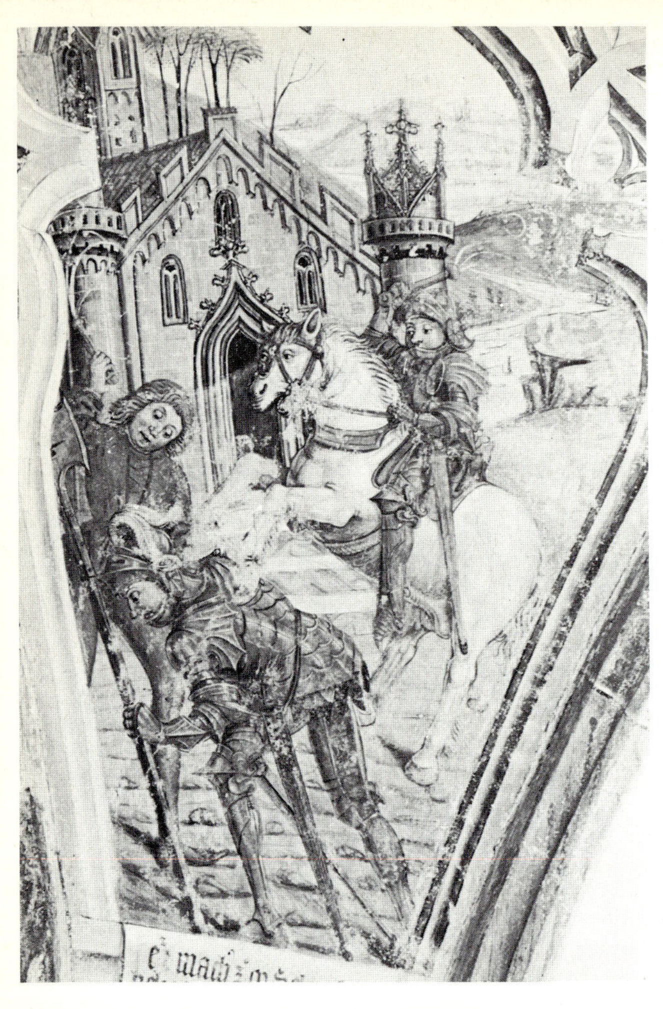

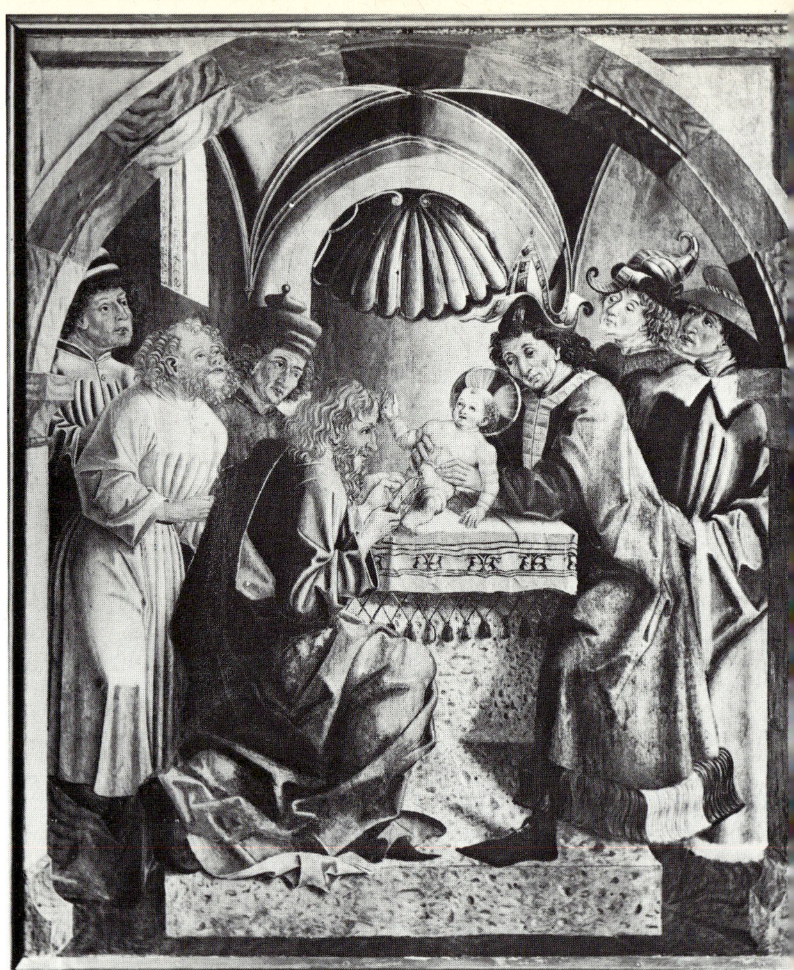

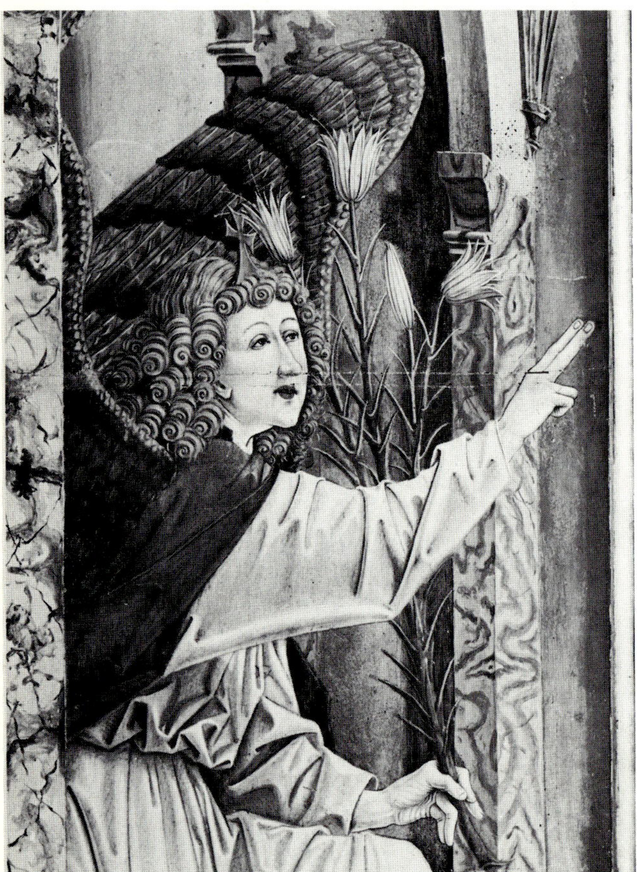

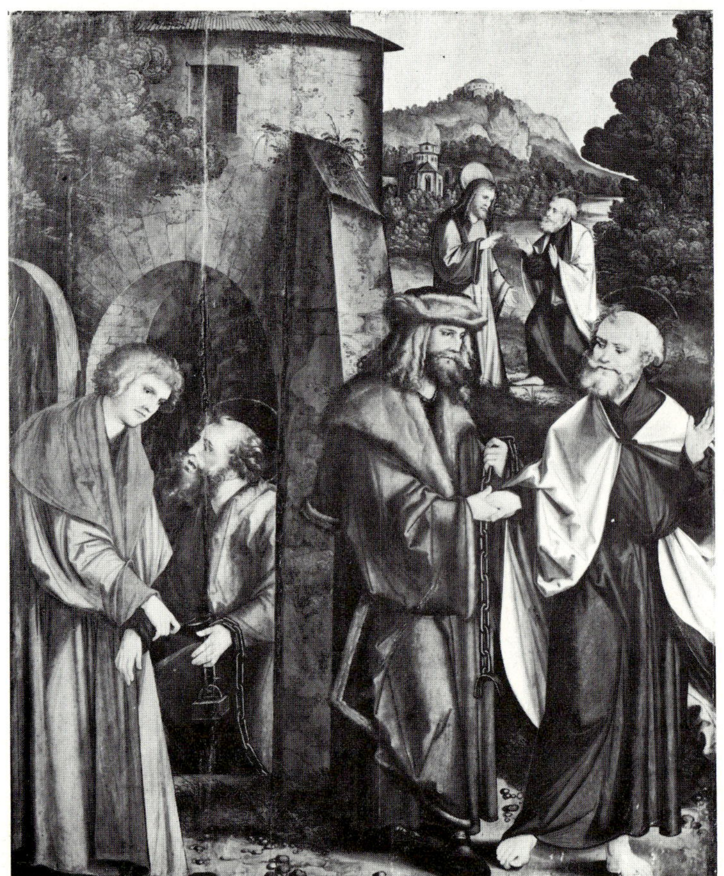

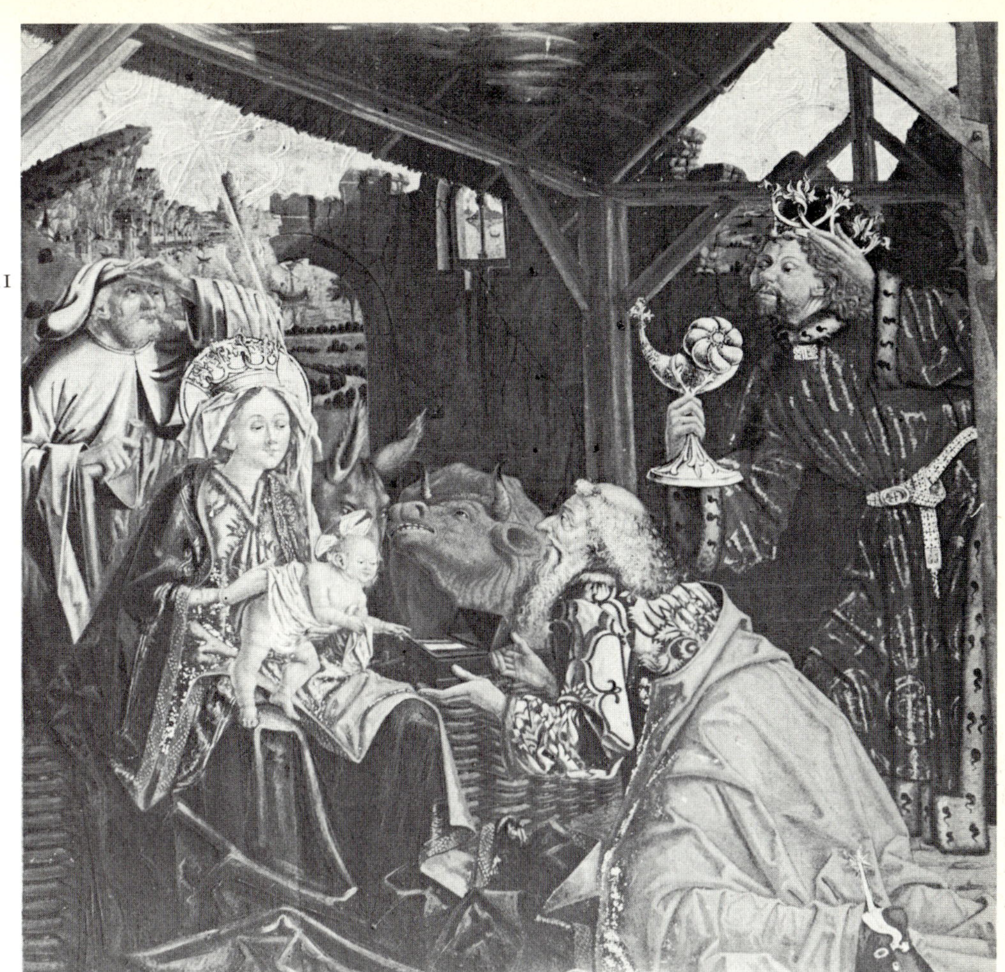

41

42

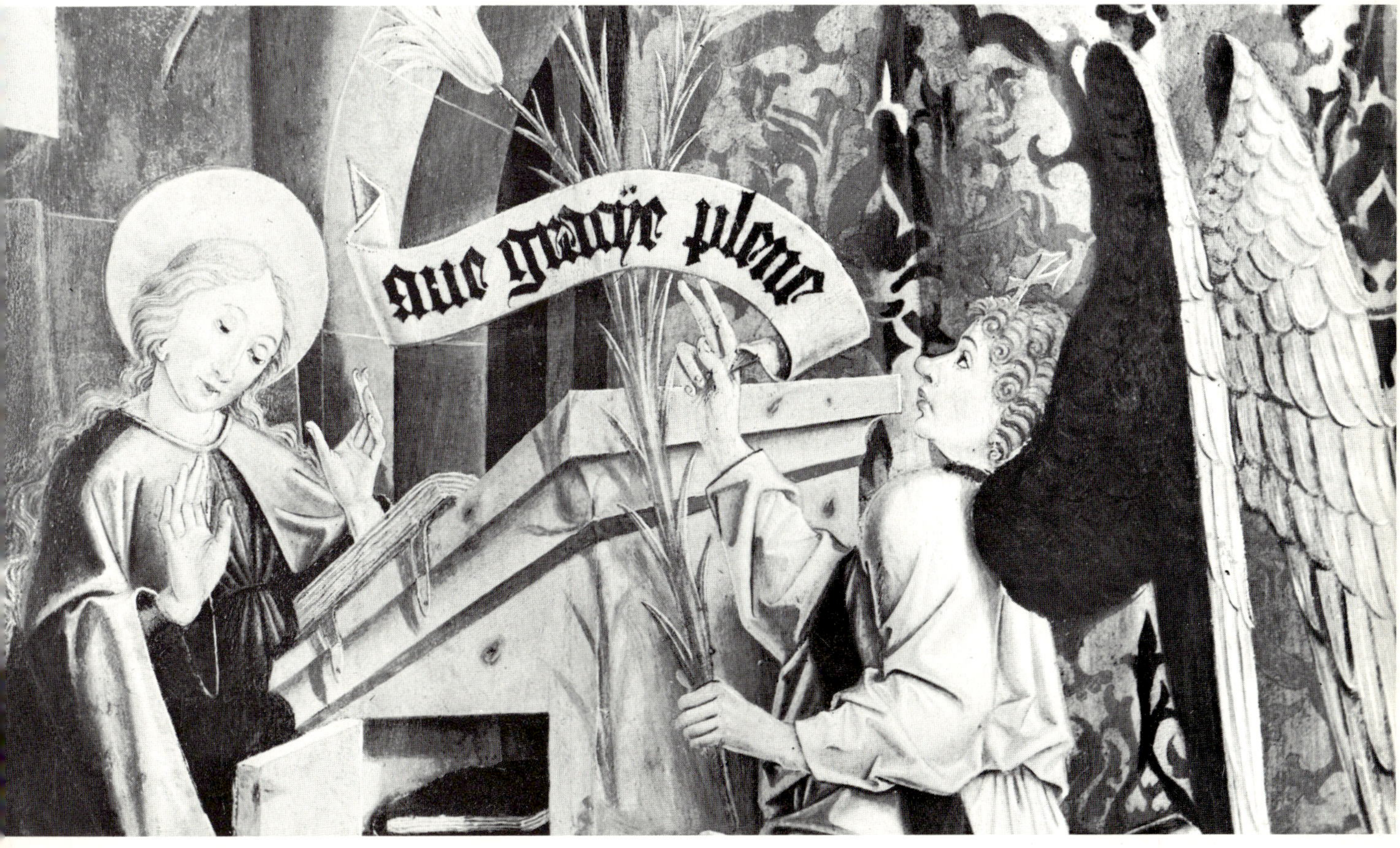

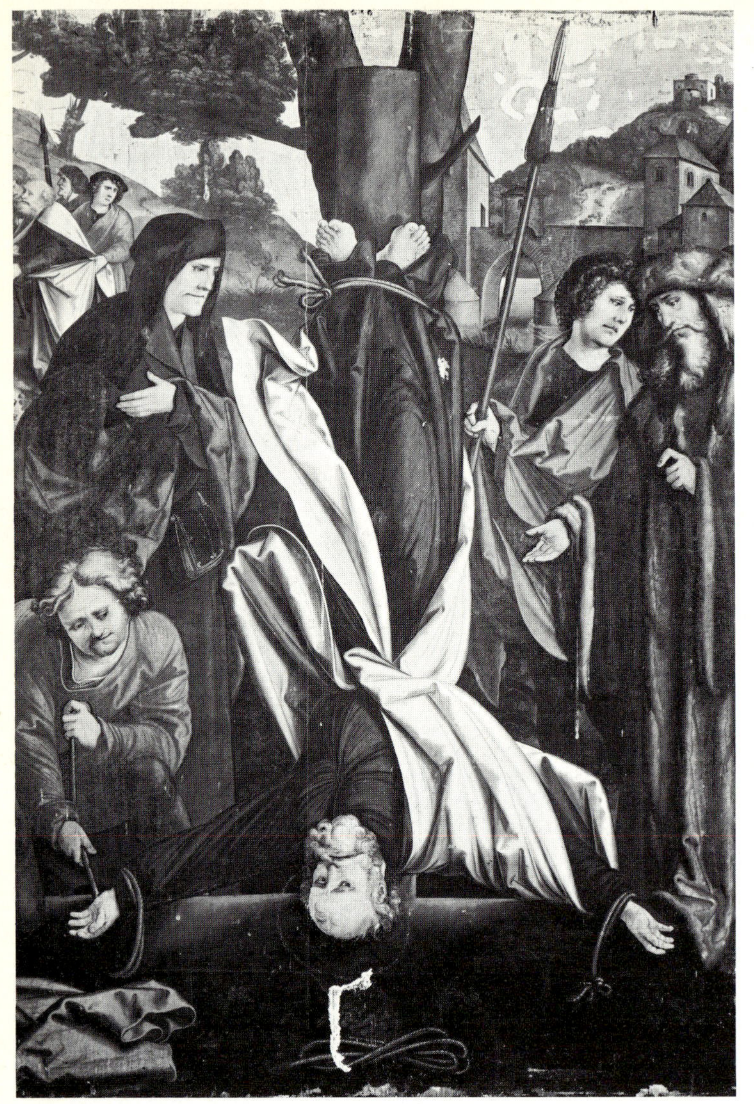

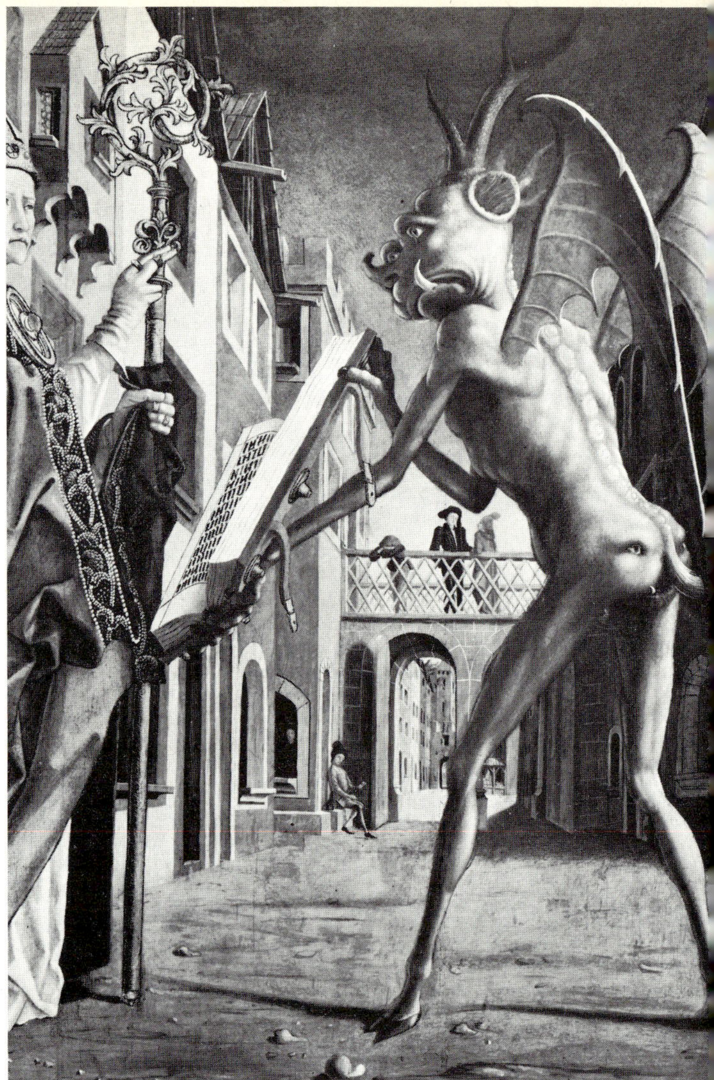

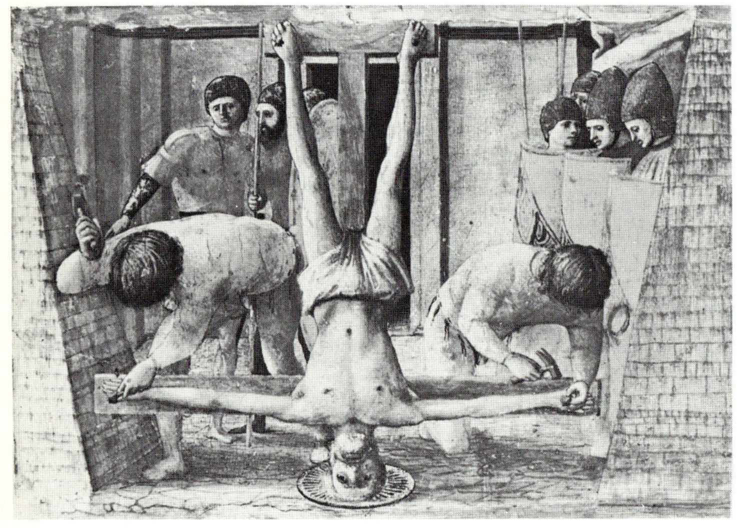

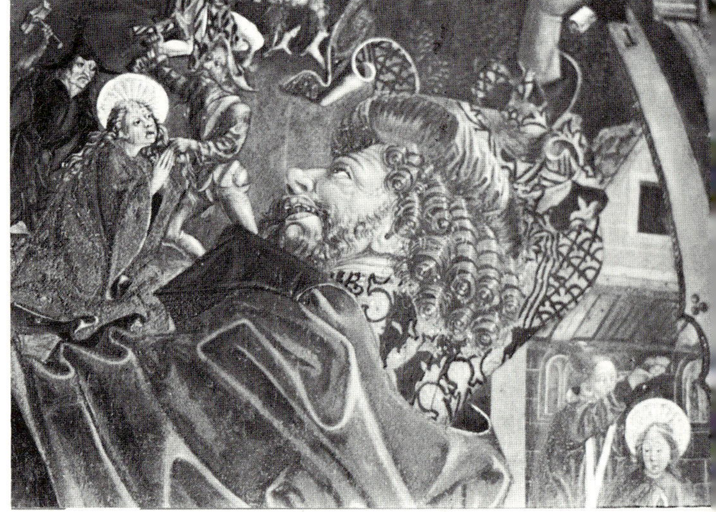

43 | 45
44 | 46

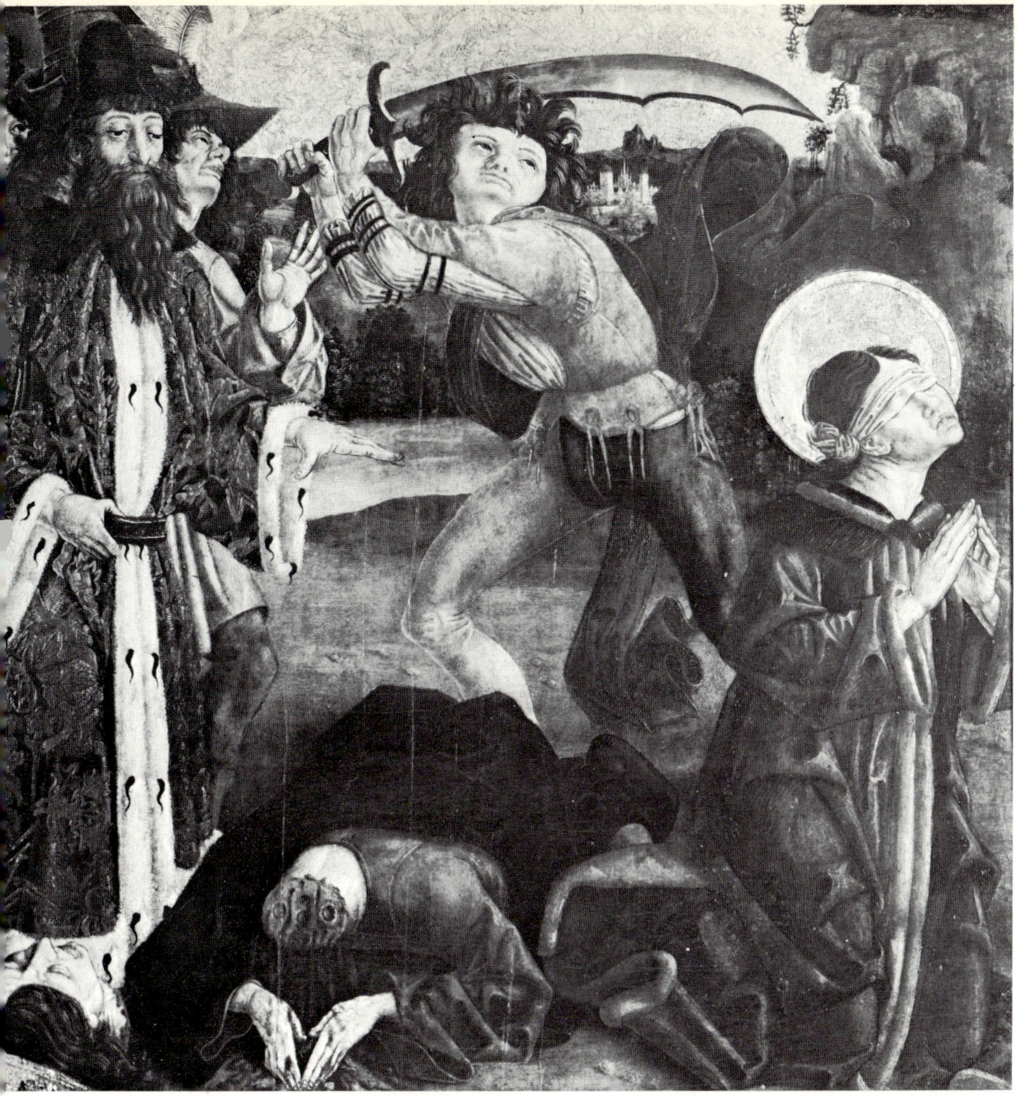

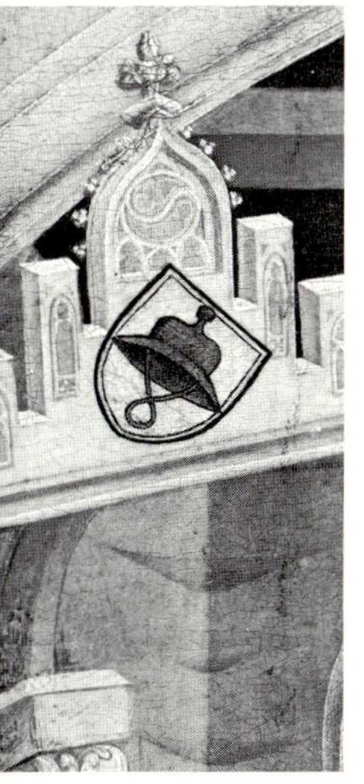

48

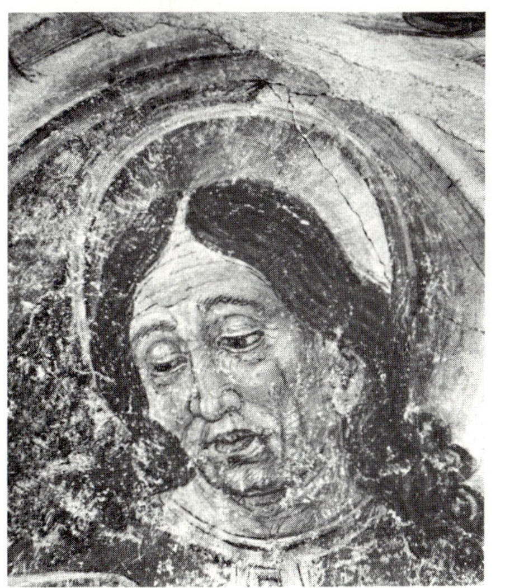

50

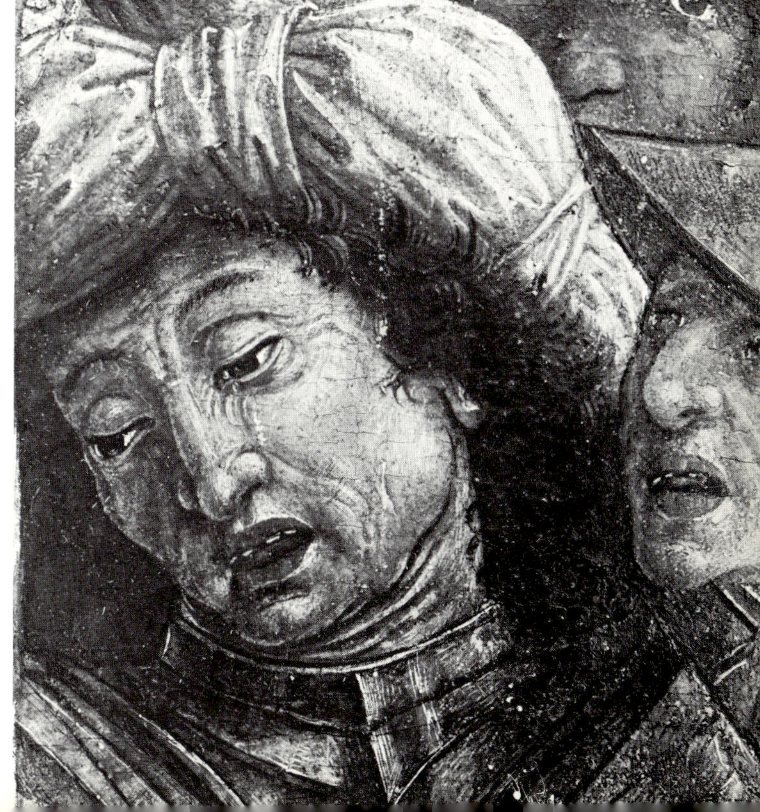

49

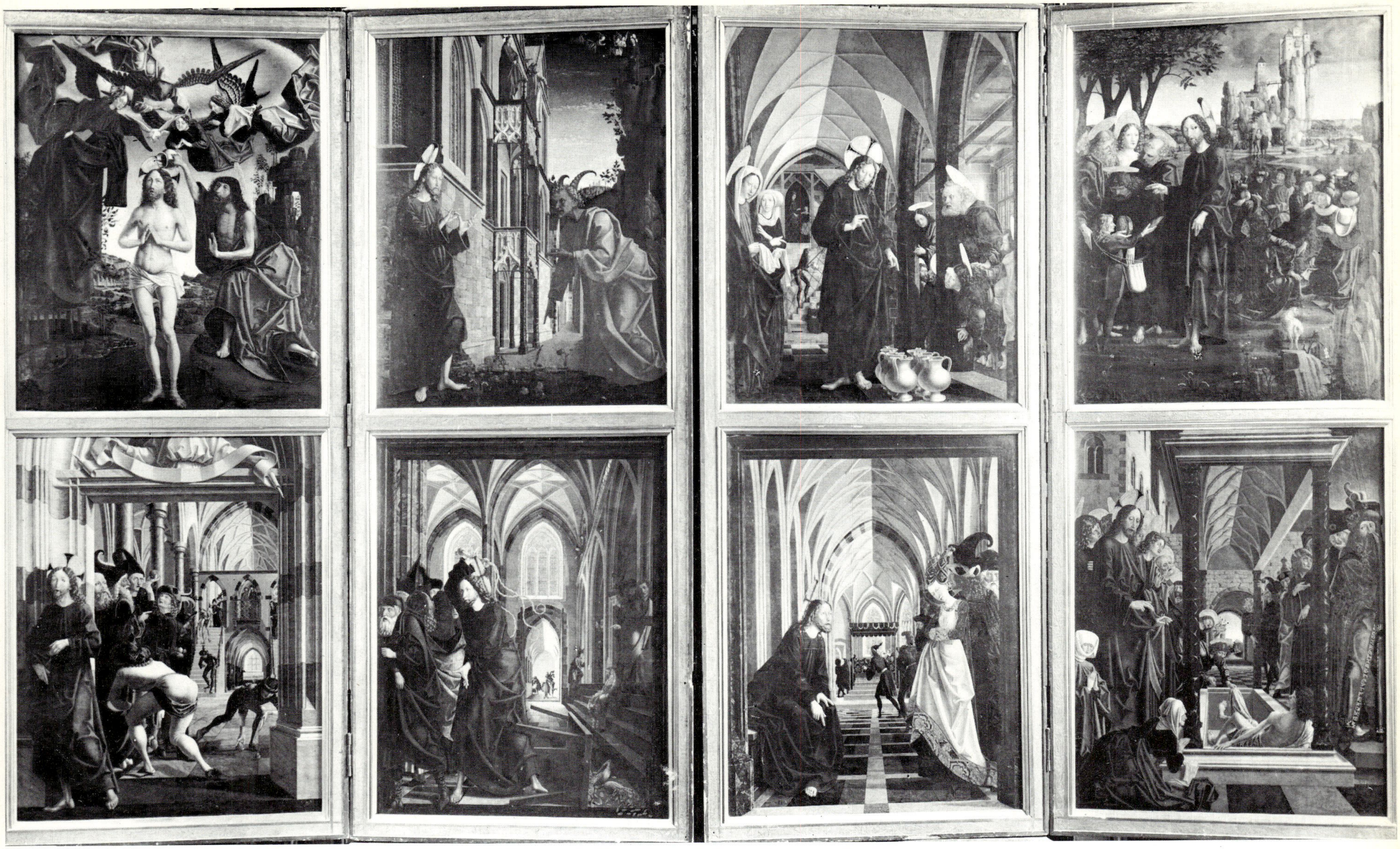

The Plates

The Sts Peter and Paul Altarpiece

Colour Plates

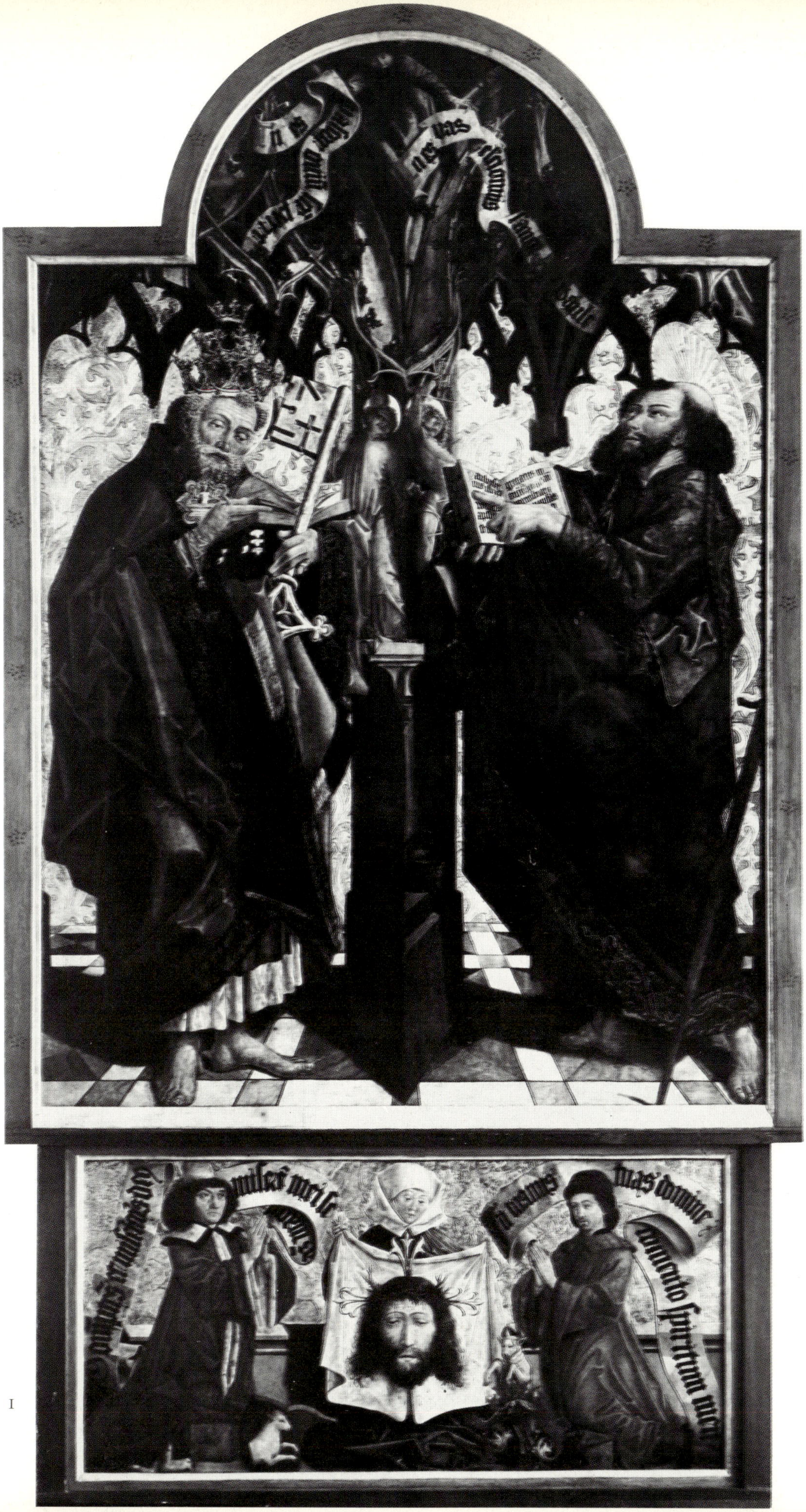

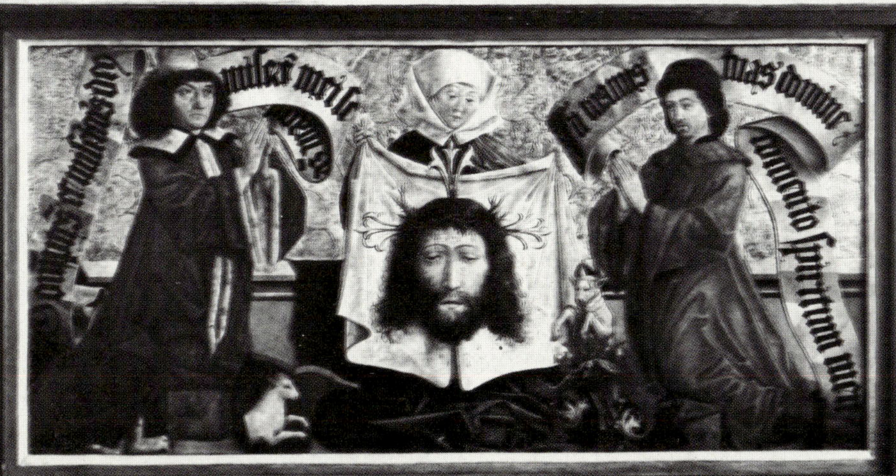

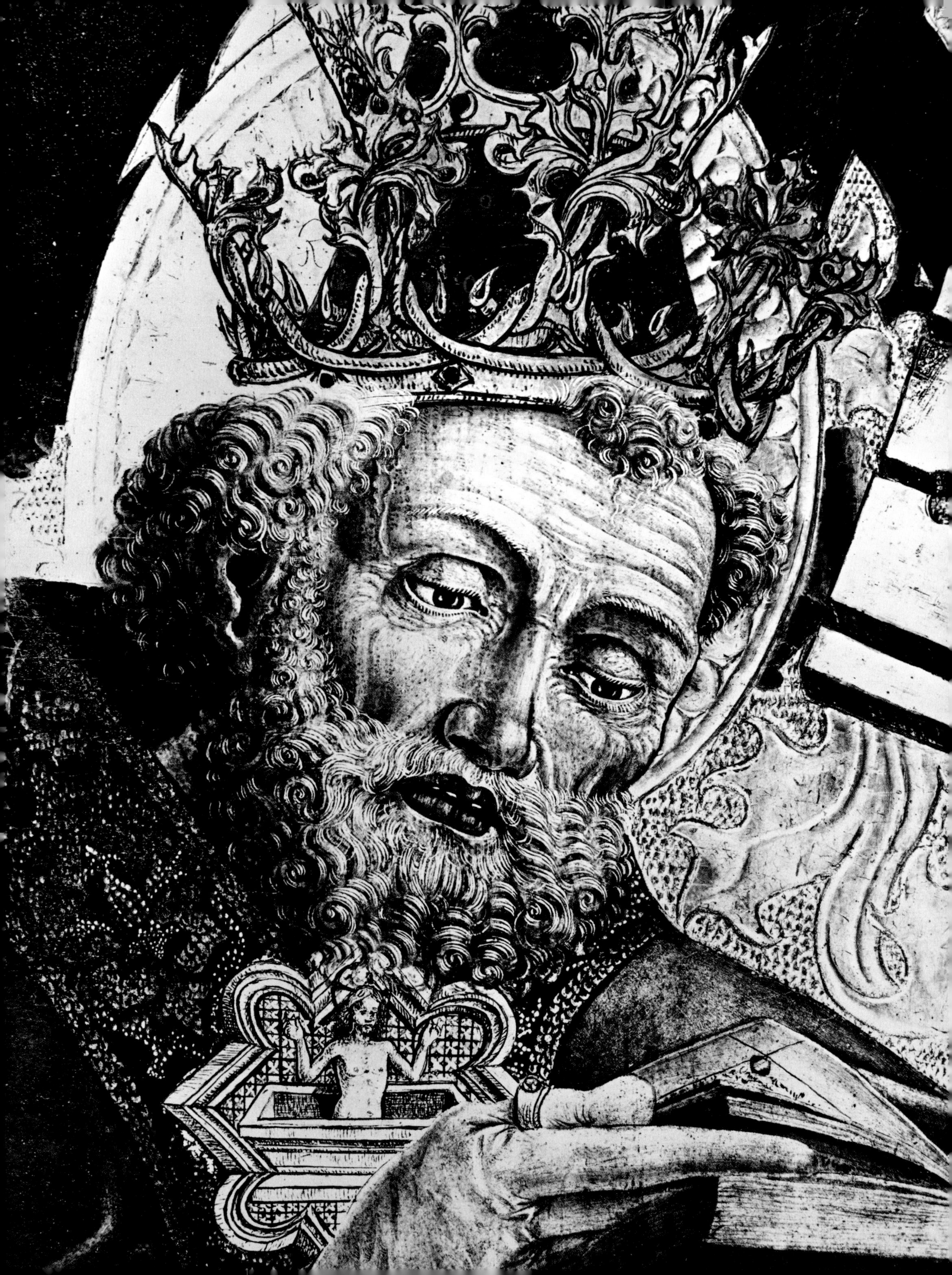

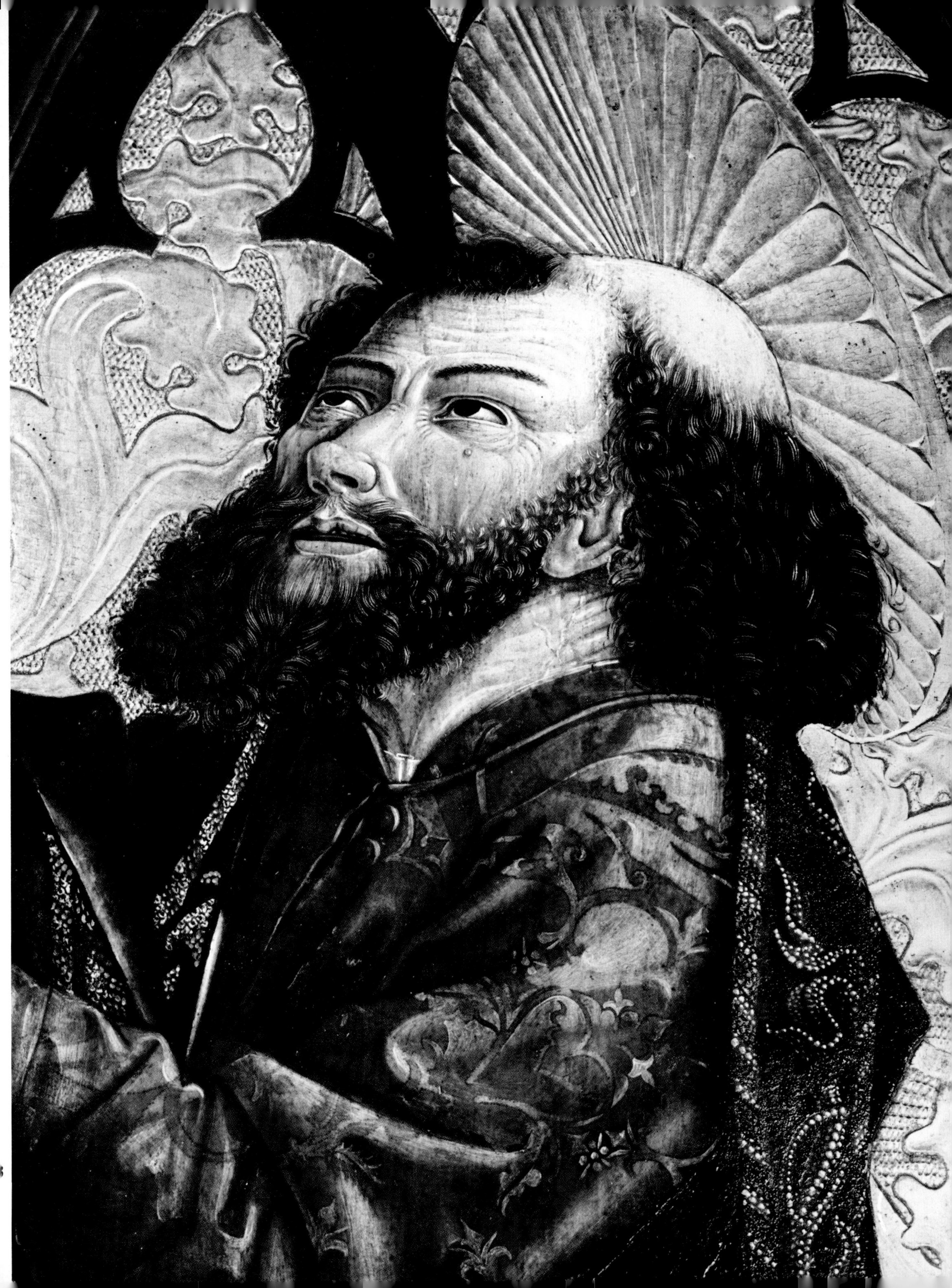

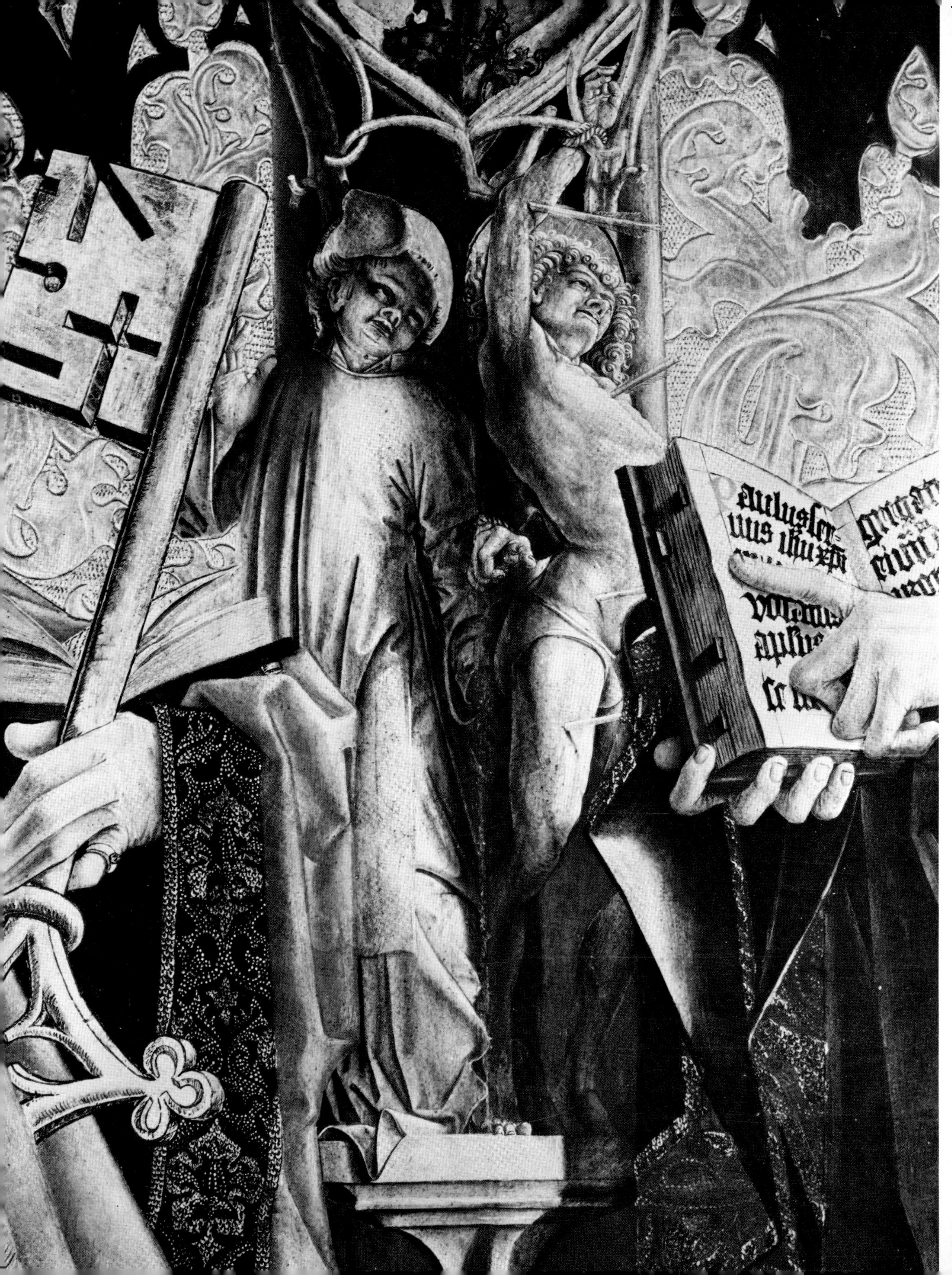
Paulus ser
uus ihu xpi
volums
apls

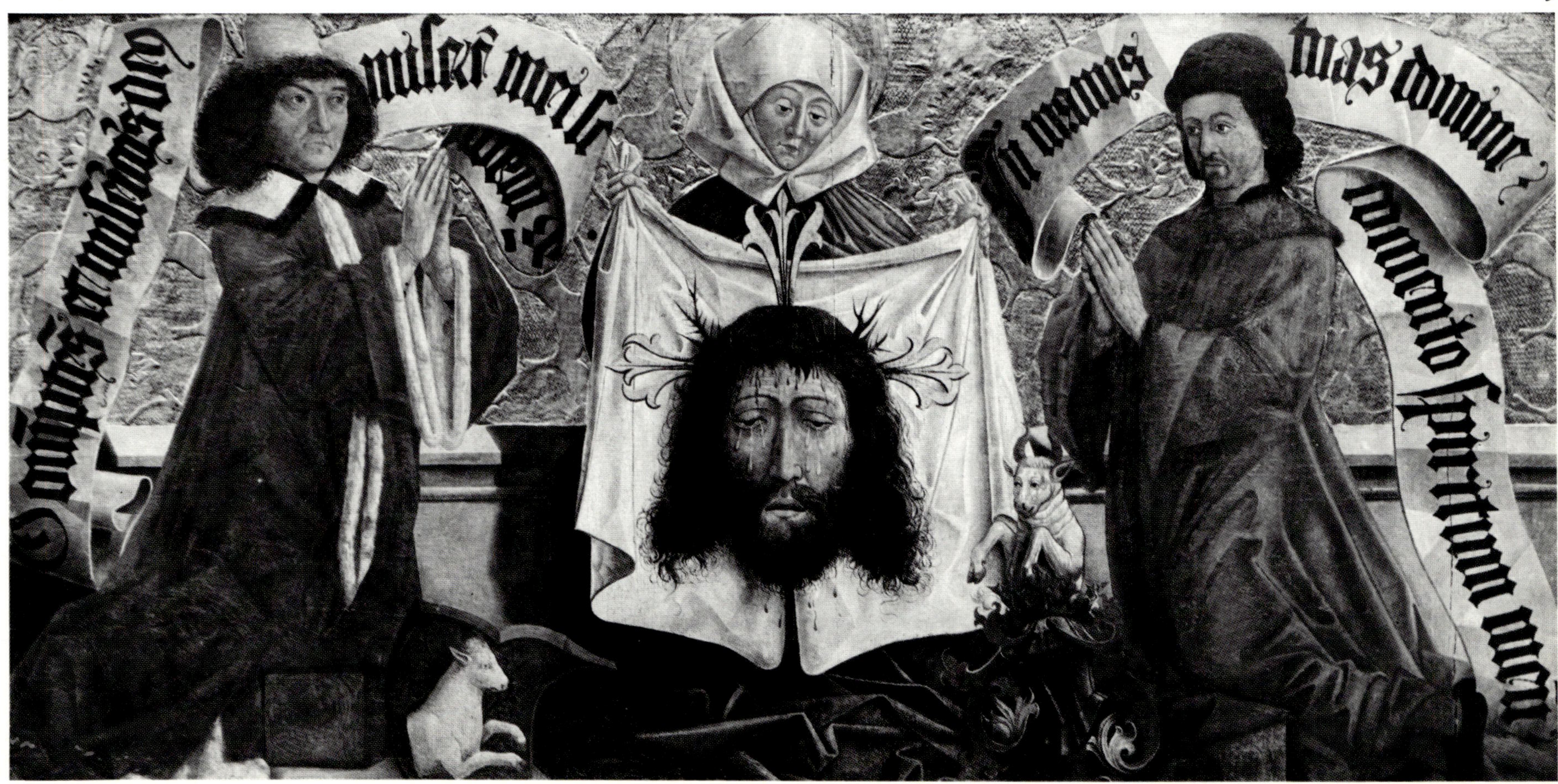

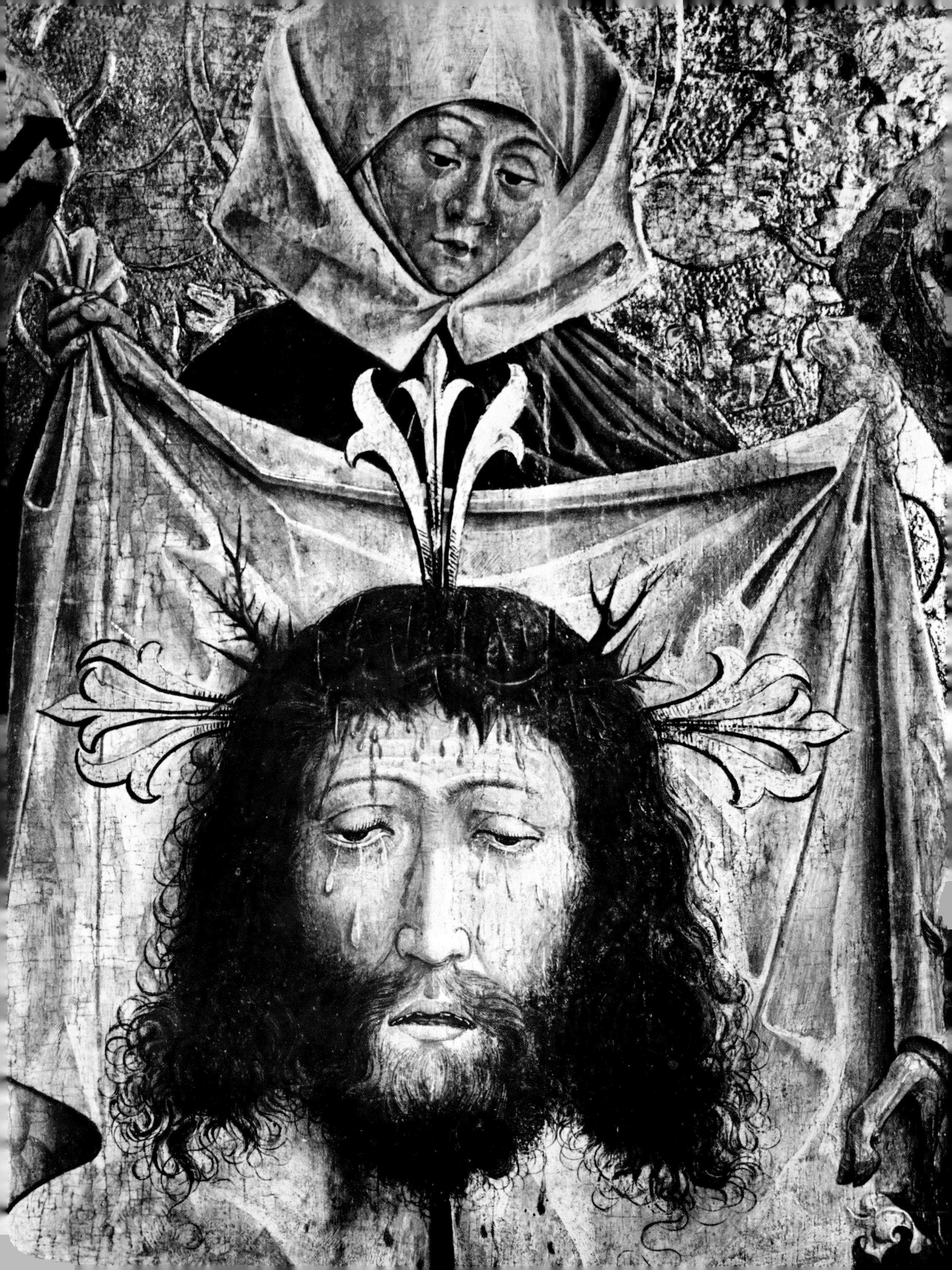

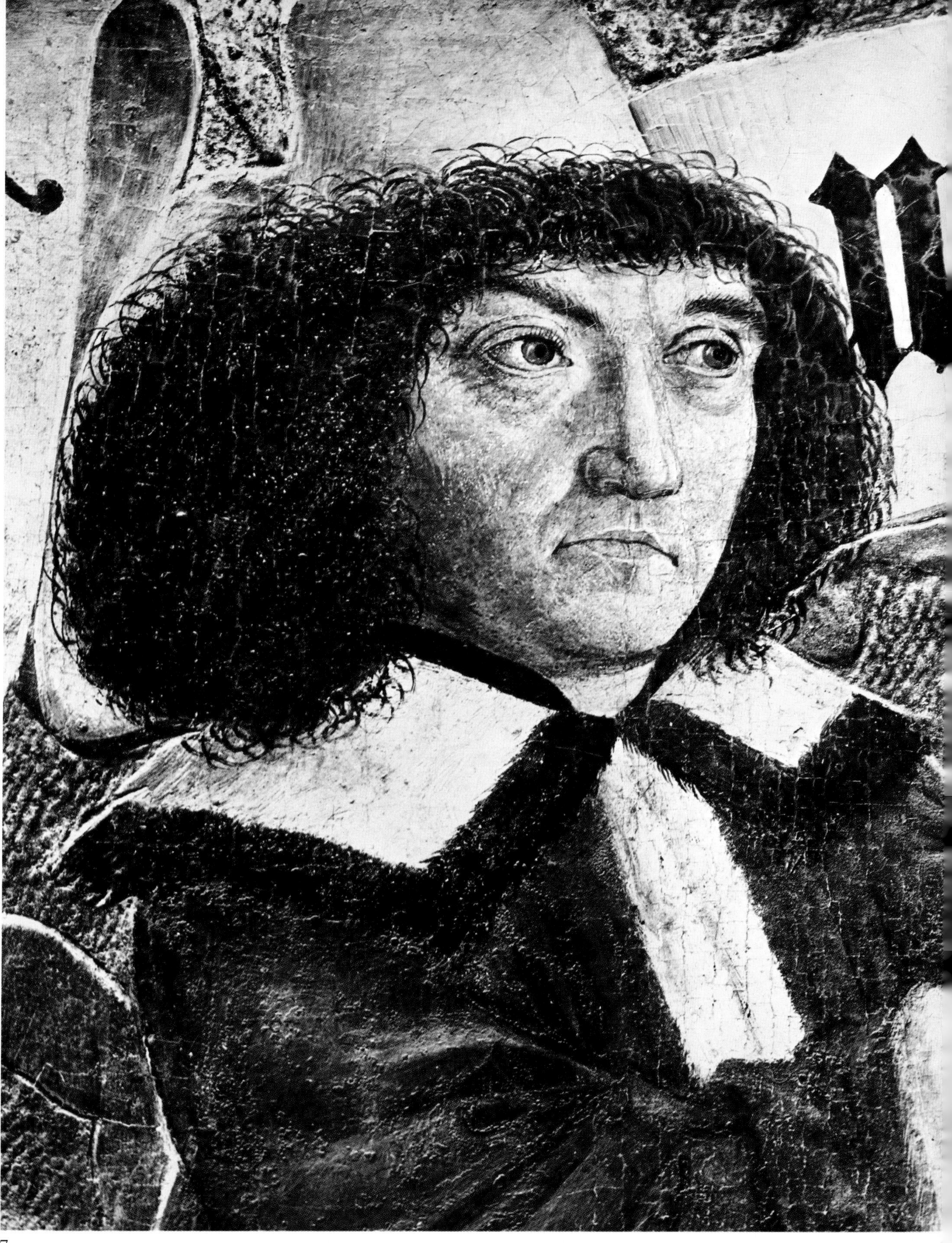

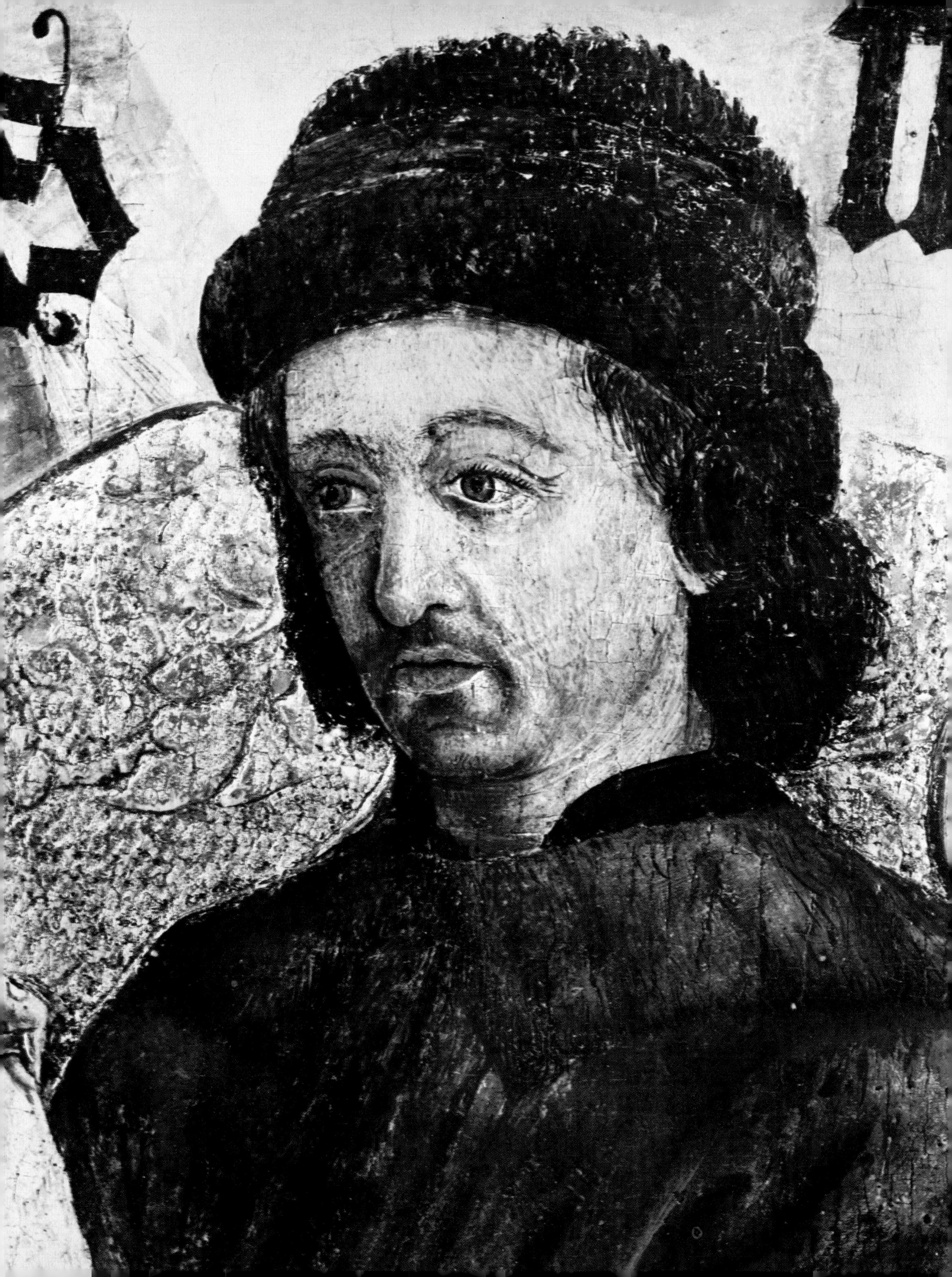

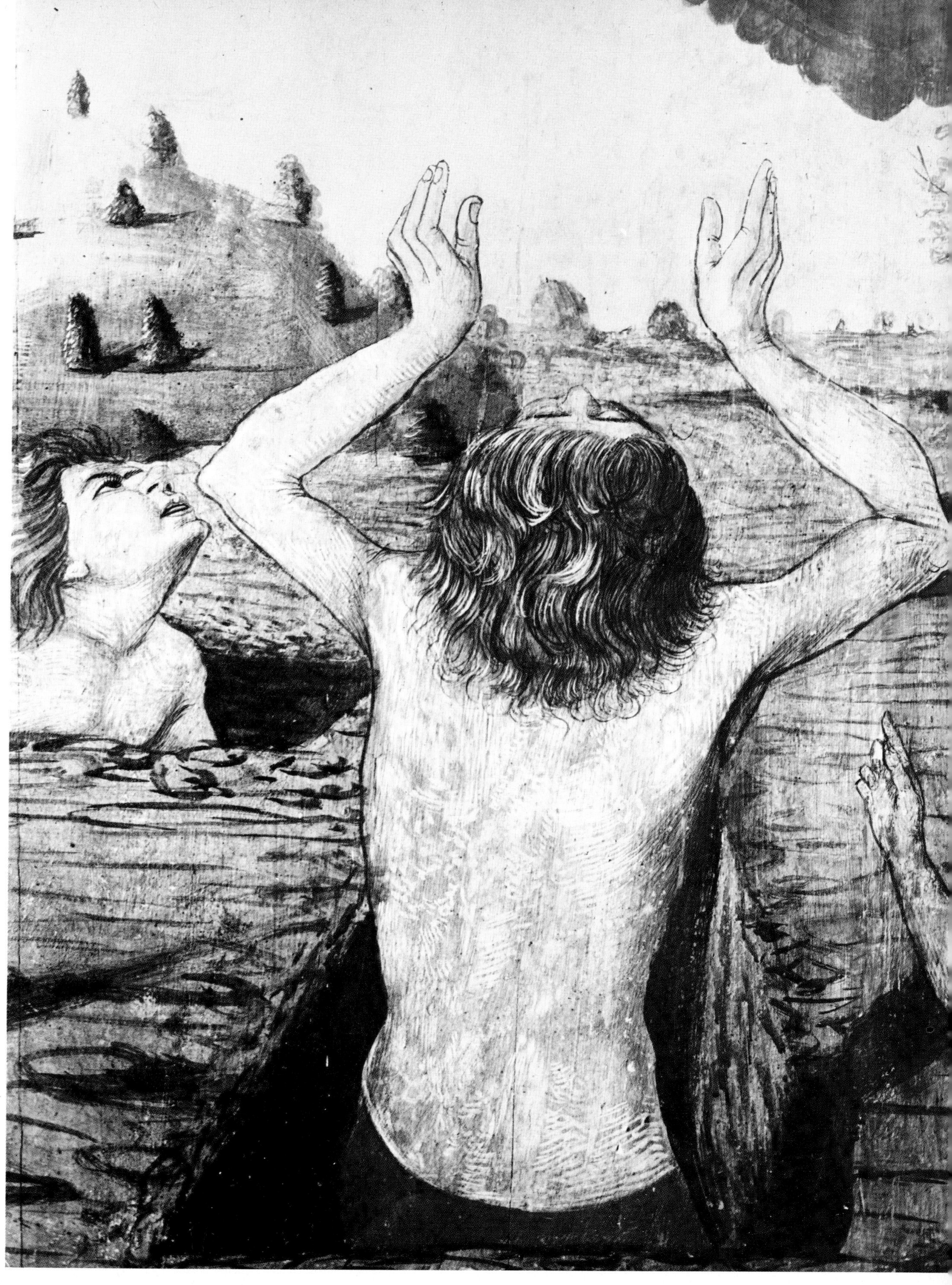

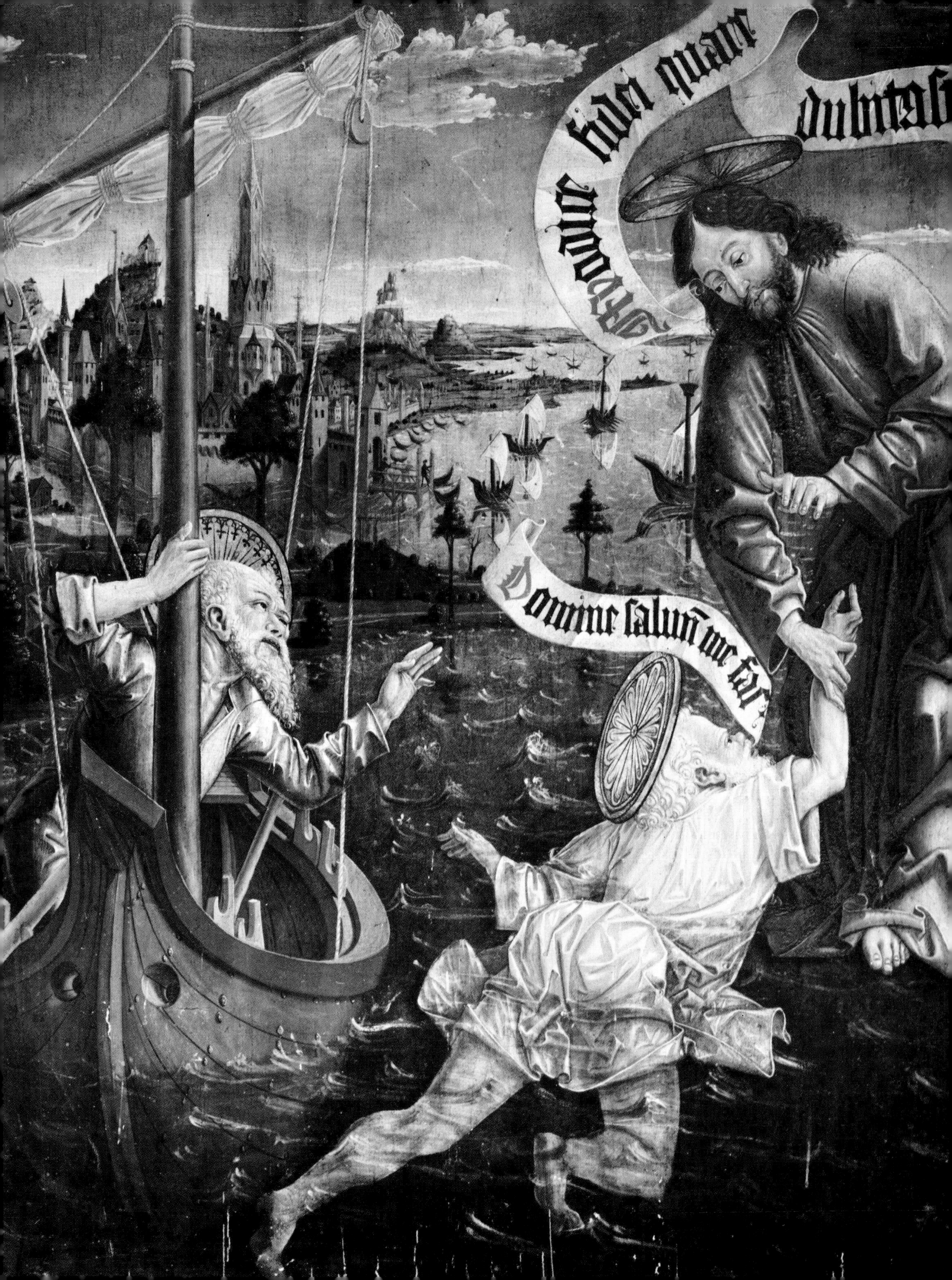
Modice fidei quare dubitasti
Domine saluum me fac

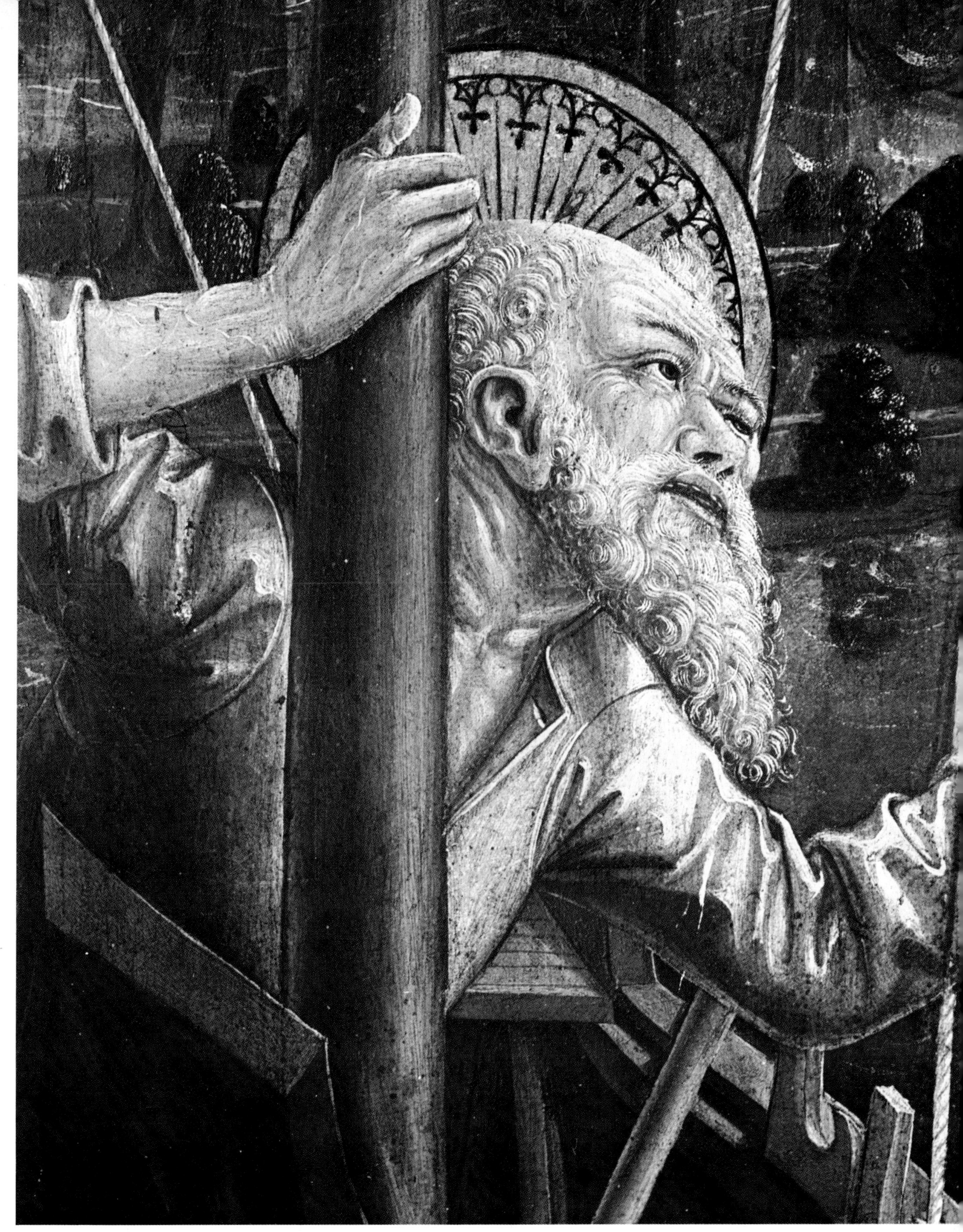

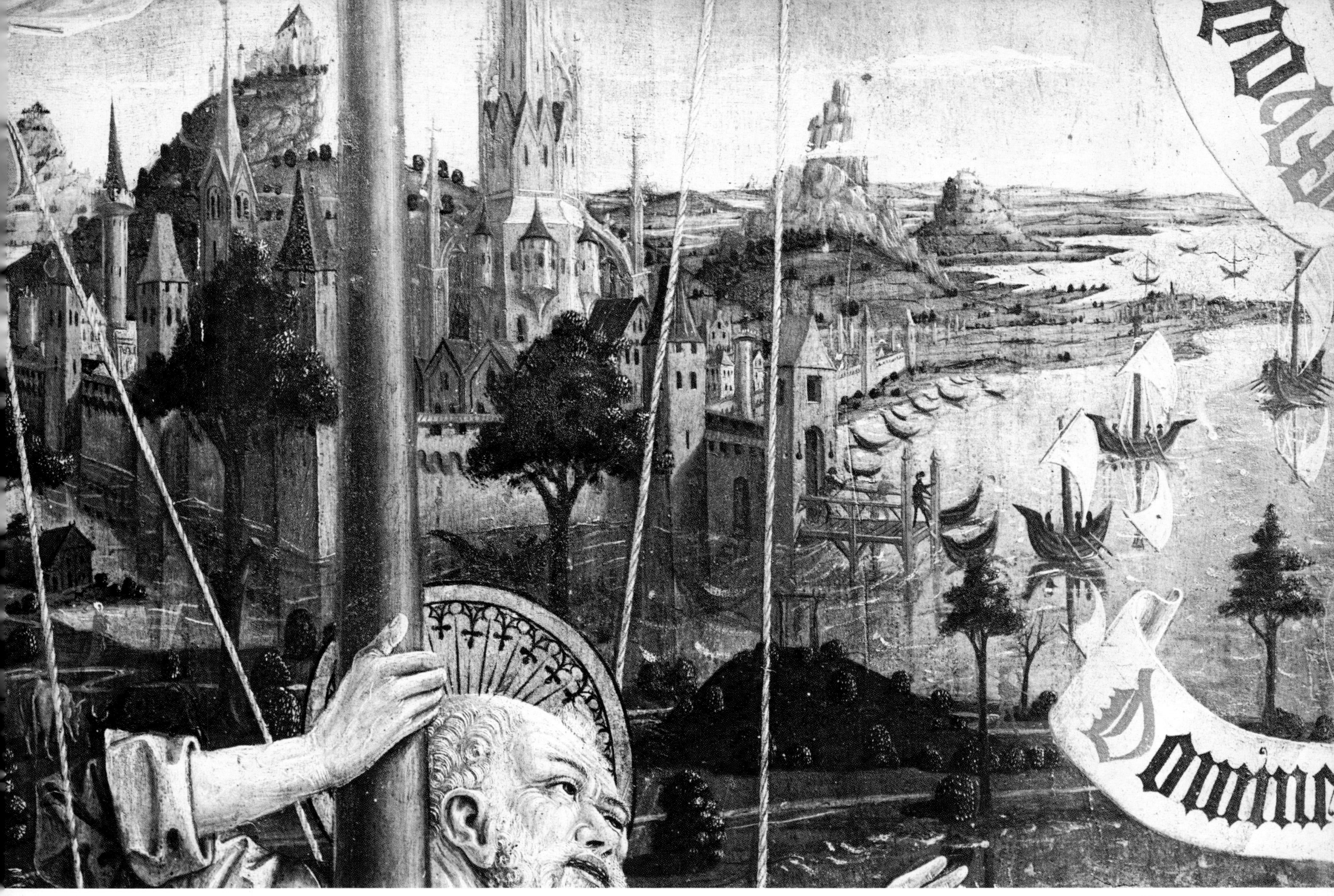

12

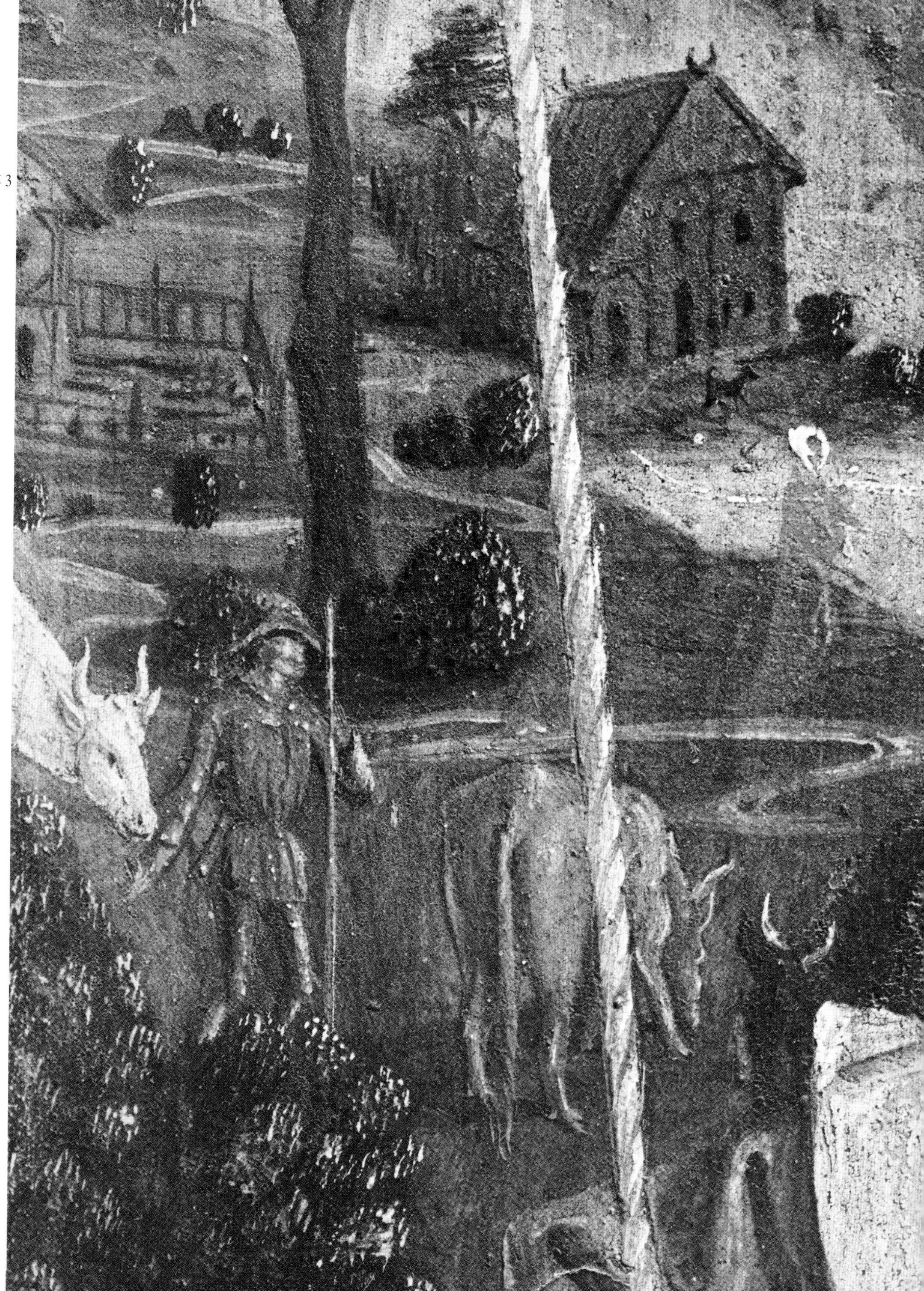

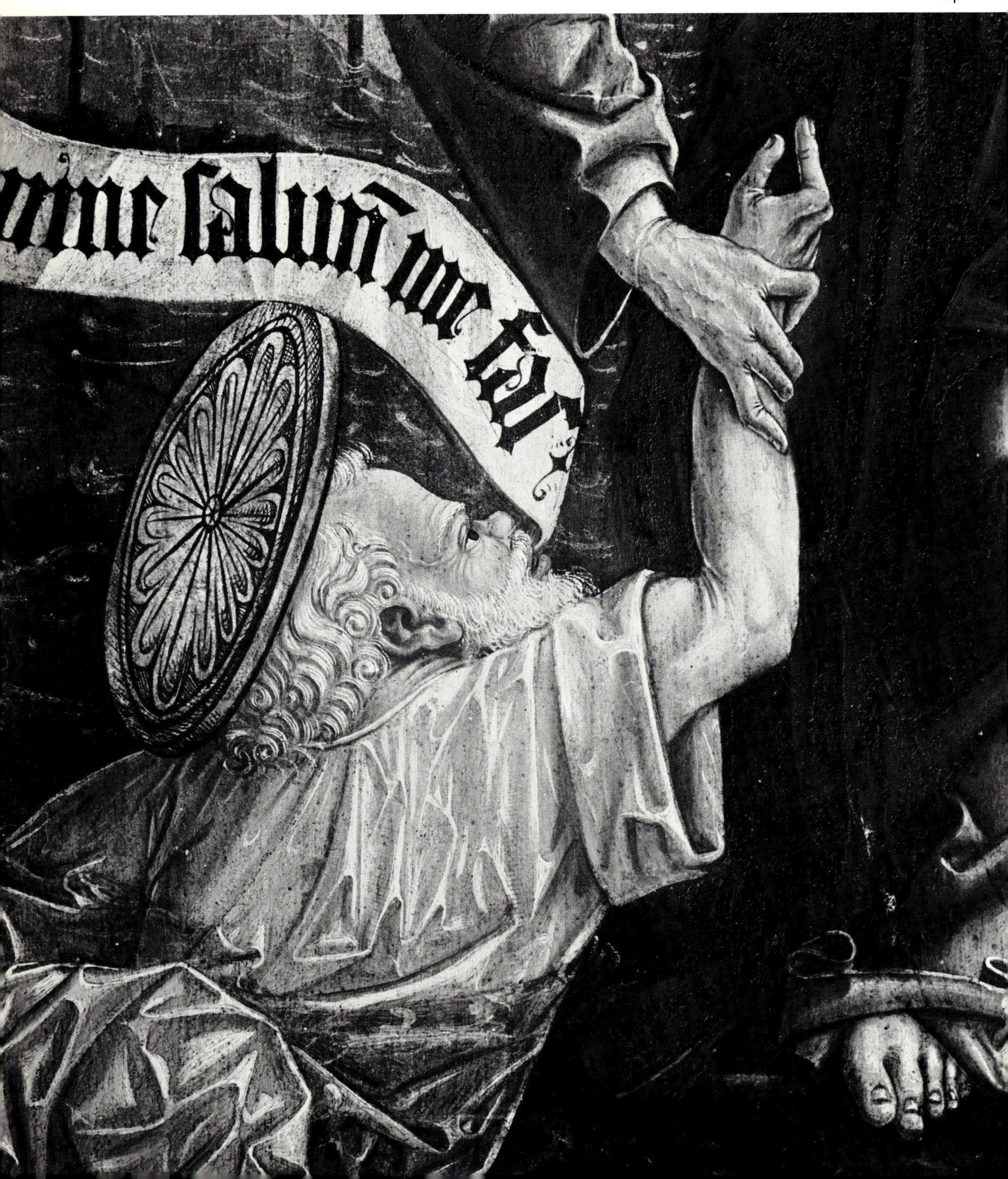
mine salum mt fa

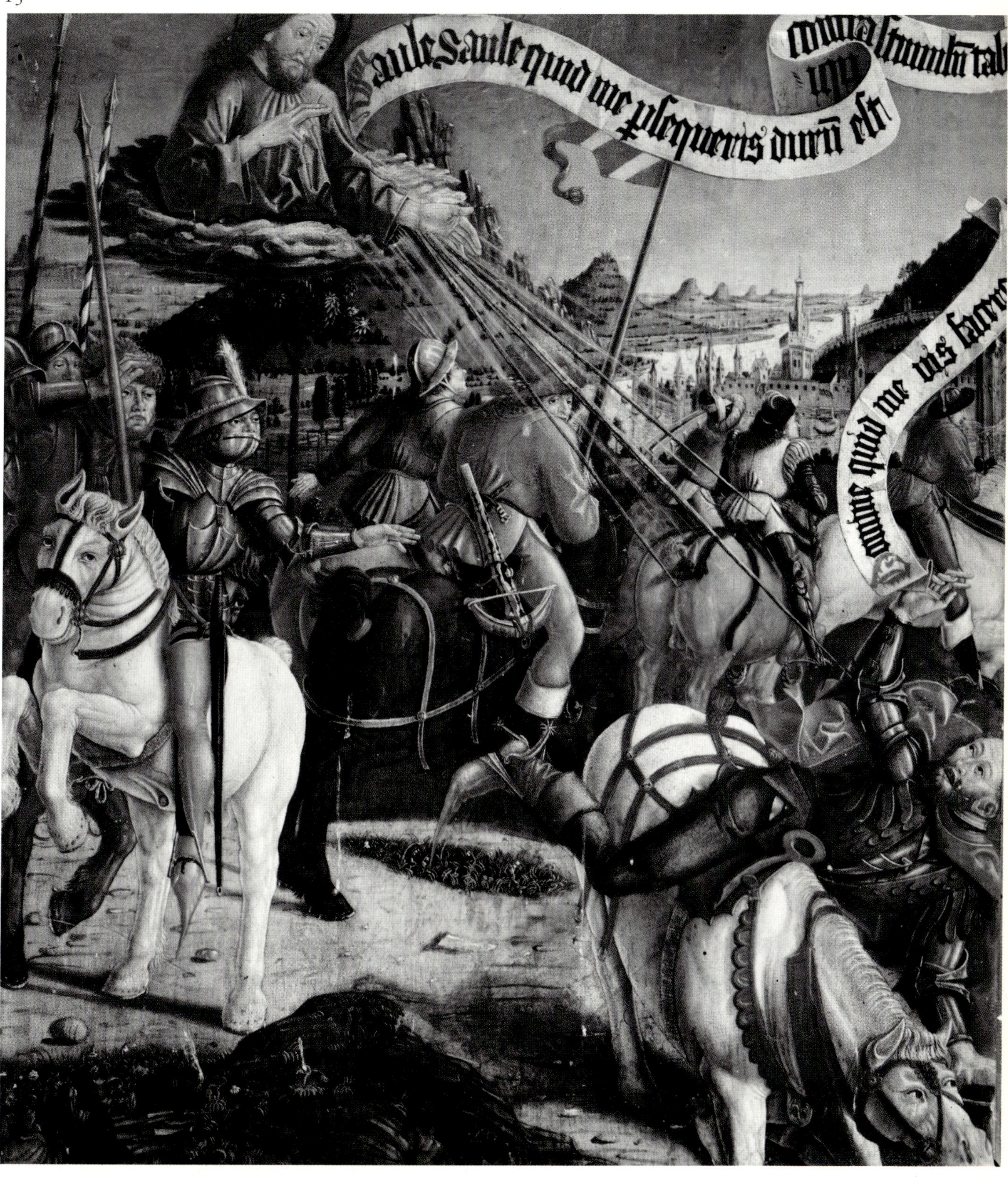
Saule Saule quid me psequeris durum est

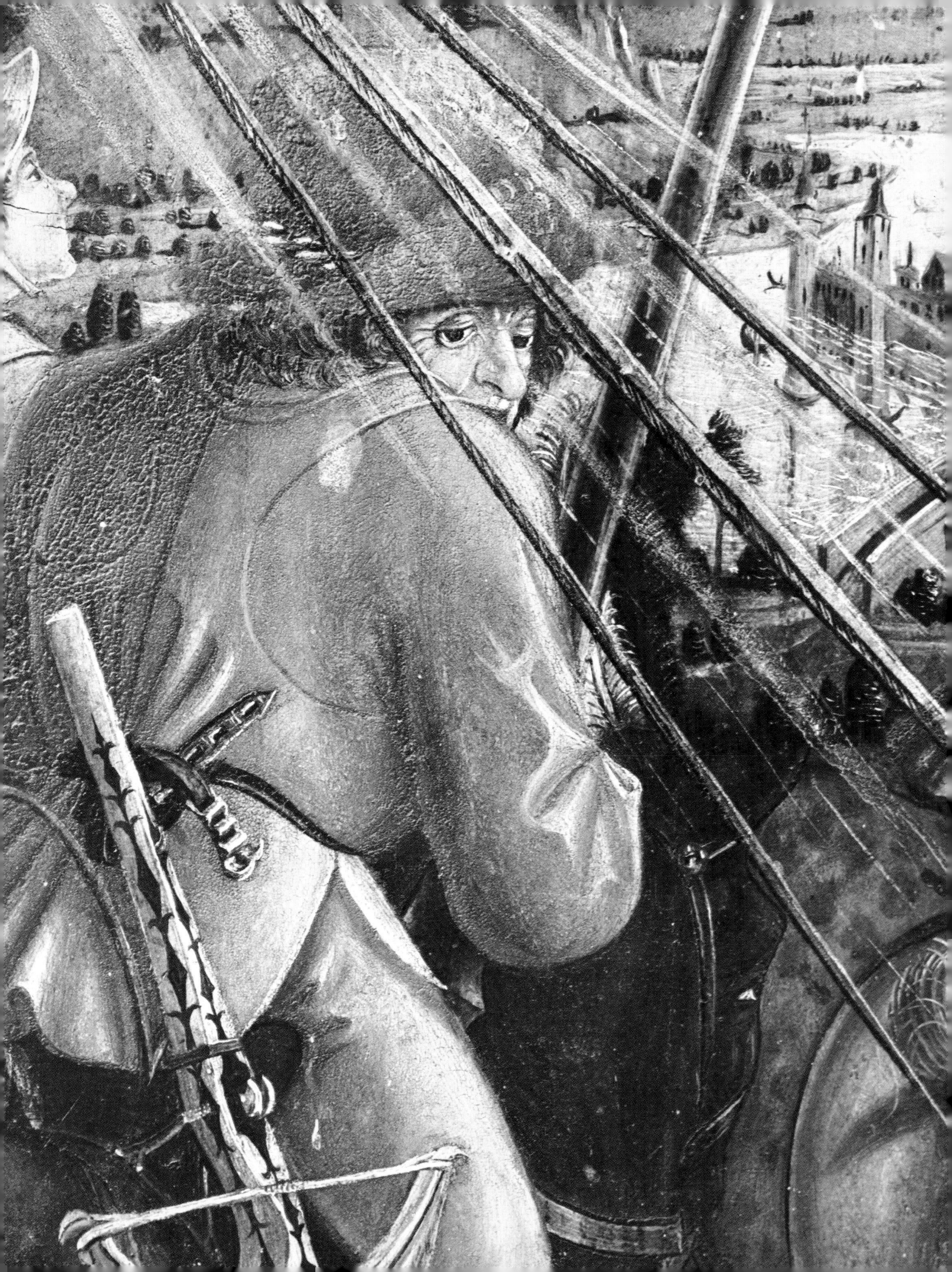

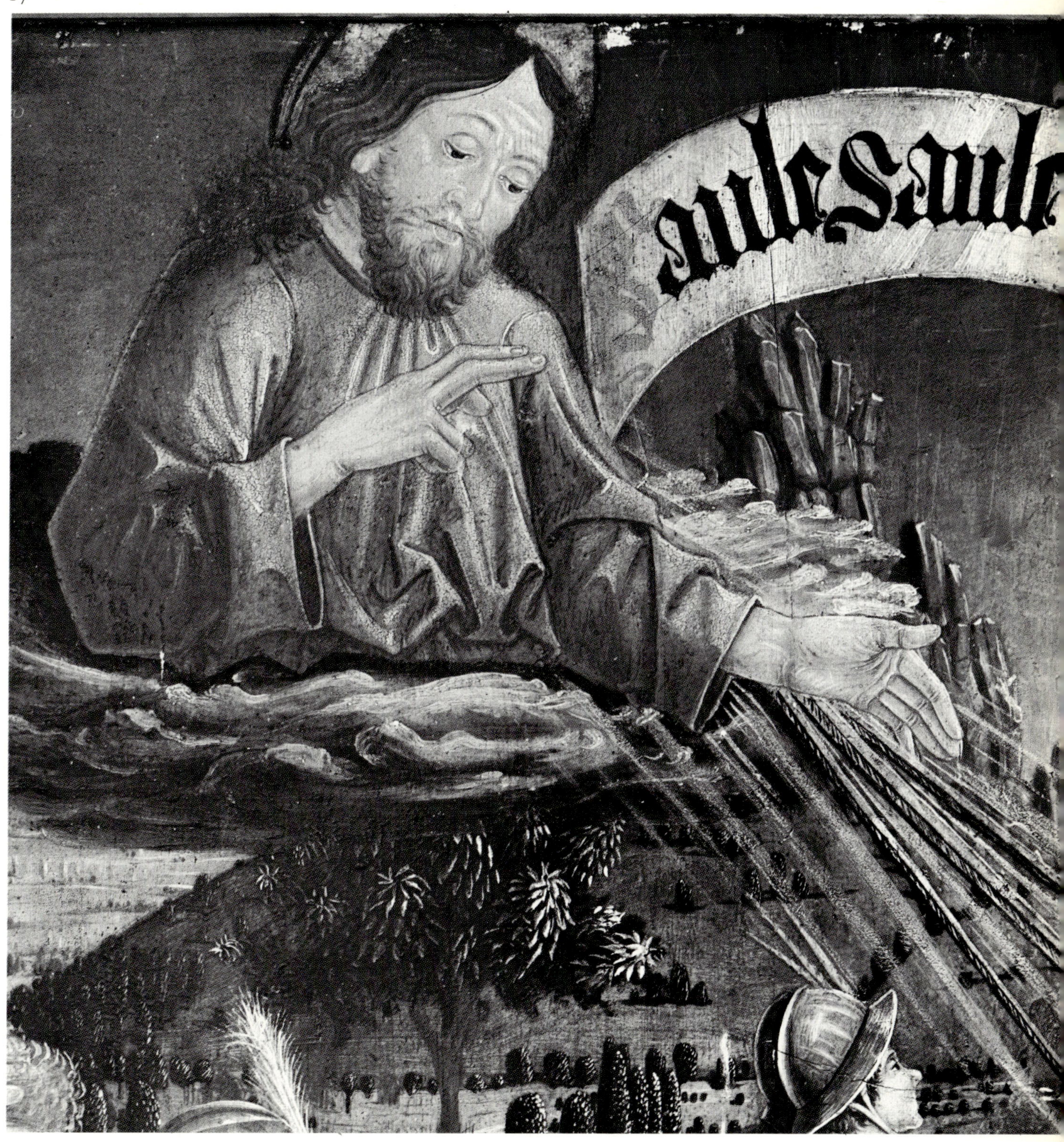
aule saule

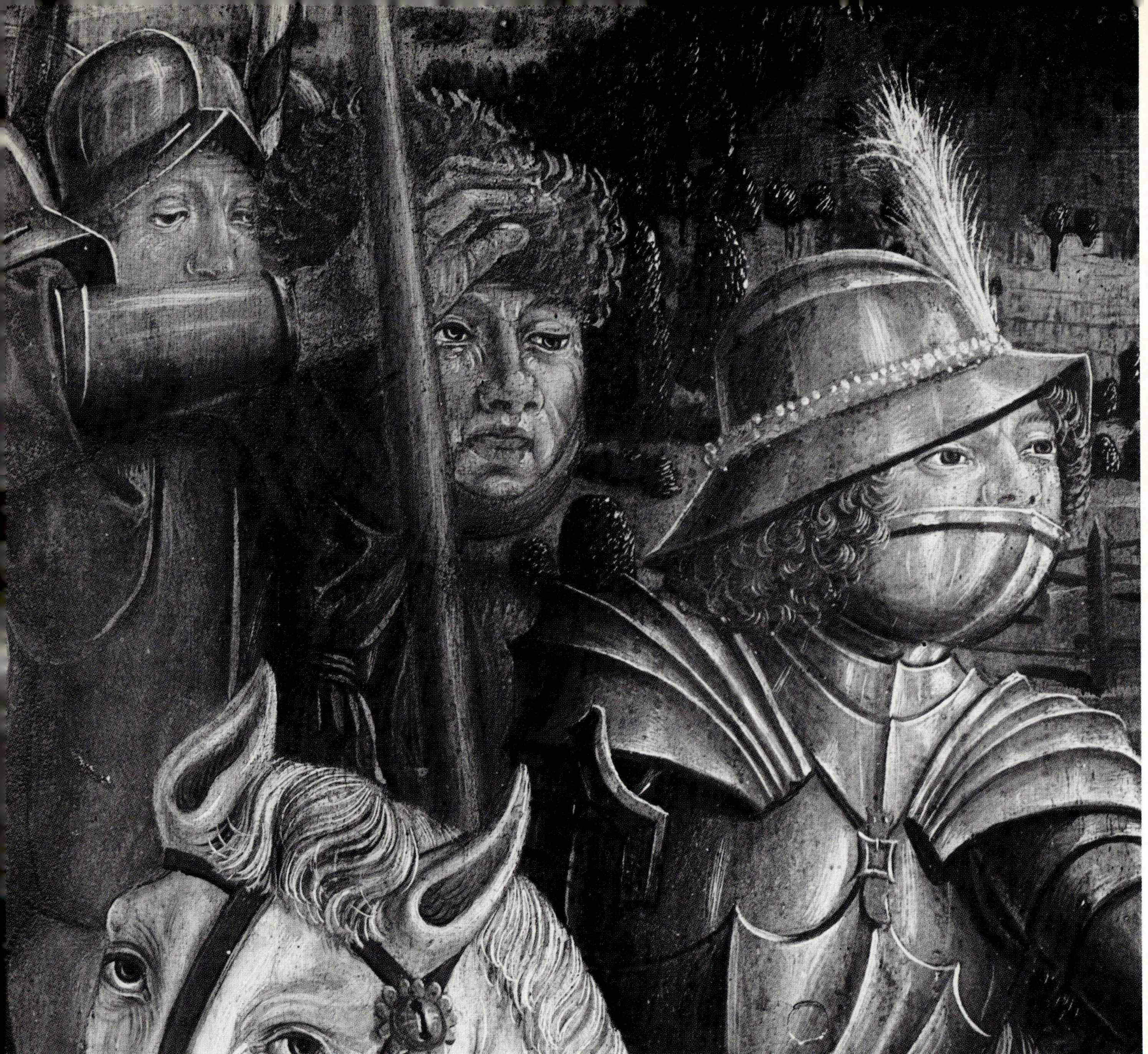

18

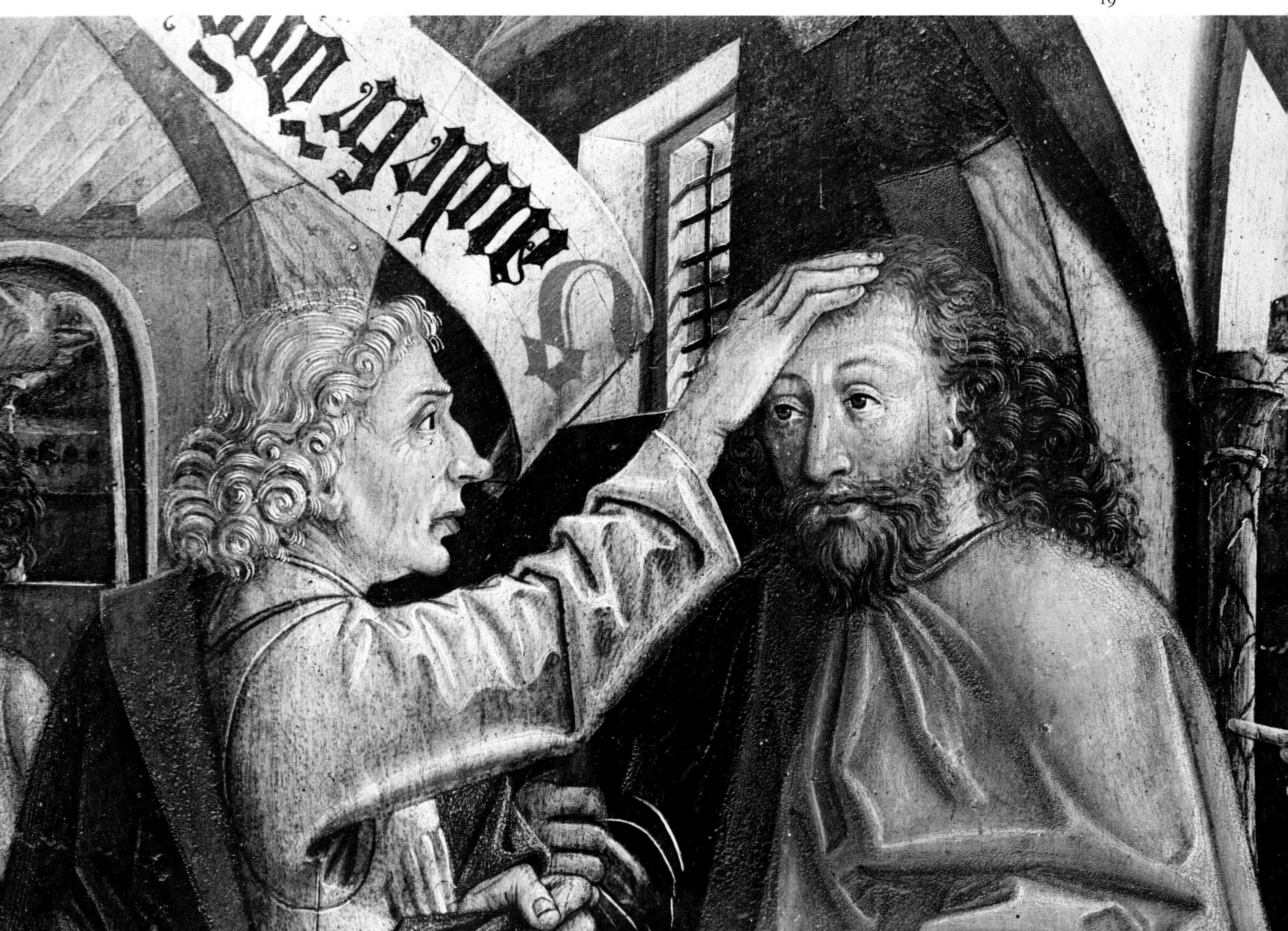

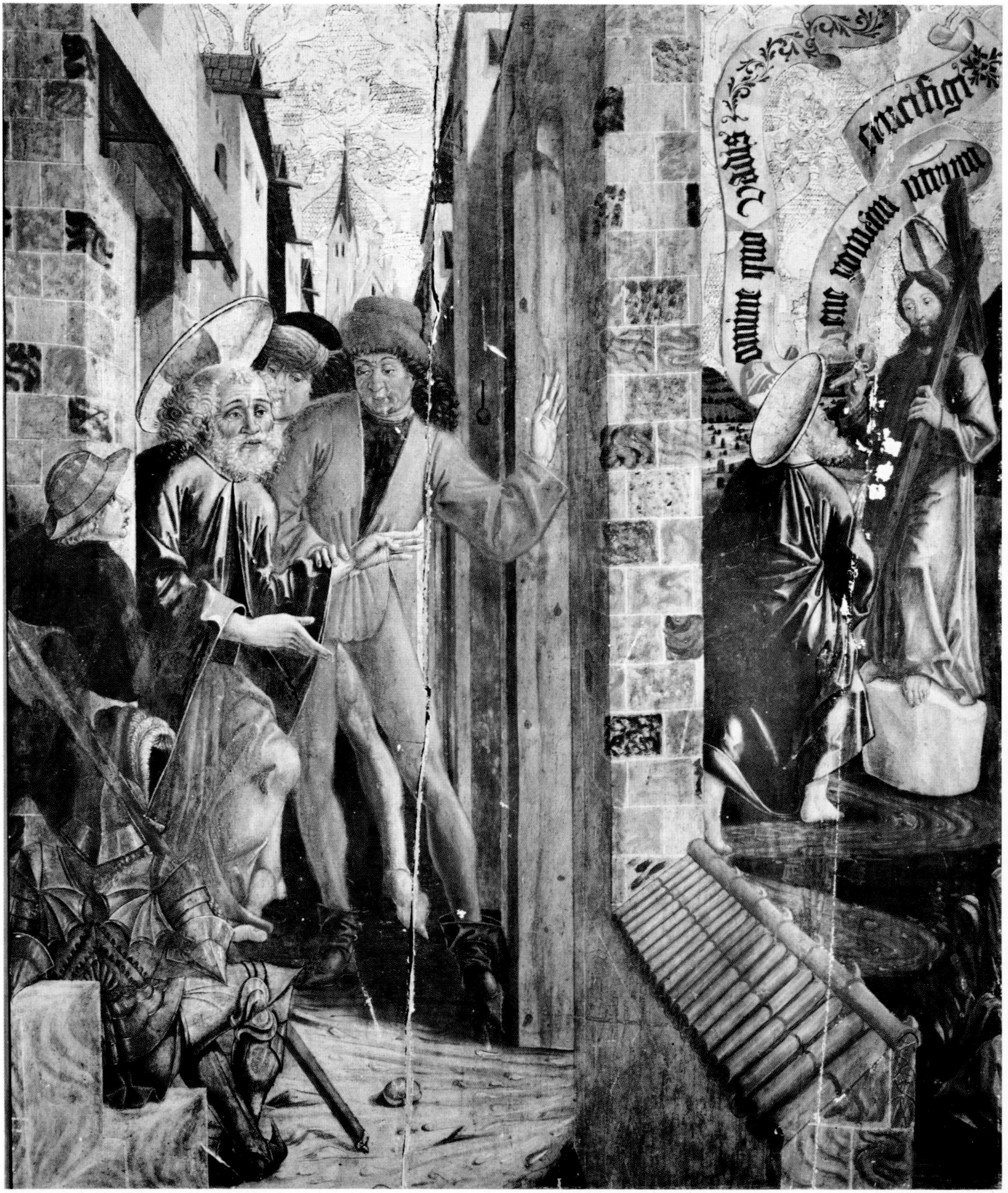

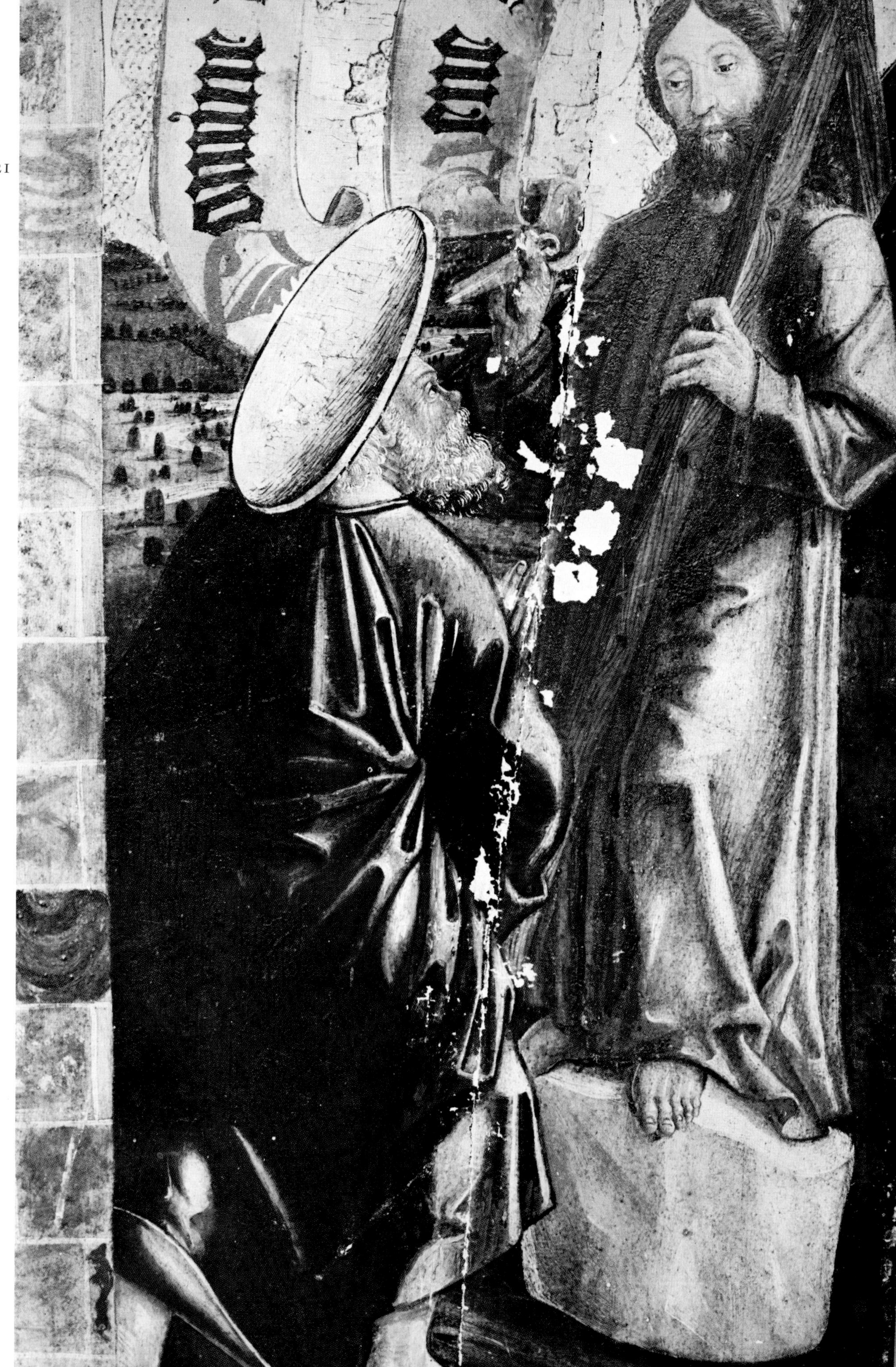

21

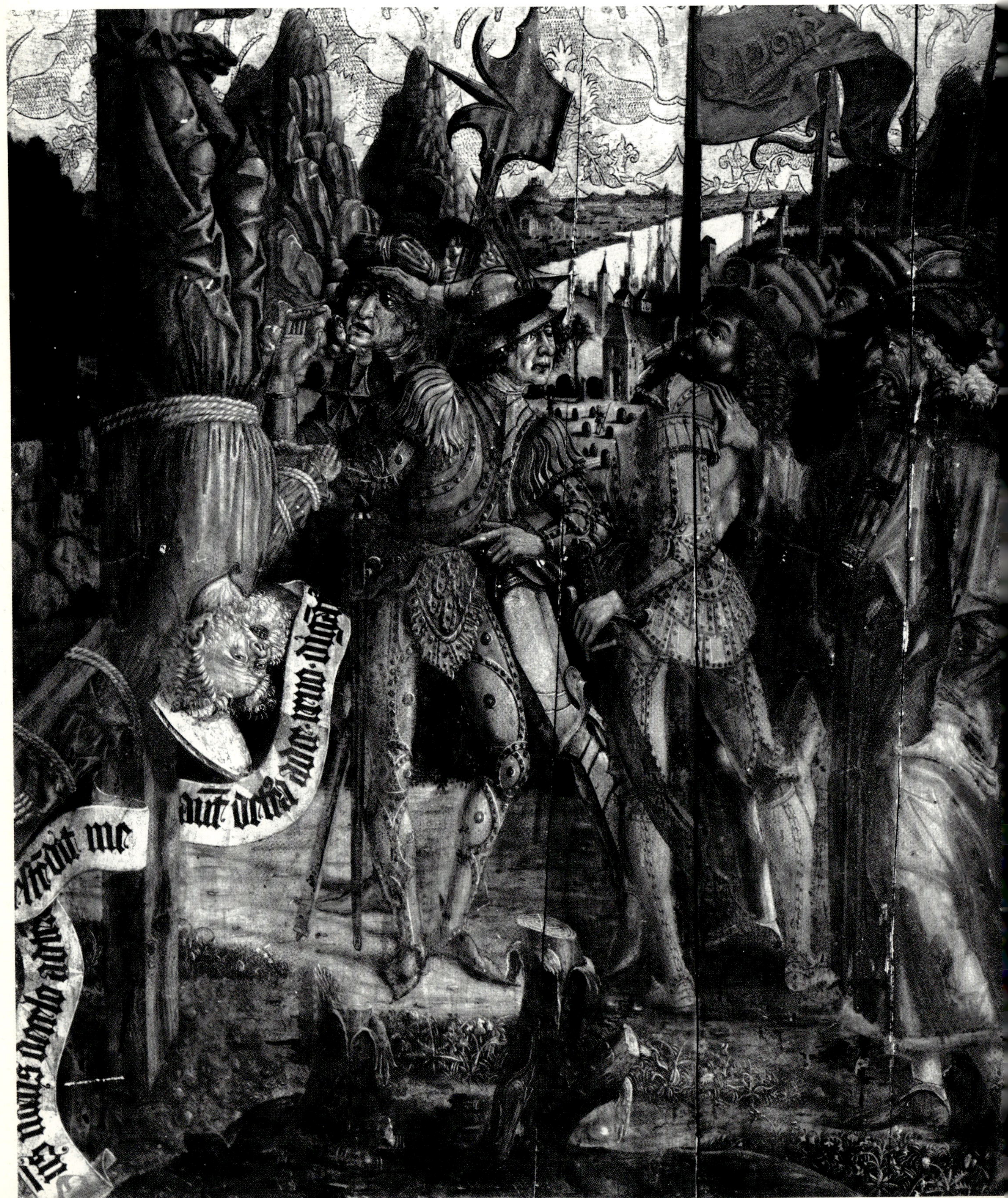

aut delta adie tevu · diġi
scivit me
Et vivis verbo adie simon en

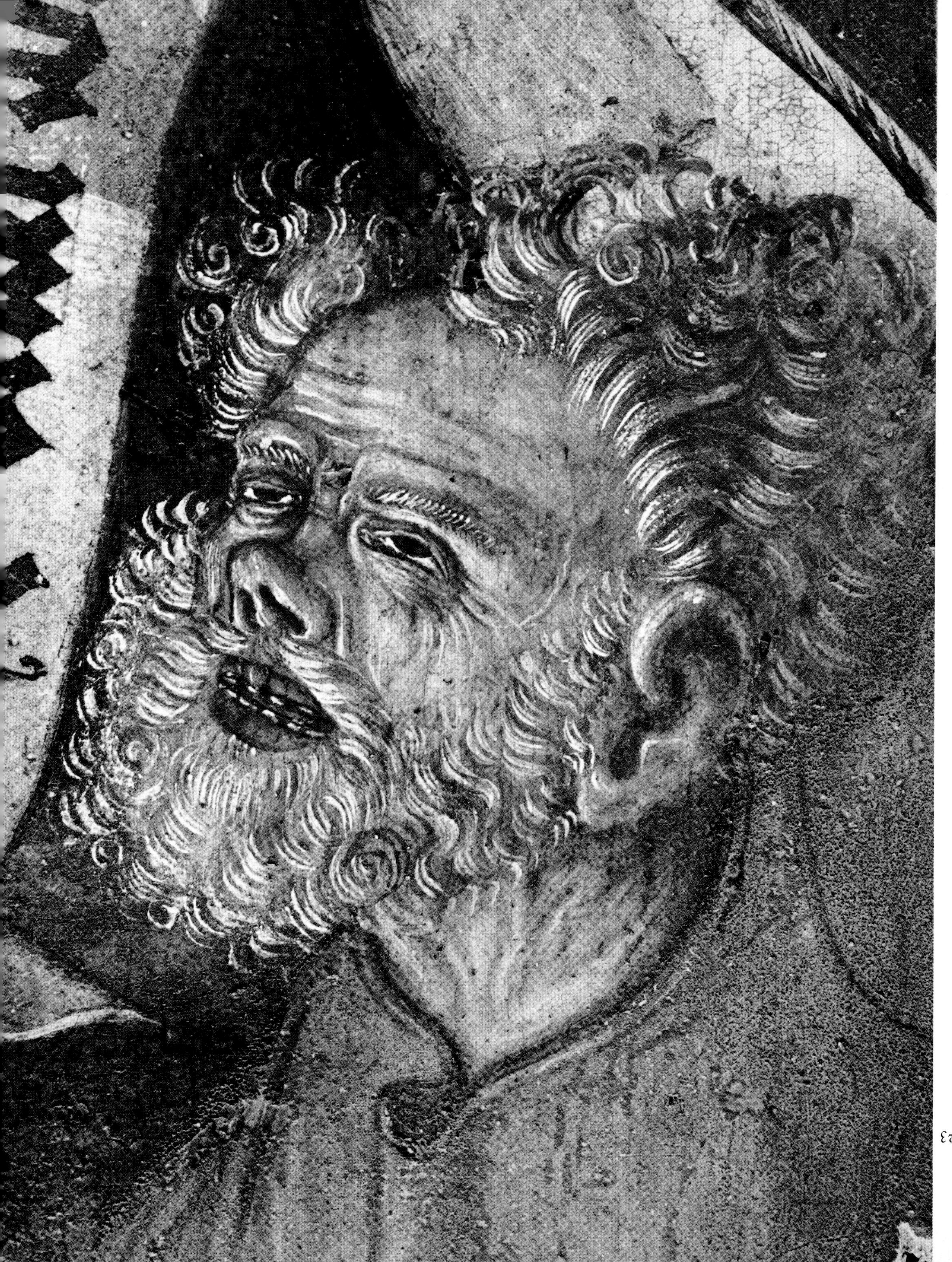

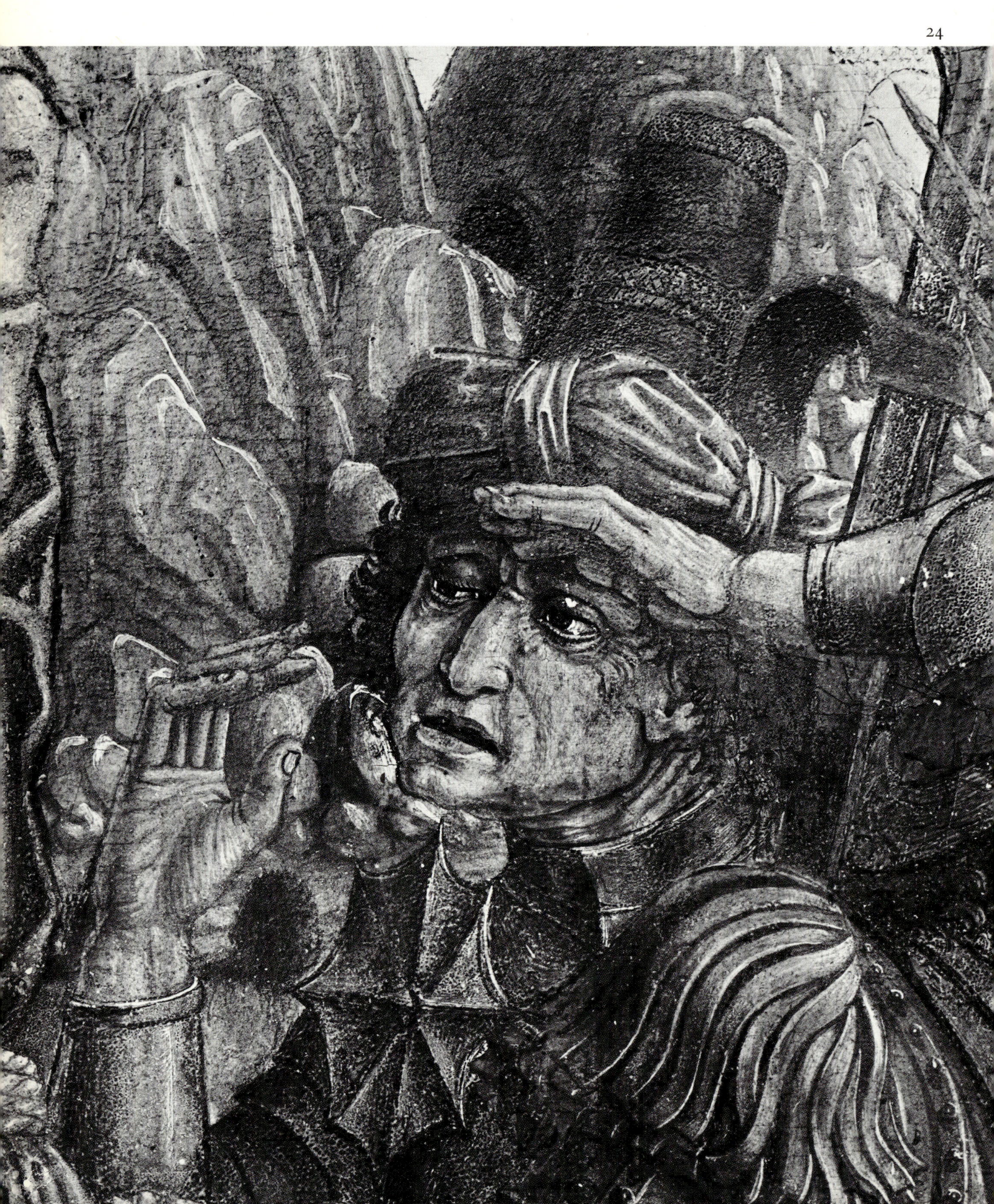

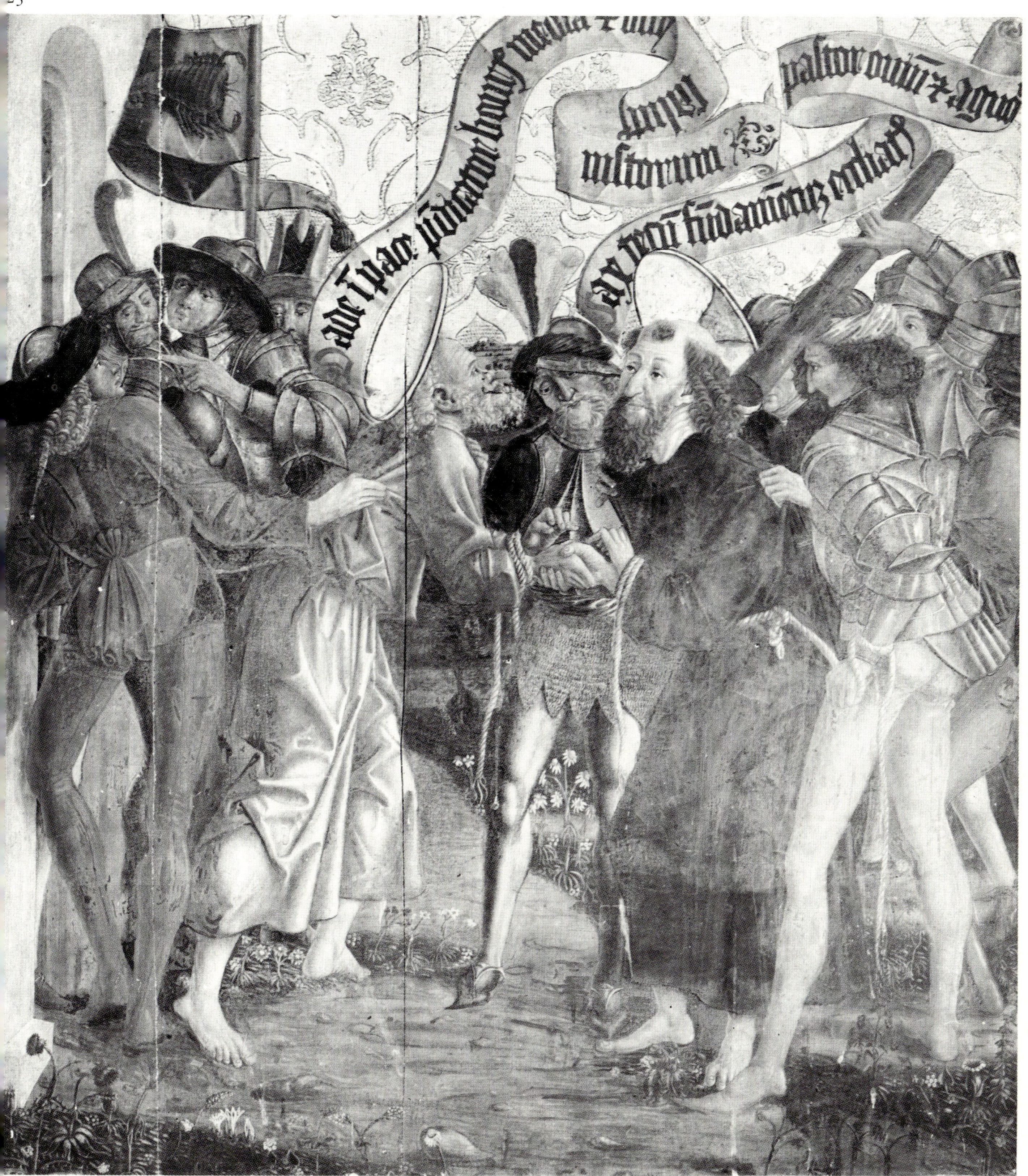

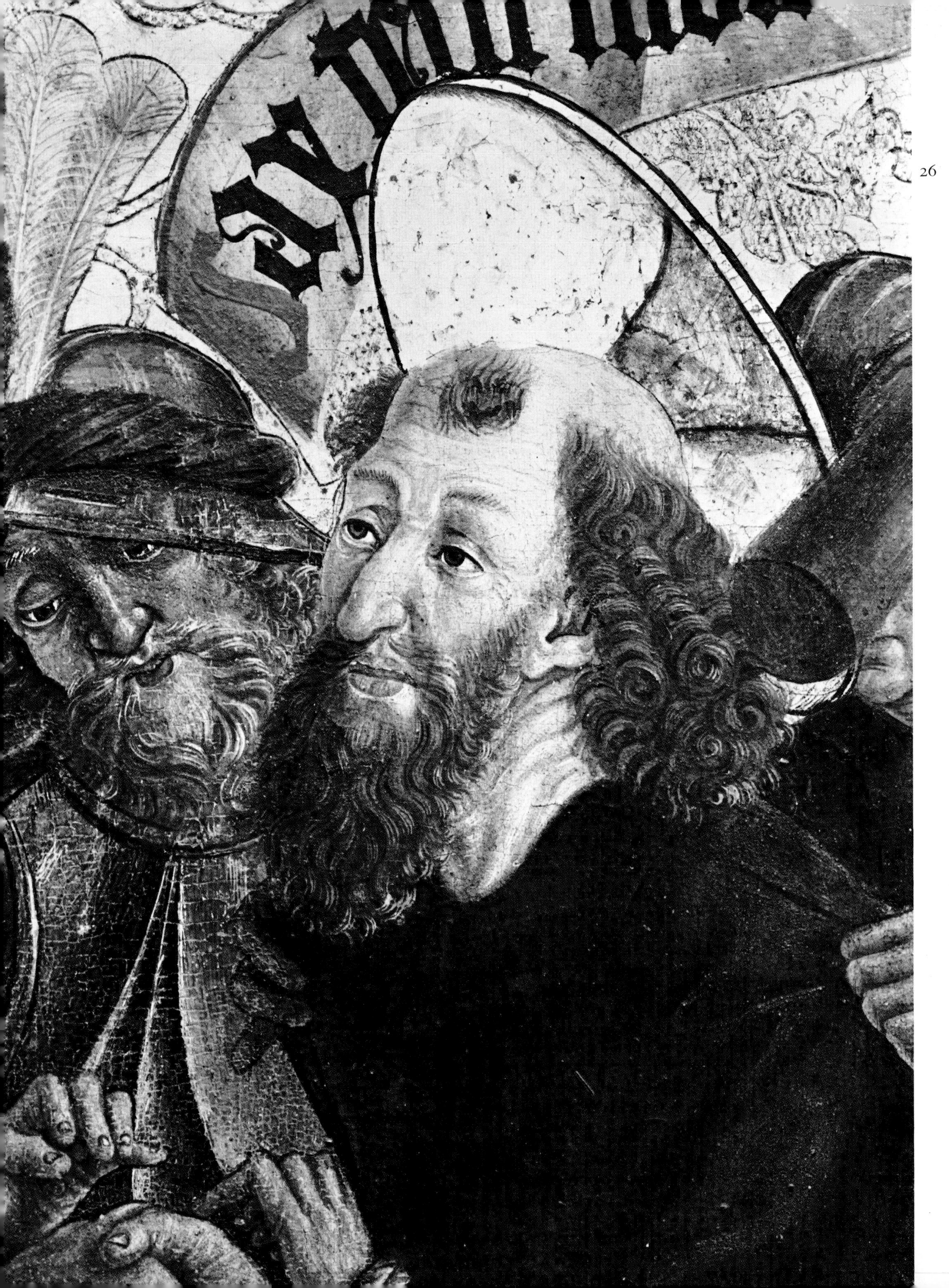

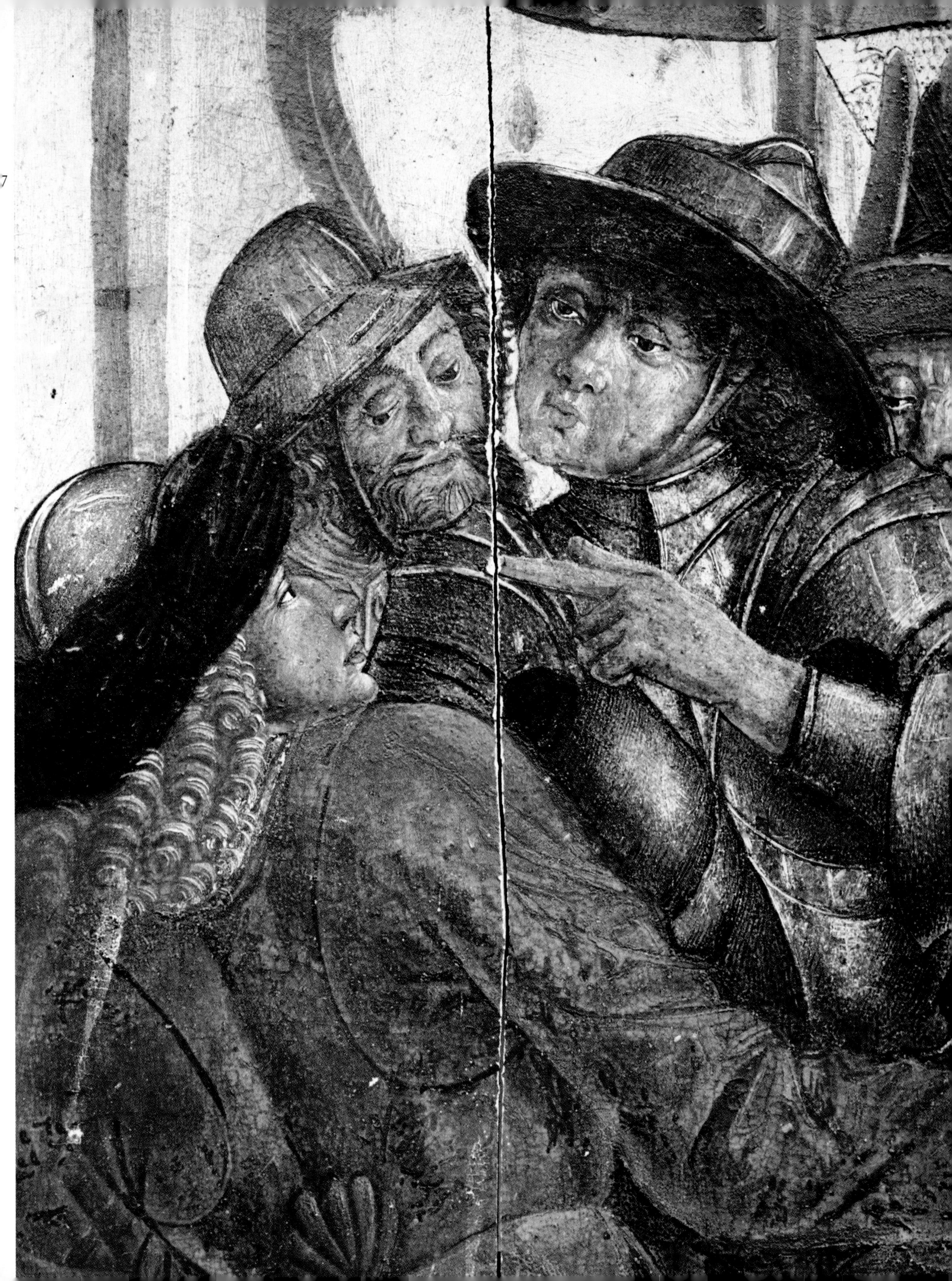

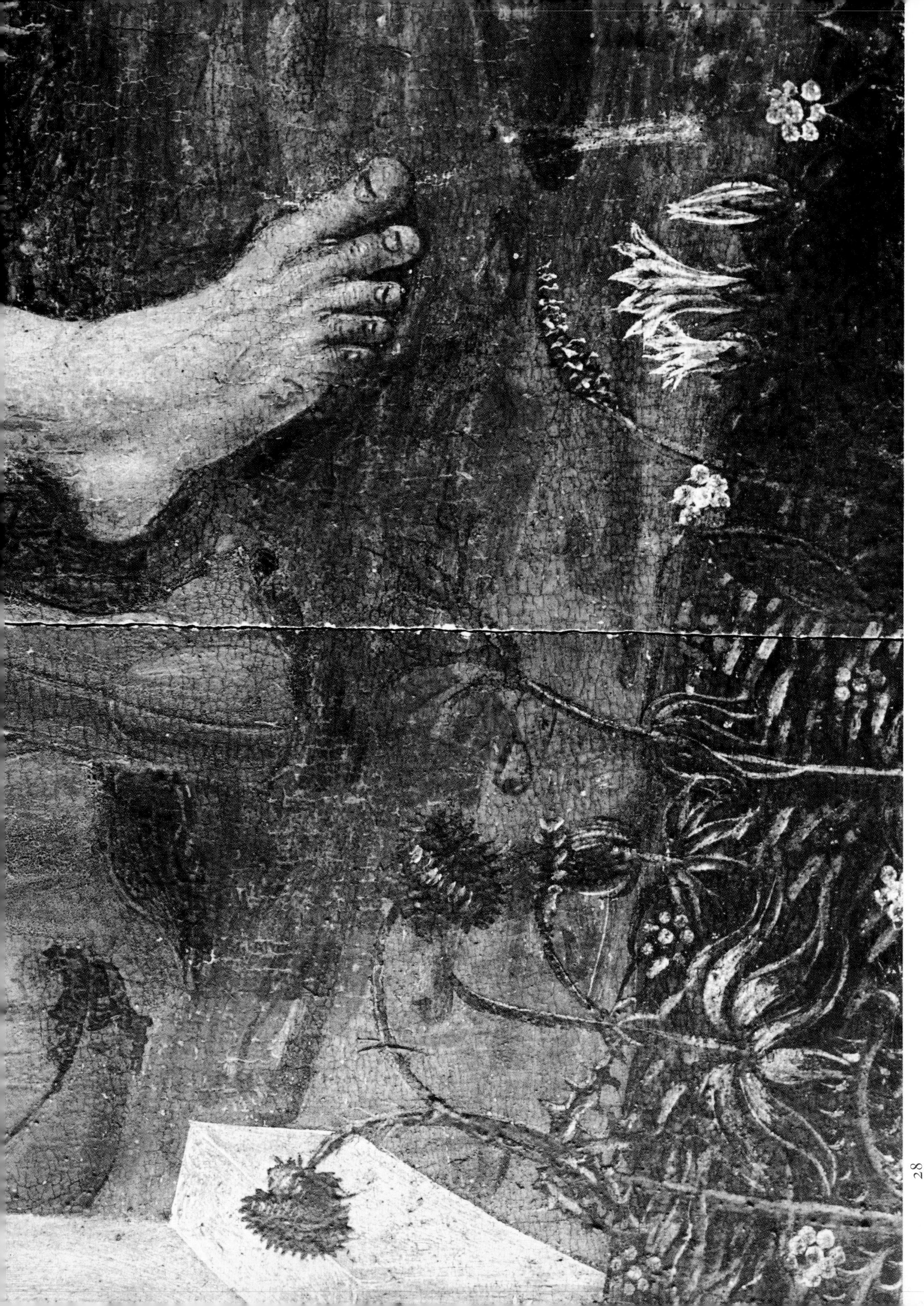

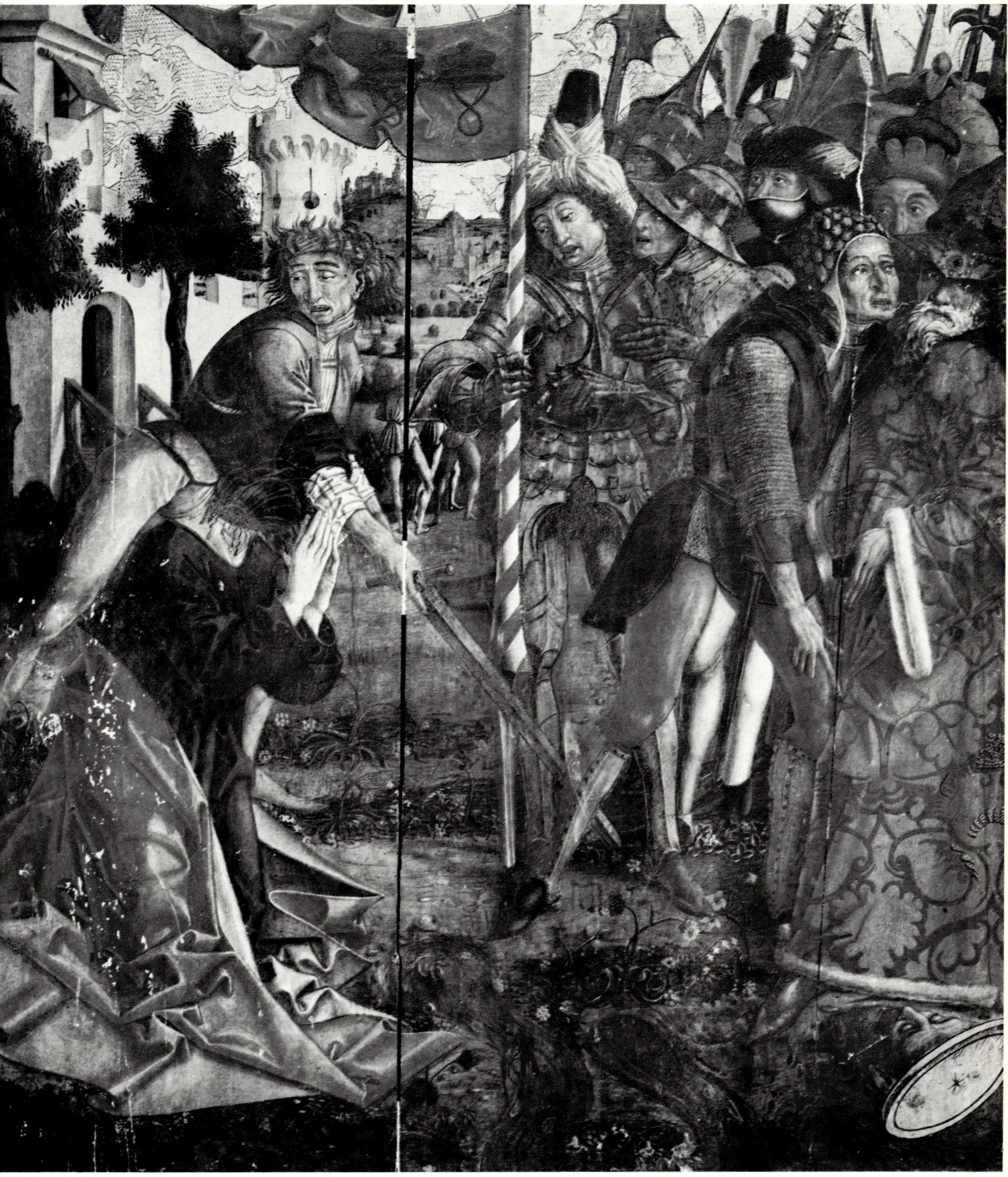

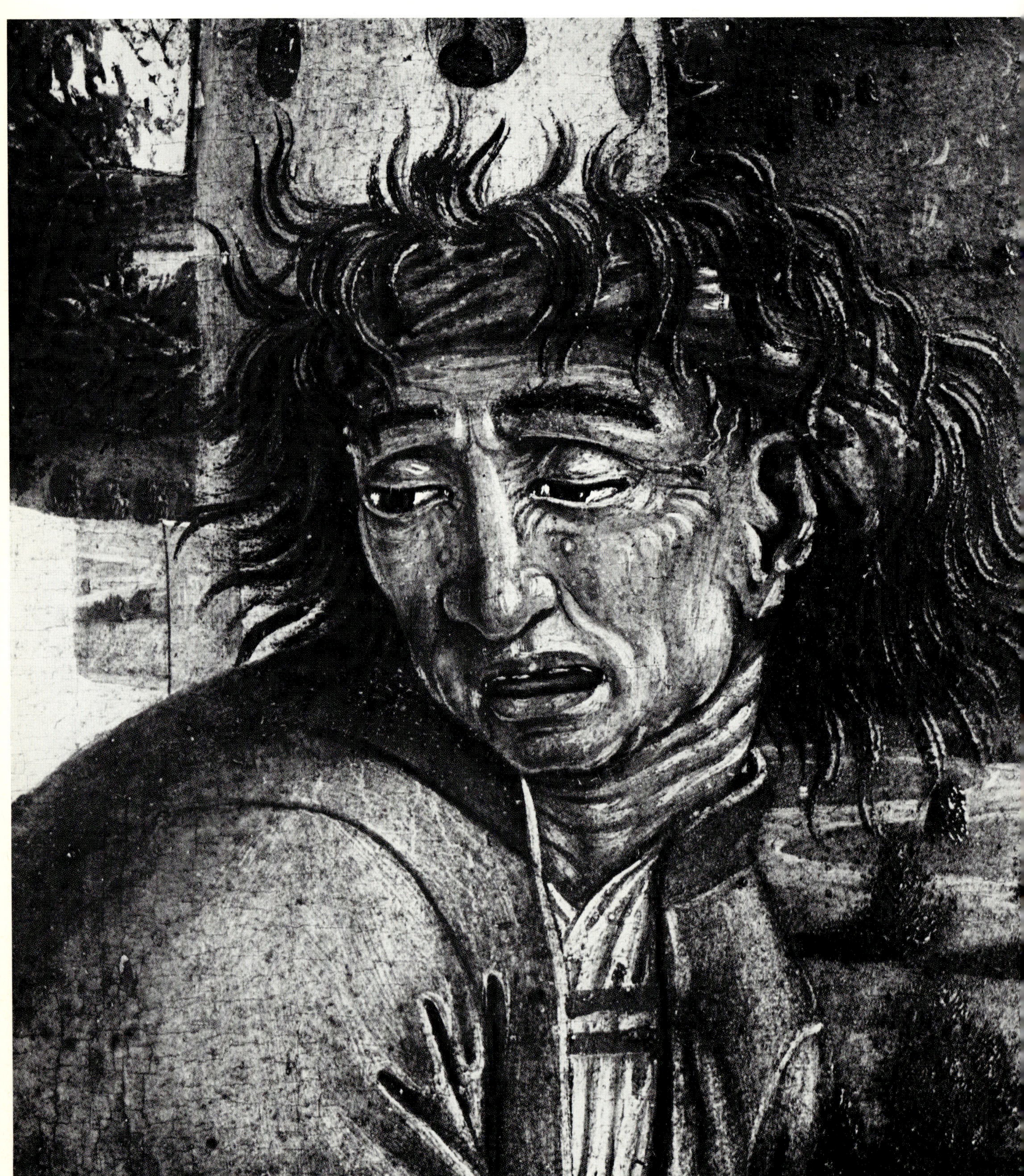

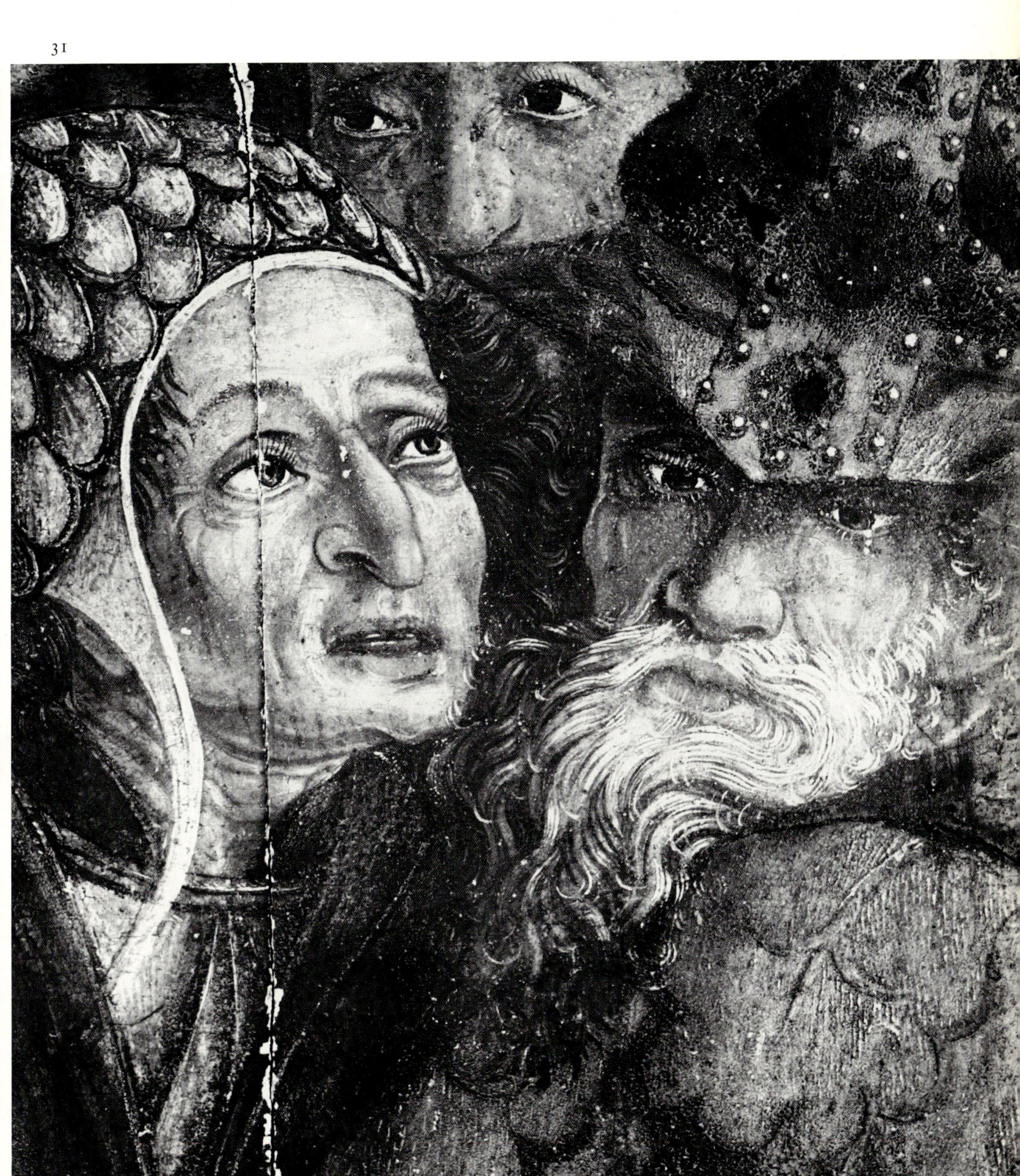

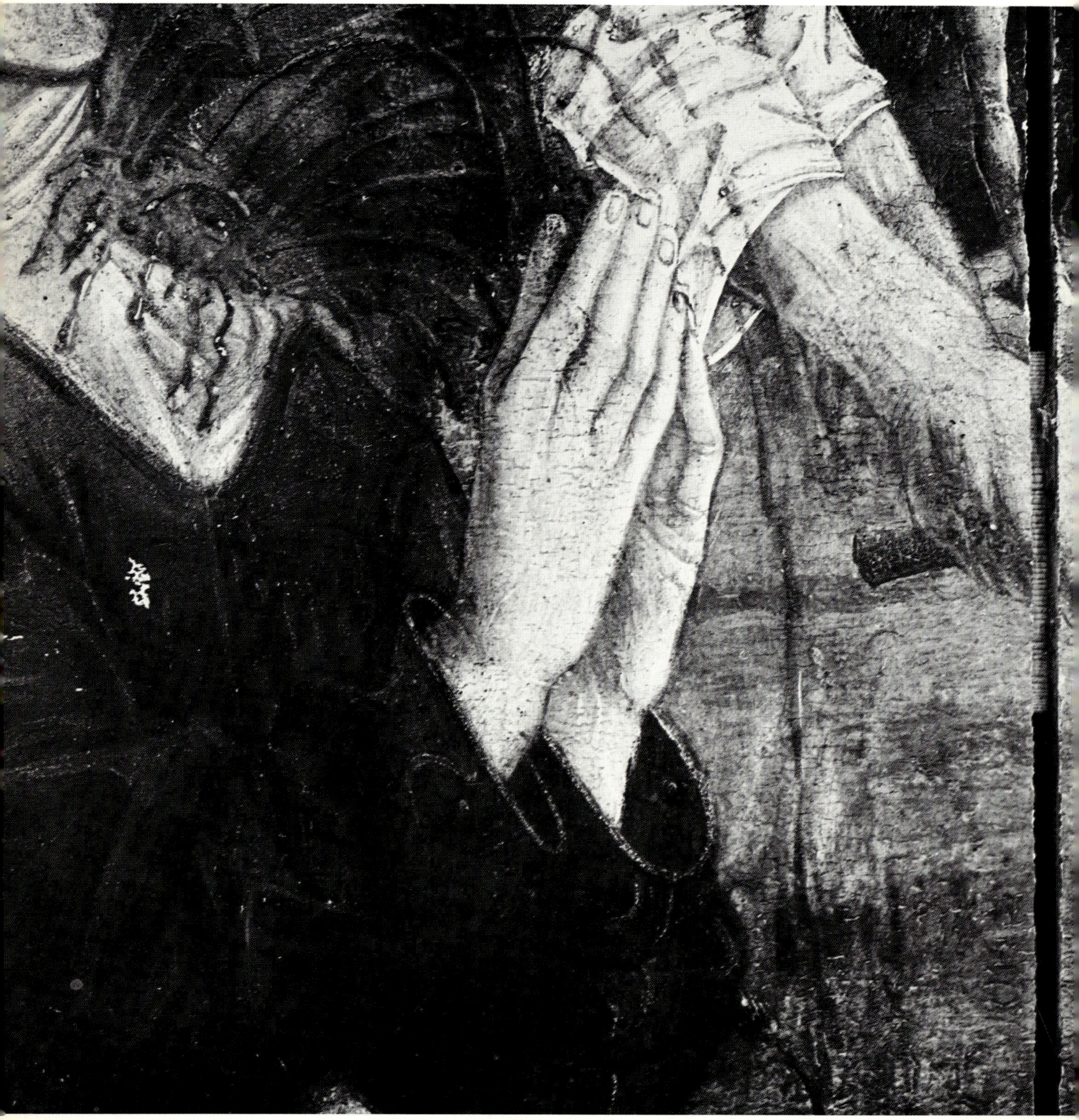

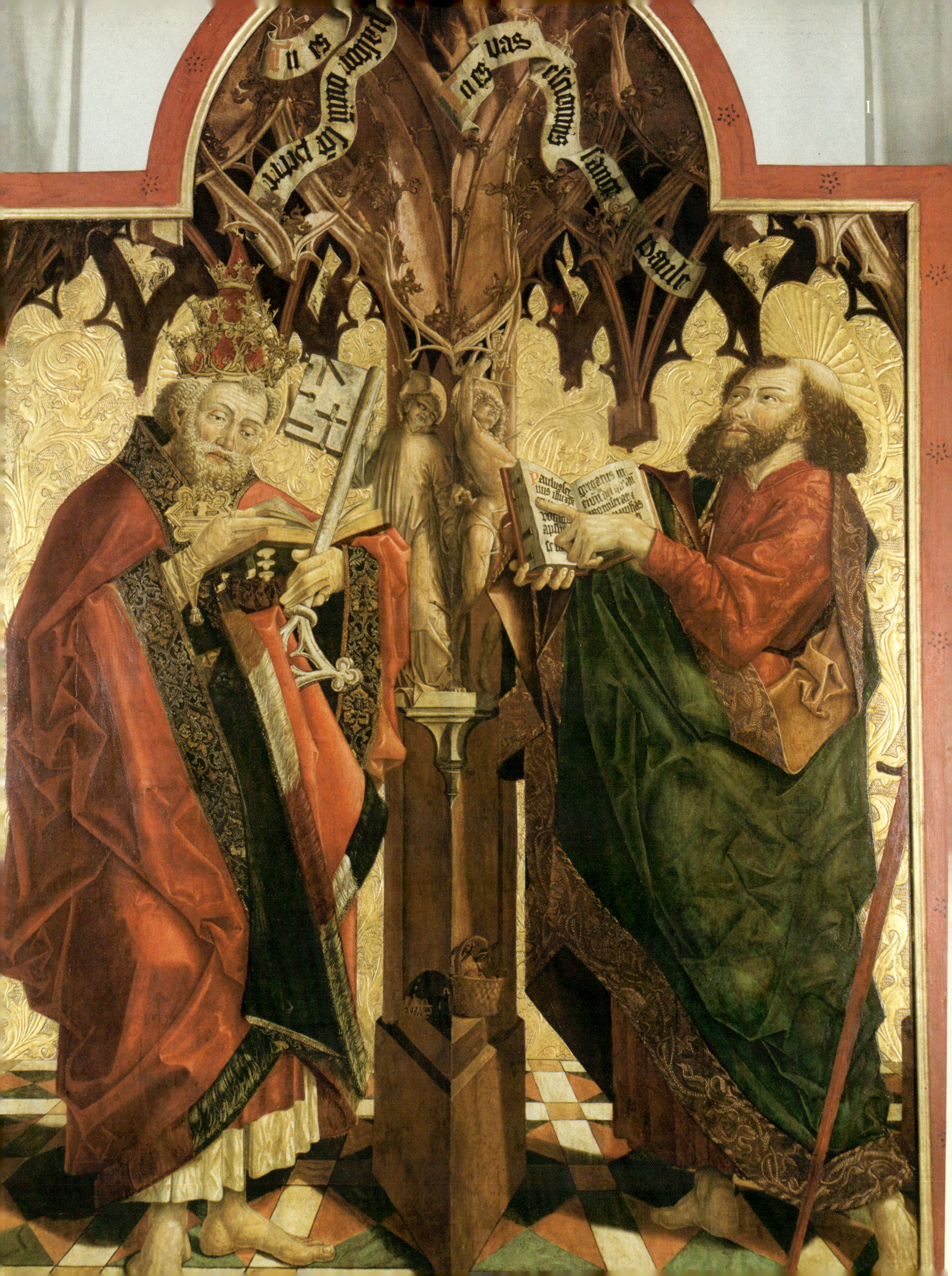

Tu es Petrus
vas electionis
sant paulus

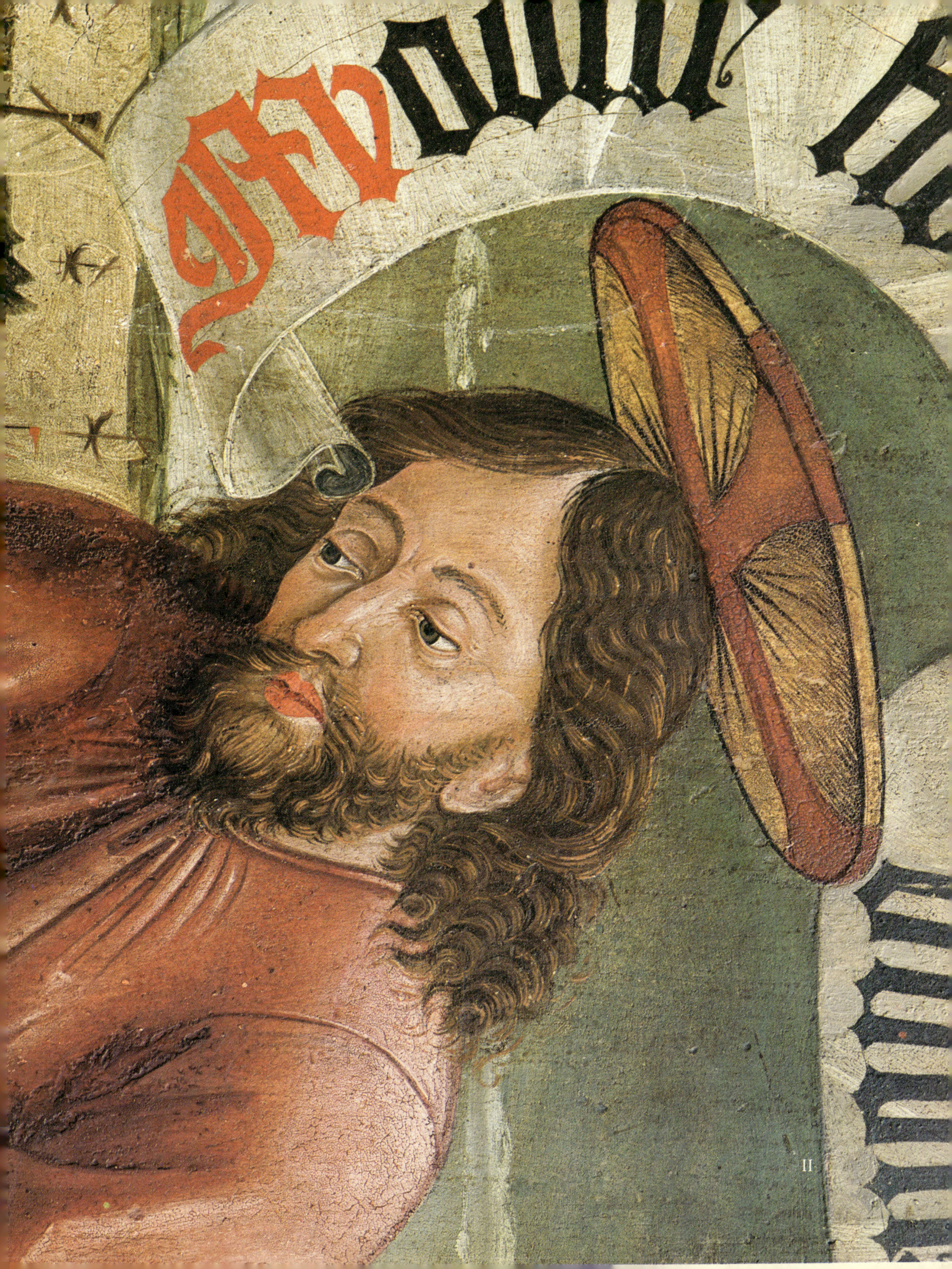

II

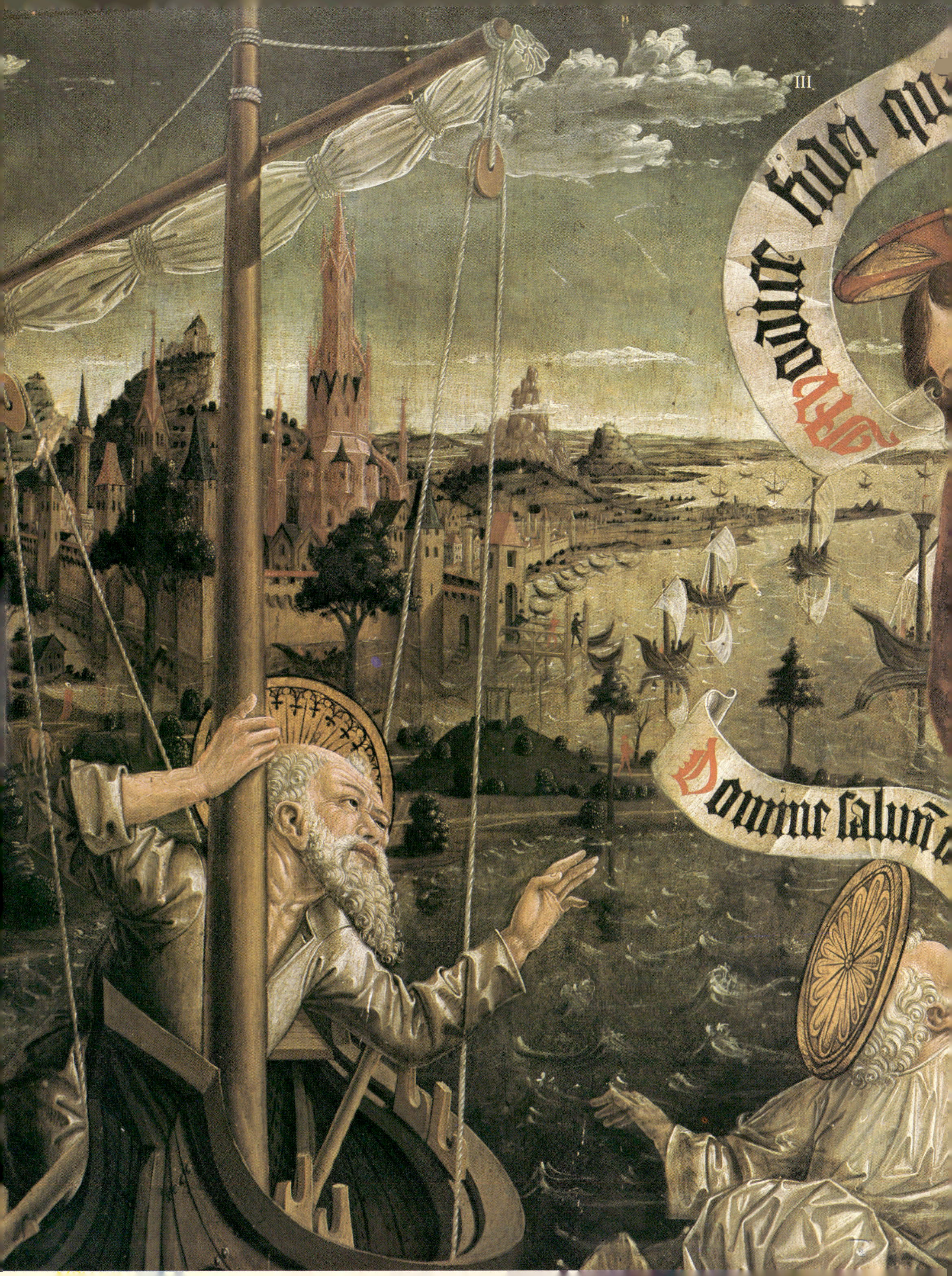
III
fidi qu
Domine saluũ

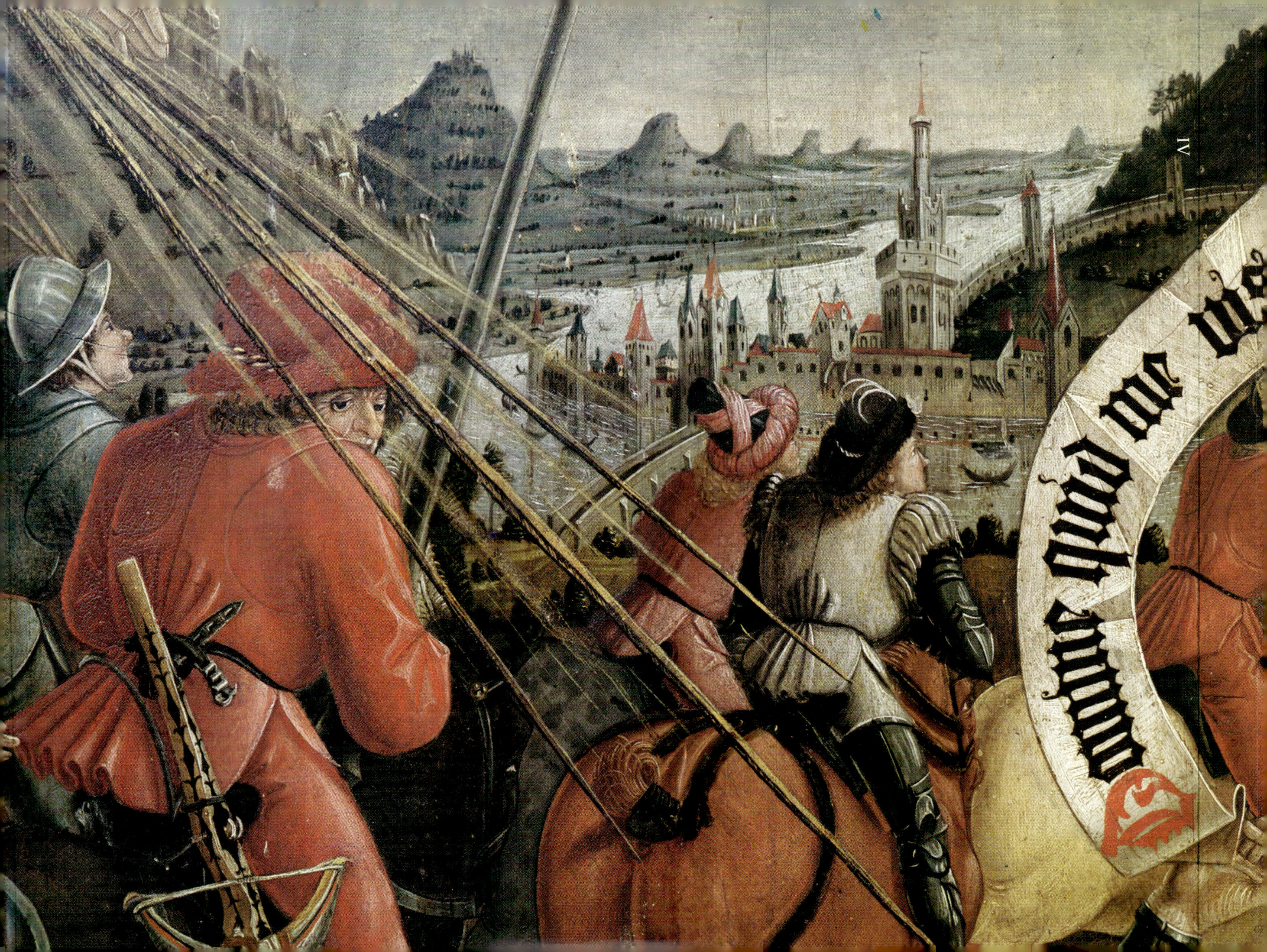

IV

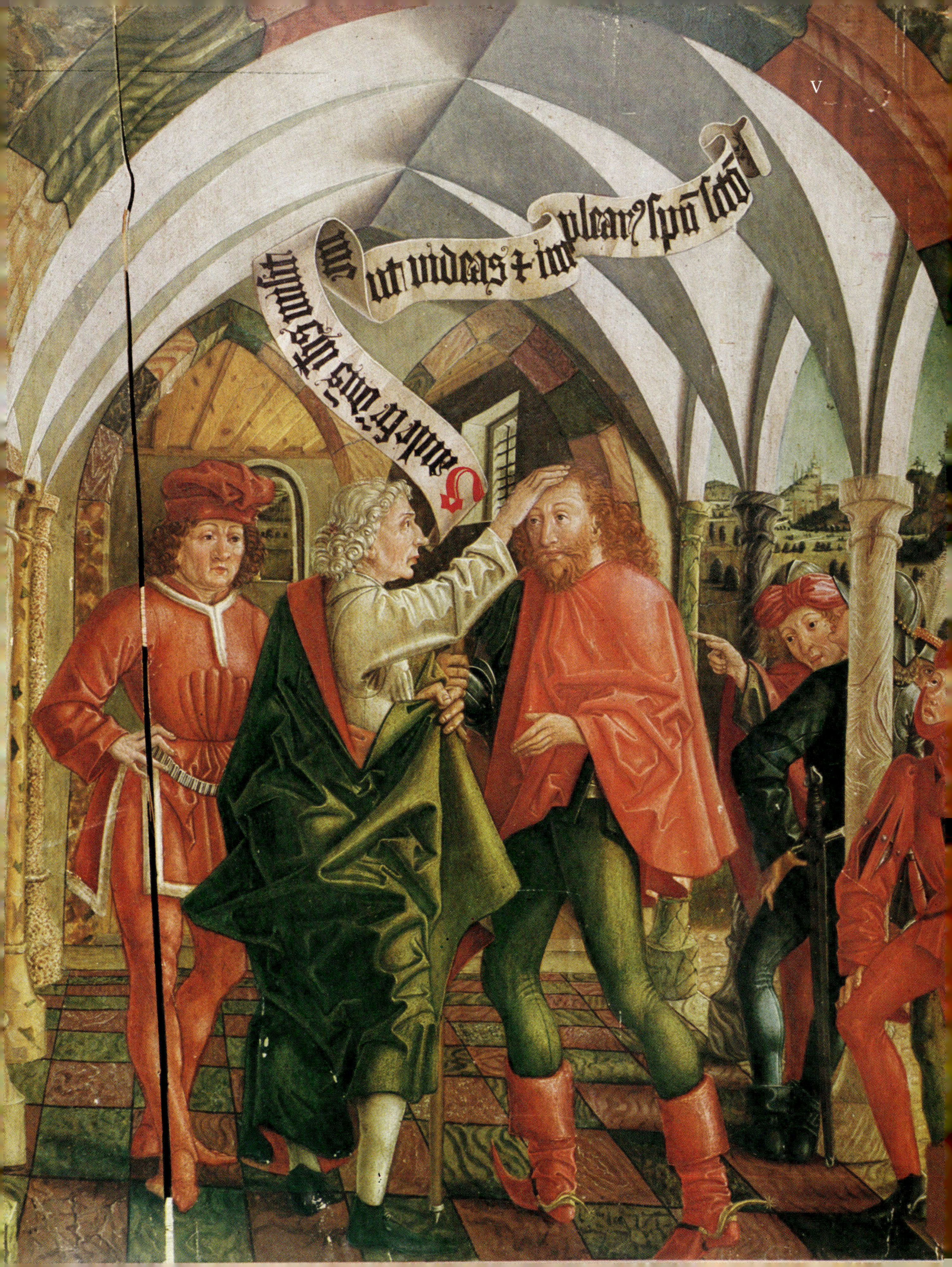
ut videas + im plearis spū scō
āte eūg suā agㄴㅅe
Sal oq̇ Anaīas

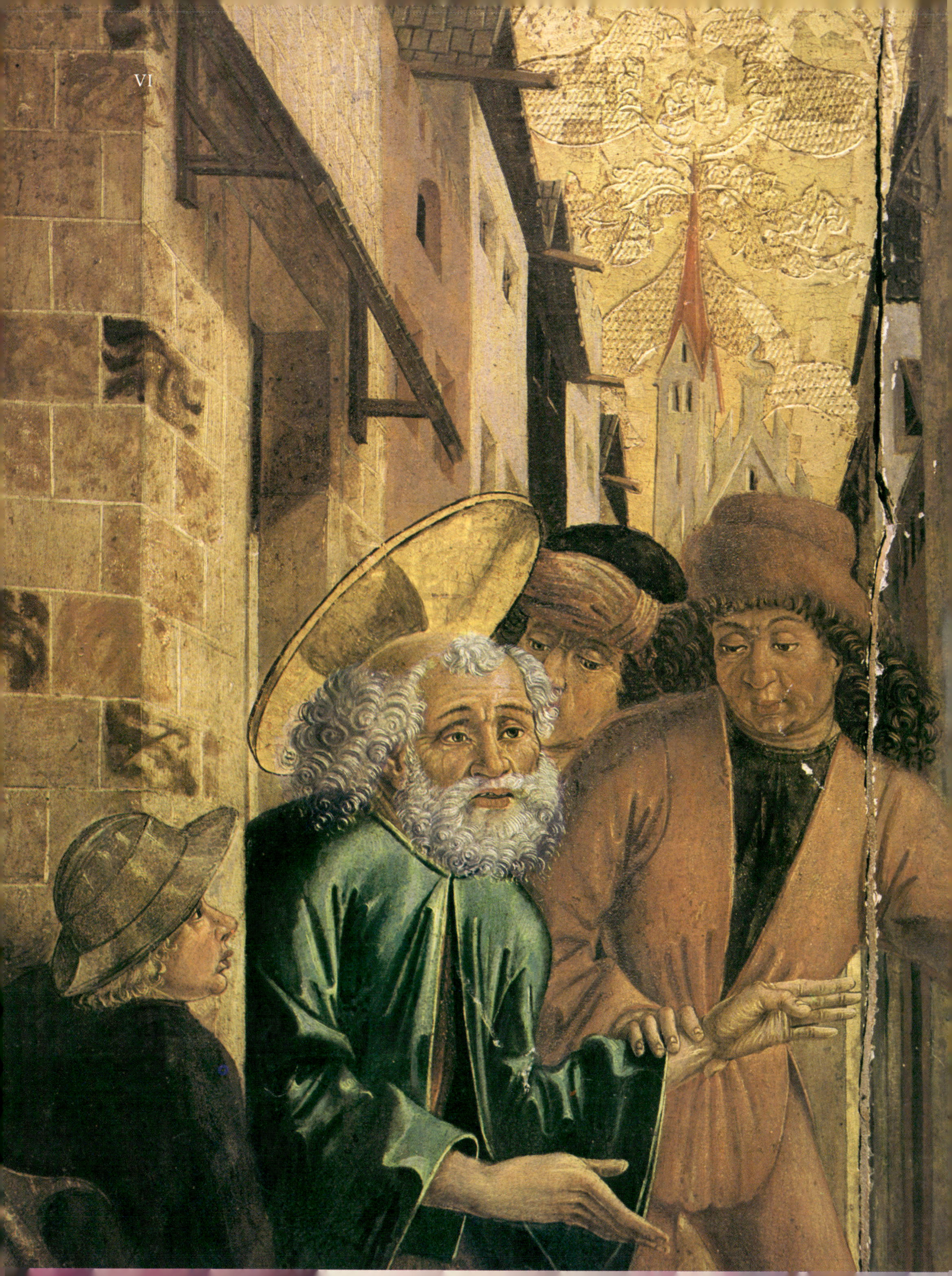

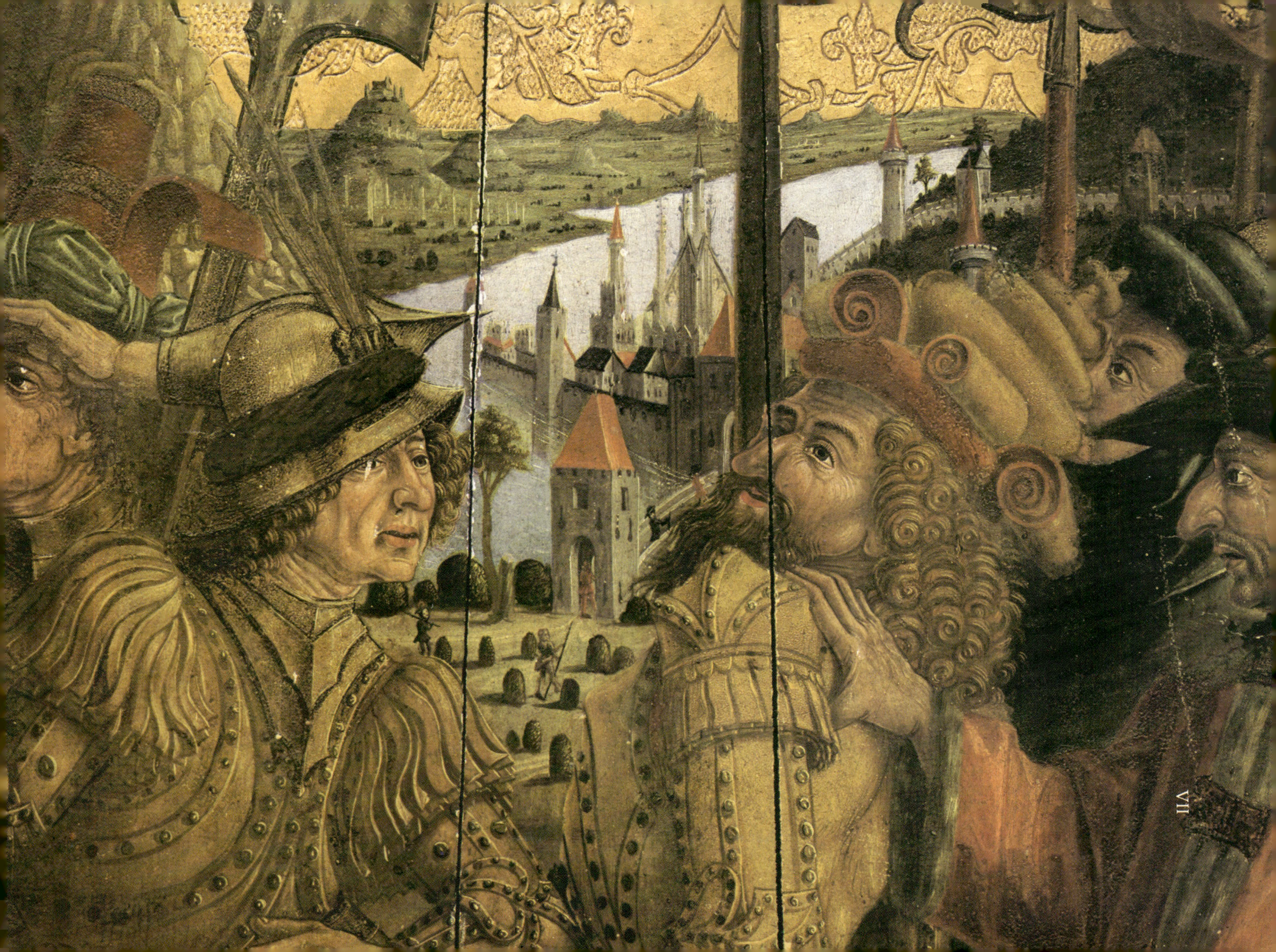
VII

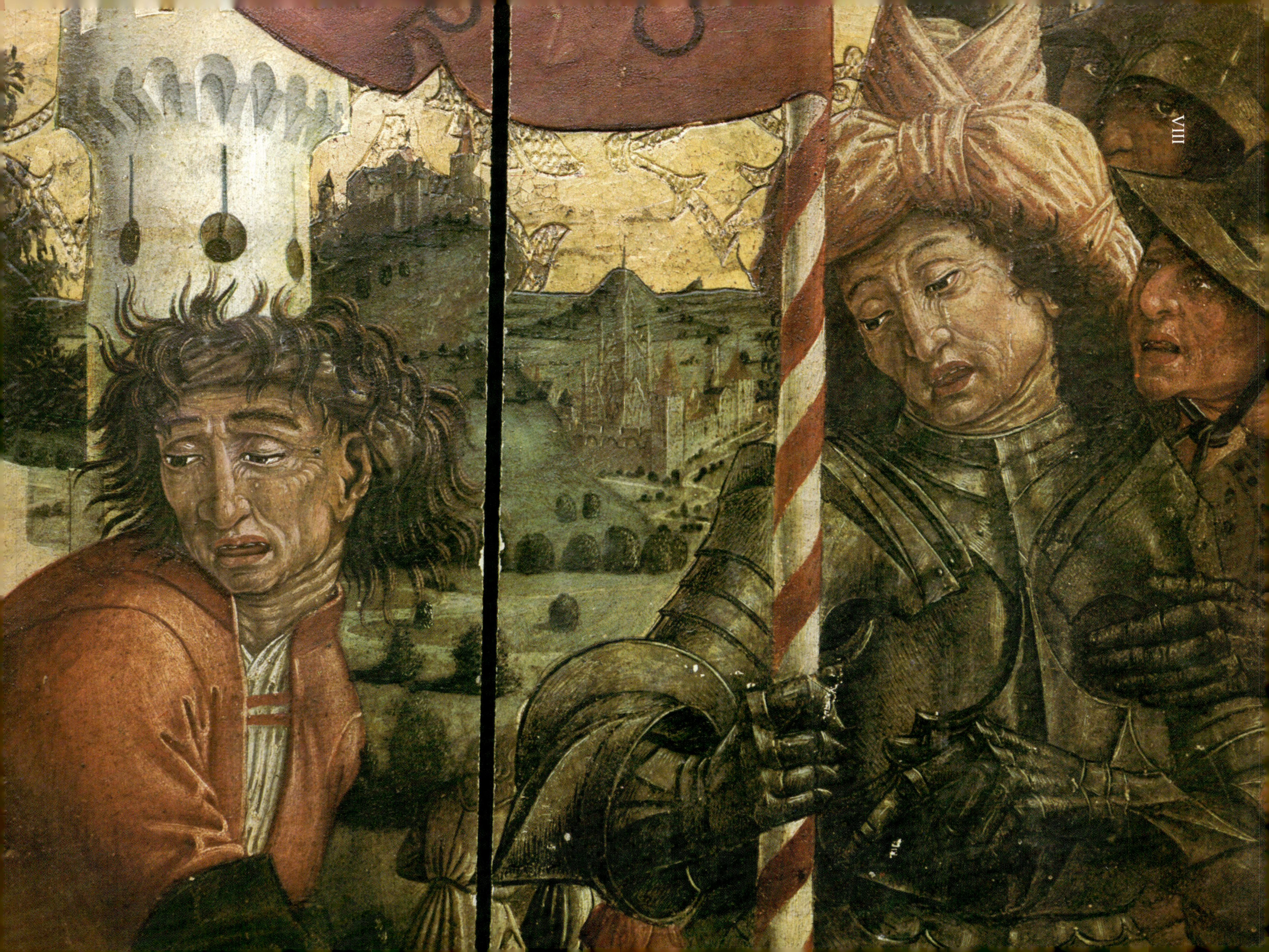
VIII

Notes

1   The history of the Jöchlsthurn is given by B. Rihl, *Die Kunst An der Brennerstrasse*, Leipzig, 1898, pp. 100–1. For a detailed account of the history of the altarpiece see Philip Maria Halm, 'Der Ehmalige St Peter und Paulus Altar in Jöchlsthurn zu Sterzing und Friedrich Pacher', *Kunst und Kunsthandwerk XV Jahg.*, Wien, 1912 (hereafter cited as *Halm*), 573 ff.; Oskar Döring, 'Neues über ein Tiroler Altar Werk des XV Jahrhunderts', *Christliche Kunst*, VIII, 1912 (hereafter cited as Döring, 1912) 301; *id.*, *Michael Pacher und die Seinen*, München – Gladbach, 1913 (hereafter cited as Döring, 1913), p. 140 (where 1464 should be corrected to 1474. The date 1455 assigned by Döring, p. 146, to Lienard's commemorative inscription on the vault of the church is probably another printer's lapse). The damaged and overpainted figures of the two Princes of the Apostles in the withered fifteenth-century fresco, which can still be seen flanking The Virgin above the modest entrance-porch of the chapel, is the only pictorial evidence to the fact that the iconography of the altarpiece accorded with its titular saints. The fresco was attributed to Michael Pacher by Walter Mannowsky, *Die Gemälde Michael Pachers*, Munich and Leipzig, 1910 (hereafter cited as Mannowsky), pp. 64–5, Pl. 32. It has been attributed to Friedrich Pacher by Halm, p. 608 ff.. See also Prinz J. Clemens von Bayern, 'Friedrich Pacher', in U. Thieme and F. Becker, eds., *Allgemeines Lexikon Der Bildenden Künstler*, Vol. 26, Leipzig, 1932 (hereafter cited as Thieme–Becker), p. 121; Alfred Stange, *Deutsche Malerei der Gotik*, Vol. X, Munich-Berlin, 1960 (hereafter cited as Stange), p. 185; *cf.* Eberhard Hempel, *Michael Pacher*, Vienna, 1931 (hereafter cited as Hempel), p. 93.

2   Stange, p. 185. A short notice on the acquisition of the Peter and Paul panel appeared in the *Veröffentlichen des Museum Ferdinandeum*, Innsbruck, Vol. 31, 1958, p. 213.

3   R. Stiassny, 'Die Pacher Schule', *Repertorium für Kunstwissenschaft*, XXVI, 1903, Berlin, p. 26, but *cf.* Halm p. 574, n.l.

4   Sepp wrote an eulogistic treatise on this Bavarian Maecenas: *Ludwig I Augustus, König von Bayern und der Zeitalter die Künste*, Munich, 1869.

5   The chief sources on Sepp's voyage to Palestine and his donation are his own writings: J. N. Sepp, *Neue hochwichtige Entdeckungen auf der Zweiter Palästinafahrt*, Vol. I, Munich, 1896, p. 198, and his biography, published anonymously, *Dr Johann Nepomuk Sepp (1816–1909) Ein Bild seines Leben nach seinen eigenen Aufzeichnungen. Xenium zum hundertsten Geburstag*, Part 1, Regensburg, 1916, pp. 81, 164, n. 34 (see also the following note); *cf.* P. Schegg, *Gedenkbuch einer pilgerreise nach dem Heiligen Lande*, Vol. II, Munich, 1867, p. 275, who cites the inscription (probably incorrectly) thus: 'HAS VII PICTURAS DONAVIT DR SEPP PROF. MONACENSIS/VITAE JESU CHRISTI AUCTOR ET SANCTAE TERRAE DEFINITOR (see also J. N. Sepp, *Jerusalem und das Heilige Land*, Vol. II, Schaffhausen, 1873, pp. 203–4 and Halm, p. 574, n. 4). The written acknowledgement of the donation was sent to Sepp only in September 1862, which might have been the real date of the arrival of the panels in Palestine. Unfortunately, the memorial tablet has disappeared from the church and the identification of the true text has remained unsolved.

6 J. N. Sepp, 'Die Kirchenväter im Besitz des Prof. Sepp', in *Repertorium für Kunstwissenschaft*, XI, 1888, 345–7 (hereafter cited as Sepp, 1888).

7 They were used by Döring, 1912 and 1913 (*see* Döring, 1912, p. 301) and Halm (p. 576, n. 1.) and as late as 1931 by Johann von Allesch, *Michael Pacher*, Leipzig, 1931 (hereafter cited as Allesch), (*see* p. 505) and by Hempel, 1931. From then, no reproduction of any of the Jerusalem panels appeared until the publication of the complete series by P. A. Picirillo O. F. M., 'Le Storie dei Santi Pietro e Paolo narrate nelle 7 tavole che si conservano nel museo della Flagellazione', *La Terra Santa*, XVII, 6–7, (Jerusalem), 1967 (hereafter cited as Picirillo), 197 ff.

8 The paintings are reported as being exhibited in the refectory in Sepp's biography (1916), *loc. cit.* See also Otto Pächt, *Österreichische Tafelmalerei der Gotik*, Augsburg-Vienna, 1929 (hereafter cited as Pächt), p. 78. As late as 1939, Salvini, following Pächt and Allesch, reported the paintings as still being in Tiberias, Roberto Salvini, 'Una nuova opera di Federico Pacher e alcune conclusioni sulla cronologia del pittore', *Le Arti*, 17, II, 1939, 189, and Allesch, p. 200. But *cf.* Thieme-Becker, p. 121; P. Bellarmino Bagatti, *Guida al Museo della Flagellazione in Gerusalemme*, Jerusalem, 1939, pp. 142–5; and Picirillo, p. 198. Stange, Vol. X, p. 185, thought that Sepp had donated the seven panels to the Franciscan convent in Jerusalem.

9 Sepp, 1888, pp. 346–7. As late as 1929, Pächt, p. 78, was still of the opinion that the general design of the central panel was due to Michael Pacher.

10 Michael Pacher is too well known to need more than a summary account here. A biography and a good, though not complete, bibliography are included in the latest monography on him, Nicoló Rasmo, *Michele Pacher*, Milan, 1969 (hereafter cited as Rasmo, 1969; English translation, Phaidon, London, 1970). Rasmo claims (pp. 13, 14, 239–40) that since no Pacher is documented in Bruneck before 1467, it should be inferred that Michael was a newcomer, arriving there from one of the surrounding localities in the Puster Valley. However, he rejects (or at least strongly doubts) the generally accepted hypothesis which proposes Neustift as Pacher's birthplace. Reverend Martin Beittner, librarian and conductor of the choir of Neustift, has kindly drawn my attention to the mediaeval *Pacherhof*, which still exists south of the monastery.

11 Maximilian Schrott, 'Michael Pacher's Verwandschaft', *Cultura Atesina*, Nos 1–4, 1966, 13–44; Rasmo, 1969, pp. 239–40.

12 Michael Pacher's earliest documented work is an altarpiece commissioned *c.* 1462 for the Church of St Lawrence (St Lorenzen) in the Puster Valley. The paintings of the shutters, now dispersed between the Munich Alte Pinakothek and the Österreichische Galerie, Vienna, show Pacher's precocious interest in linear perspective and problems of rational representation of space. As for his role in the history of German painting as the *avant-garde* master of his times, see G. Bonsanti, 'Il Michele Pacher del Rasmo', *Arte Veneta*, 24, 1970, 275.

13 Robert Stiassny, 'Ein Mitteldeutscher Alpenkünstler', *Deutsche Rundschau*, No. 12, 1897, 20, was the first to observe that the paintings of the *St Wolfgang Altarpiece* were executed by several different hands. He was also the first to have ascribed the eight scenes on the external wings to Friedrich Pacher ('Urkundliches über Friedrich Pacher', *Repertorium für Kunstwissenschaft*, No. XXIII, 1900, p. 39). His study was later developed by Mannowsky, pp. 77–82, Pls 43–51; H. Semper, *Michael und Friedrich Pacher*, Eszlingen, 1911 (hereafter cited as Semper, 1911), pp. 30, 210, 238 ff., 293; Halm, p. 597 ff.; Döring, 1913, p. 156; Hempel, pp. 26, 49 ff., 92–3; Thieme-Becker, p. 121; Stange, p. 172 ff.; Rasmo, 1969, p. 136 ff.; W. Böck, 'Der Anteil Michael und Friedrich Pachers an den Gemälden des Altars in St Wolfgang', *Festschrift Luitpold Dussler*, Munich, 1972, p. 177 ff. Opinion as to the extent of Friedrich's collaboration, as well as that of the other assistants of Michael Pacher, varies from one author to another. Some members of Michael Pacher's circle, particularly his son Hans (Stiassny, *loc. cit.*; Semper, 1911, p. 30, n. 2; Rasmo, 1969, p. 140) have been suggested as being responsible for the execution of diverse parts of the altarpiece; but

to date not one of these suggestions has been proven.

14 Documents related to Friedrich Pacher were first published in 1878 by D. Schönherr, cited by G. Dahlke, 'Michael Pacher', *Repertorium für Kunstwissenschaft*, VIII, 1885, p. 30 ff. and later in 'Urkunden und Regesten aus dem k. k. Statthaltereiarchiv', *Jahrbuch der Kunsthistorischen Sammlungen d. Allerh. Kaiserhäuser*, II (1884), XVI ff. (republished by the Kunstfreund, 1893), p. 59. A documentary history of Friedrich Pacher's life and civil career is by R. Stiassny, *op. cit.*, 1900, p. 38 ff. Further documents were brought to light by M. Schrott and partly published by E. D. Theil-Salmoiraghi, Michael Pacher in Neustift, Milan, 1946, p. 52. M. Schrott, in *Cultura Atesina*, 1966, *loc. cit.*; K. Wolfsgruber, 'Beiträge zur Pacher–Forschung', *Der Schlern*, 43, 1969, 132.

Semper, 1911, has remained the only book which includes in its title the name of Friedrich Pacher. A bibliographical summary is given in Thieme-Becker, pp. 120–1. See also Allesch, pp. 43 ff.; Hempel, p. 22; Stange, p. 181 ff. Vincenz Oberhammer *et al.*, *Gotik in Tirol* (Catalogue of the Exhibition at the Ferdinandeum, Innsbruck), 1950 (hereafter cited as Oberhammer, 1950), p. 45, believes that Friedrich Pacher must have been born *c.* 1430–5; Rasmo (1969), p. 111, post-dates his birth as late as *c.* 1450. Most other datings fall between these two.

There is no documentary evidence for the collaboration between the two Pachers. Neither the problem of chronological precedence in age and in artistic activity nor that of their presumed kinship has been satisfactorily solved. For some disputed views, see the above-mentioned authors and Semper, 1911, pp. 16 ff., 40, *passim*; Döring, 1913, p. 156 ff.; N. Rasmo, *Nuove Acquisizione alla conoscenza dell'arte medioevale dell'Alto Adige*, Bolzano, 1952, reprinted from *Cultura Atesina*, IV, 1950 (hereafter cited as Rasmo, 1950 [1952]), p. 16 ff., 1969, pp. 111, 195, 239 ff.; Pächt, p. 48 ff.; Hempel, 1931, pp. 21, 26, 27; R. Salvini, *Sulla posizione storica di Michele Pacher*, Bolzano, 1937, p. 14 ff.; Stange, p. 181 ff.; Rasmo, 1969, pp. 239–40 and 110–22, where a hypothetical chronology is given, though some points in it are open to serious doubts. According to Rasmo, the collaboration probably began around 1468 and

ended in 1481. He claims (contrary to our opinion) that Friedrich Pacher established his own workshop in Bruneck only after he had concluded his work on the St Wolfgang shutters in 1481.

15 The *Baptism* is mentioned in all writings on Friedrich Pacher and in many on Michael. The most important references are: Semper, 1911, pp. 17 ff., 209 ff., Fig. 7; Halm, pp. 591 ff., Pl. 13; Döring, 1913, p. 138 ff., Pl. 75; Hempel, p. 22 ff., Fig. 29; Allesch, p. 115, Pl. 29; Oberhammer, 1950, p. 46, Pl. 55; Rasmo, 1950 (1952) p. 19 ff.; Stange, p. 182, Pl. 289. The *Baptism* was transferred from its original location to Landshut and from there in 1809 to the Klerikalseminar in Freising. The original shutters and the predella (if, indeed, there was one) have not survived.

16 A list of works appears in Thieme-Becker, pp. 120–1 and Stange, p. 182 ff. Friedrich's works are also mentioned in the other bibliographical sources cited throughout this essay. Recent attributions and illustrations are included in Oberhammer, 1950, p. 45 ff.; N. Rasmo, *Arte Medievale nell'Alto Adige*, Bolzano, 1949 (Exhibition Catalogue), p. 34 ff., n. 108–14; *id.*, 1969, p. 110 and *passim*. Good illustrations (frequently assigned to anonymous artists of Friedrich Pacher's circle) appear in Semper, 1911; Halm; Doring, 1913; and Allesch.

17 Mannowsky, p. 77.

18 Whenever such backgrounds appear in the scenes of the *St Wolfgang Altarpiece*, they probably indicate the active participation of Friedrich Pacher, even when the general design is not his. The castle on the right in the skyline of the Munich *Baptism*, however, seems to have been borrowed from Michael's 'Flight into Egypt' in the predella of the *St Wolfgang Altarpiece*.

19 One of these two scenes, the 'Temptation of Christ' in the *St Wolfgang Altarpiece*, does not belong to the scenes executed by Friedrich Pacher and his assistants. However, one is tempted to think that either he or a member of his workshop was invited to participate in the execution of the plants and flowers in the foreground of this scene.

20 *Cf.* the ruined fresco of the *Baptism* in the Dominicans' Cloister, Bozen, where God is represented in
the same way.

21 Halm, p. 596, considers these script-rolls as 'Friedrich's signature'. This may be too far fetched.
Script-rolls similar to those used by Friedrich
Pacher appear in the dismembered *Altarpiece
of St Stephen*, attributed to his important rival,
the Uttenheim Master. The numerous frescos,
painted mainly during the fourteenth and fifteenth
centuries, which decorate the cloister of Brixen
Cathedral abound in inscriptions and script-rolls.
However, script-rolls with the same neat triangular
folds as in Friedrich's works appear only in a well-
defined group of scenes, all of which
were apparently painted by the same master,
variously identified as Jacob Sunter or Leonard
von Brixen. These include the 'Nativity', 'Christ
among the Doctors', 'The Coronation of the
Virgin', 'The Resurrection'. Their enigmatic creator was probably Friedrich's only real precursor
in the Brixen school of painting. *Cf.* Hempel,
1931, p. 11., Fig. 8.

   With the rise of realism in the later fifteenth
century, script-rolls gradually became obsolete
and old-fashioned. They persisted, however, around
the turn of the century, and even later, in works of
art of a more popular character (popular art
has been always conservative), such as prints, illustrations in early block-books and incunabula,
tapestries, etc. The fact that not a single inscription
appears in the paintings of the *St Wolfgang Altarpiece*
(even in those in which Michael Pacher was
assisted by Friedrich) might serve as further
proof of the fact that Friedrich's responsibility,
as far as their general design was concerned,
was rather limited.

22 See n. 71. Döring, 1913, pp. 129, 130, Fig. 72 has
proven that the direct source of inspiration for the
architectural frame of the *Baptism* was an engraving
by the Master E. S. (1467) reworked by Israhel
Van Meckenem. See M. Lehrs, *Geschichte und
Kritische Katalog des deutschen, niederländischen und
Franzosischen Kupferstiches um 15. Jahrhunderts*,
Vol. II, No. 57, Vienna, 1910 (works by Master
E. S. will hereafter be cited according to their
numbers in Lehrs' list). This is a sophisticated

version of an earlier phase of the same print
(Lehrs, No. 56). A double arch, which is half-
way between these two versions and is likewise
enclosed by a rectangular window appears in
the *Birth of the Virgin* (Germanisches National
Museum, Nürnberg) and in the *Annunciation*
(Bayerische National Museum, Munich) by the
Uttenheim Master.

23 As to these frescos, see N. Rasmo, *Il Chiostro
monumentale di S. Domenico a Bolzano*, Bolzano,
1953, p. 38; Rasmo, 1952 (1950), p. 20, n. 37.

24 The closest example is *St Jerome in His Study*
by Antonello da Messina (National Gallery, London). The attribution to Antonello,
though universally accepted in recent studies, is still
somewhat problematic. So is the dating, which
is generally accepted as *c.* 1475. Antonello's influence on one of Michael Pacher's compositions was
noted by Rasmo, 1969, p. 104. Other analogies
to the 'window frame' may be found in Mantegna's
St Mark (Staedel, Städelsches Kunstinstitut, Frank-
furt); in Carlo Crivelli's *Annunciation* of 1486
(National Gallery, London); and *Madonna and
Child* (Accademia Carrara, Bergamo), and in
other Venetian and Paduan works. *Cf.* Rasmo,
1952, pp. 19, 20, n. 37.

25 See n. 14, 26. The first author who held that Friedrich was influenced by Michael Pacher was J.
Sighard, 'Friedrich Pacher, Maler von Brunecken',
*Mittheilungen des K. K. Central Commission zur
Erforschung und Erhaltung der Baudenkmäle*, IV,
1, 1859, n. 7, 223–4, who went so far as to think
that Friedrich was Michael's son.

26 Works now generally ascribed to Friedrich Pacher
and his workshop were ascribed by earlier authors
to various anonymous masters, i.e., the 'Master
of the *St Katherine Altarpiece*, the 'Master of the
St Barbara Altarpiece (both works are in the Neustift Gallery) or of the *St Magdalen Altarpiece*
(St Korbinian, Thal), or the 'Master of St Korbinian
(named after the *Altarpiece of St Korbinian* (or
of Sts Peter and Paul) in the church of that name
in Thal [Fig. 11]). While Allesch considered
these presumed individual artists as precursors of
both Michael and Friedrich Pacher, they were

considered by other authors as either members of their circle or as followers of Friedrich. See Halm, p. 604 ff.; Semper, 1911, pp. 242, 253 ff.; O. Benesch, 'Der Meister von St Korbinian', *Zeitschrift für bild. Kunst.*, 61 Jg., 1928/9, 153 ff.; Allesch, pp. 13 ff., 218; Thieme-Becker, pp. 121–2; E. Hempel, in Thieme-Becker, Vol. XXXVII, p. 246; Salvini, 'Una Nuova opera di Federico Pacher . . .', *Le Arti*, II, 1938/9, 190; Rasmo, 1949, p. 35; Oberhammer, 1950, p. 47; Rasmo, 1952 p. 2 ff., 18–20; N. Rasmo, 'L'Altare di S. Barbara a Novacella ricomposto', *Cultura Atesina*, VII, 1953, n. 1–4, 160; Stange, pp. 188–9.

27 Halm, p. 604 ff.; Hempel, 1931, p. 93; Thieme-Becker, pp. 121–2; Rasmo, 1950 (1952), pp. 14, 18, n. 37; and Stange, p. 181 ff., arrange Friedrich's works in a conjectural chronological order which follows the presumed dates of his principal works and the hypothetic evolution of the artist's style.

28 As to the various hypotheses concerning the dating of the *Peter and Paul Altarpiece*, see Stiassny, 1903, p. 26; Semper, 1911, p. 248; Halm, p. 590 ff.; Döring, 1912, p. 309; 1913, p. 149; Pächt, p. 78; Benesch, 1929, p. 121; Hempel, p. 22; Thieme-Becker, p. 121; Rasmo, 1949, p. 37; Rasmo, 1950 (1952), p. 14; Oberhammer, 1950, p. 46; *cf.* n. 40.

29 For some of the rules which determine the scheme of the German altarpiece, *see* E. Panofsky, *The Life and Art of Albrecht Dürer* (4th edition), Princeton, 1955; W. Pilz, *Das Triptychon als Komposition und Erzählform*, Munich, 1970, *passim*; J. Braun, *Der Christliche Altar*, Munich, 1924. Typical examples of altarpieces with five scenic representations of episodes from the life of a single saint, all of them seen when the altarpiece is open (i.e., two pairs of scenes painted on the inner sides of the wings and one scene on the central panel) are Friedrich Pacher's own works – the altarpieces of *St Barbara* and *St Katherine* (Neustift [Figs. 29–33]), and the *Altarpiece of the Magdalen* (St Korbinian, Thal-Assling). On the outside of its wings, the first has a Man of Sorrows and a Virgin (damaged); the closed wings of the other two show a painted Annunciation.

30 The *Legenda Aurea* by Jacopo (Jacobus) da Voragine (or *da Varazze*, d. 1264) (*The Golden Legend*, tr. G. Ryan and H. Ripperger, New York, 1969) has served as the principal literary source for the representations of the lives of the saints and their attributes in European art since the fourteenth century. Surprisingly enough, not one of the previous authors has ever mentioned this source in connection with the *Peter and Paul Altarpiece*, though most of the excerpts from the earlier sources, which are claimed by Halm and Döring as the direct sources for the iconography, are cited in the *Legenda Aurea*. *Cf.* Döring, 1912, p. 306; Halm, p. 581 ff.

31 Döring, 1912, pp. 306–7; 1913, pp. 141, 144, and Halm, pp. 574, 590, Figs 11, 12, attempted a reconstruction of the original arrangement of the scenes on the shutters, presuming that it was mainly dictated by the principle of iconographical parallelisms between the two cycles. They arrived at the erroneous conclusion that the missing scene from the life of St Peter must have been the second one.

The original shutters were of the same height and half the width of the central panel. Halm, basing his graphic reconstruction on incorrect measurements of the central panel, wrongly thought that the wings must have reached only the height of its 'shoulders', forgetting that these were created by the mutilation of the central panel in the eighteenth century. These errors are corrected in our reconstruction, Figs 7, 8.

32 Oberhammer, 1950, p. 46. The new frame covers the margins of the painting. For earlier and different measurements, probably with the frame, *cf.* Mannowsky, p. 84; Döring, 1913, p. 140; Halm, p. 574; Pächt, Pl. 66; Allesch, p. 200. See also n. 31.

33 To illustrate by using three German examples, the *St Korbinian Altarpiece* by Friedrich Pacher (Fig. 11), where the sculpture of the saint (not executed by him) is flanked by the painted panels of Sts Peter and Paul; the *Peter and Paul Altarpiece* by Hans Süss Von Kulmbach (Uffizi, Florence), an iconographical program which is similar, though not identical, to that of our work; and

the *Peter and Paul Altarpiece* from Rangersdorf (1426), now in the Diozesanmuseum, Klagenfurt. See Stange, Vol. XI, 1961, p. 83 ff., Pl. 124; *Kärenten Kunst des Mittelalters aus dem Diozesanmuseum*, Klagenfurt, Österreichische Galerie in Oberen Belvedere (Exhibition Catalogue) No. 1, Vienna, 1970, p. 101.

34 In Paleo-Christian and Byzantine art, Peter's head and forehead are generally covered with thick, short, curly hair, while Paul's head is bald and his beard is usually dark, long and pointed. In German painting, Peter is often bald. See Fig. 25 and A. Shestack, *Master E. S.*, Five Hundredth Anniversary Exhibition, Philadelphia Museum of Art (Catalogue), No. 29, 1967. *Cf.* Hans Holbein the Elder's *Basilica di San Paolo Fuori le Mura* (Gemäldegalerie, Augsburg).

35 Paul's escape, hidden in a basket, appears in the background of *The Conversion of Saul* (c. 1500, Neustift Gallery [Fig. 36]) and of the *Basilica di San Paolo* by Holbein the Elder. The subject appears in the ninth-century frescos at Naturns (Naturno) in South Tyrol. *Cf.* also the twelfth-century Byzantine mosaics at Palermo (Cappella Palatina) and Monreale Cathedral. The objects on Peter's side were thought by Halm (p. 588) to be some 'writing utensils'. I have not found a better interpretation.

36 The pose of St Sebastian recurs in the only surviving shutter from the *Altar of the Trinity with Sts Mark and Anthony* by Friedrich Pacher (Österreichische Galerie, Vienna). One is tempted to detect in the figure of St Stephen the softer touch of Marx Reichlich, who is thought to have been Friedrich Pacher's follower.

37 A very similar decorative design appears on the gold-brocade grounds of the *St Blasius* by Friedrich Pacher (Ferdinandeum, Innsbruck), the predella shutters of the *St Thomas Altarpiece* by Michael Pacher (Joaneum, Graz) and the *Coronation of the Virgin* (the so-called *Ambraser Tafel*, Alte Pinakothek, Munich), arguably attributed to Michael Pacher – in which, incidentally, the figures are related to the background in much the same way as they are in the Peter and Paul panel. *Cf.*

Rasmo, 1969, p. 201 ff. A complete bibliography on the *Coronation of the Virgin* is given in C. A. zu Salm and G. Goldberg, *Alte Pinakothek München*, Katalog II, Altdeutsche Malerei, Munich, 1963, p. 161 ff. See further on p. 17 and n. 60.

38 The same ornamental scheme of the two papal tiaras recurs in the crowns of *St Dorothy* (Joaneum, Graz) and of the young king in the *Adoration of the Magi* in Mitterolang (Valdaora di Mezzo [Fig. 41]), South Tyrol, generally ascribed to Friedrich Pacher (but *see* Rasmo, 1950 (1952), p. 21). The combination of the three motifs – a quadrilobed fibula with a representation of the Man of Sorrows on a papal gown (though each in itself is a frequent iconographical theme in German art) – is too rare to allow for the possibility of a mere coincidence. The only other quadrilobed fibula with the same inconographic motif known to me in a German fifteenth-century painting appears on the gown of a bishop, *St Candidus* (Collegiate Church, Innichen) attributed to Michael Pacher but possibly executed by Friedrich Pacher. It appears again on a bishop's gown, in an Italian painting, *St Augustin* by Piero della Francesca (from the *Altarpiece of St Augustine*, Lisbon).

39 Rasmo, 1969, p. 99, claims that this and the other three scenes which originally belonged to the outside of the shutters of the *Altarpiece of the Fathers of the Church* represent scenes from the life of St Augustine.

40 *The Altarpiece of the Fathers of the Church* (Fig. 9) is thought to have been ordered by Leonard Pacher for the Church of Neustift. The majority of modern students of Michael Pacher believe that it was executed after the completion of the *St Wolfgang Altarpiece* (1481), i.e., towards the end of Leonard Pacher's activity as provost of Neustift .(1483). Hempel, pp. 16, 59 ff.; *id.* in Thieme-Becker, p. 123 ff.; Oberhammer, 1950, p. 39; Rasmo, 1949, p. 34; Rasmo, 1950 (1952) p. 15; Salm and Goldberg, *op. cit.*, p. 163 ff. Taking this date as a starting point and accepting 1475 as the date of the *Peter and Paul Altarpiece*, Rasmo (*ibid.* p. 18 ff.) claimed that the *Altarpiece of the Fathers of the*

Church could not have served as a source of inspiration for the Peter and Paul panel. He related it instead to the much earlier *Altarpiece of St Lawrence*. Later (1969, pp. 79 ff, 98) Rasmo dated the *Altarpiece of the Fathers of the Church c.* 1475–9. This new dating might corroborate our thesis, which apparently is now also accepted by Rasmo (1969, p. 198), but *cf.* p. 195, where 1478 is implicitly given as a *terminus postquem* for the altarpiece. Leonard Pacher apparently also invited both Michael and Friedrich Pacher to work on the decoration of the vaults of the church and the sacristy of the convent rebuilt by him, so here we might have all three Pachers working together. Friedrich's *Altarpiece of St Katherine* (Figs 29–33) was also painted for the Church of Neustift (now in the Gallery). The altar for which it was painted was consecrated as early as 1465. There is no reference in documents to the dates of these works.

For the dating of the rebuilding of the choir and the sacristy, see Rasmo, 1969, pp. 97 ff., 195. As to the still-disputed date of the *St Katherine Altarpiece*, see Stiassny, 1903, p. 24; Semper, 1911, pp. 226–7; Halm, p. 601 ff.; Döring, 1913, p. 124; Stiassny, *Michael Pachers St Wolfganger Altar*, Vienna, 1919, p. 198 ff.; *Gotik in Österreich* (Exhibition Catalogue), Krems A. d., Donau, 1967, (the painting section, W. Buchowiecky), p. 120; Thieme-Becker, p. 121; Hempel, pp. 16 (n. 4), 21, 93; Rasmo, 1949, p. 38; Oberhammer, 1950, p. 49; Rasmo, 1950 (1952), p. 19; Stange, 1960, pp. 186–7.

41 The low vanishing point of this floor is probably inspired by Mantegna. *Cf.* the *St Luke* (Brera, Milan), and *St Zeno* (Verona) altarpieces.

42 Gothic ornamentation based on naturalistic plant forms, rather than on abstract geometric ones, appear on Michael Pacher's two major sculptural works in Gries and St Wolfgang (Fig. 18). Friedrich was probably inspired here by him, though he used the motif more freely.

43 Mategna's famous *Dead Christ* (Brera, Milan) is a typical example of this stylistic feature. *Cf.* Carlo Crivelli's *Demidoff Altarpiece* (1476, National Gallery, London) and his *St Roch* (in the Wallace Collection).

44 Golden haloes designed in gilt-gesso reliefs is another characteristic feature of Friedrich's traditionalism. He applied this device in other panel paintings (*The St Barbara Altarpiece*, [Neustift], the so-called *Small Katherine Altarpiece* [Bayerische National Museum], etc.) and in many of his murals (Bozen, Neustift, Taufers, etc.). Significantly, the ornamentation of this type of halo in Friedrich's paintings is invariably of a radial design similar to that used in the Peter and Paul panel. Here again, Friedrich could have drawn from the same traditional sources of the fifteenth-century frescos in the cloister of Brixen.

45 Reichlich's *Sts James and Stephen Altarpiece* (Fig. 10) once belonged to J. N. Sepp, who also owned the Jerusalem panels. Curiously, Sepp, 1888, p. 347, attributed this work to Andreas Haller and believed the Peter and Paul panel to be a clumsy work of Haller's school. Semper, 1902, Pl. VIII, attributed Reichlich's work to the school of Michael Pacher. The relation between the composition of this work and the Peter and Paul panel has already been pointed out by several authors, but they have generally ignored the architectural frame and its relation to the Innsbruck panel in its original state and to Friedrich Pacher's frescos. See Oberhammer, 1950, p. 46 (n. 116); Rasmo, 1969, p. 197; Salm and Goldberg, *op. cit.*, p. 174. Significantly, the twisted top ends and the pinnacles of the little canopies which shelter the saints on the sides of the architectural frame are stylistically akin to analogous details in Friedrich's *Baptism* and in the Peter and Paul panel. They, too, are directly inspired by engravings by the Master E. S. (Lehrs, 35 and 56).

46 Pächt, p. 78; Rasmo, 1949, p. 38 (n. 113), Pl. 102; *Gotik in Österreich*, pp. 120–1, n. 38. The reverse is painted with the figure of the Magdalen, which is closely related to those of the female saints in the altarpieces of The Virgin, St Katherine, St Barbara and St Magdalen by Friedrich Pacher and his workshop.

47 *Cf.* 'Sts Sebastian and Roch' (1513), 'Sts Nikolaus and Erasmus' (1522; side panels of an altarpiece signed by Matheis Stoberl, both in the Ferdinandeum, Innsbruck), E. Egg, *Tiroler Landesmuseum*

Ferdinandeum, Innsbruck, 1964, p. 17; Semper, p. 99 ff.), and the Sts Peter and Paul flanking the Virgin and Child in an altarpiece in Neustift Gallery (Rasmo, 1949, p. 52).

48 Vischer's description is an interesting evidence regarding the state of knowledge of the two Pachers in that year: '*Paulus und Petrus, zwei grosse flügelgemälde von Meister der vier Kirchengelehrten in der Augsburger Galerie* [there Michael Pacher's *Fathers of the Church* had been before it was transferred to Munich] *halb mantegnesk, halb deutsch spätgotisch.*' *Studien für Kunstgeschichte*, Stuttgart, 1886, p. 458. *Cf.* Semper, 1911, p. 103, where a similar information is still given on the Peter and Paul panel.

49 *Cf.* Halm, pp. 587–8. The central panel of Conrad Von Soest's *Altarpiece of the Virgin* (Marienkirche, Dortmund) and Hans Pleydenwurff's *Crucifixion* (Alte Pinakothek, Munich) suffered a similar mutilation in their upper part for a similar reason. The width of the missing central longitudinal section can be calculated by subtracting the width of the mutilated yellow tile in the centre foreground from that of an undamaged one on any of its sides.

50 *Cf.* R. Muther, *Die Deutsche Bücher Illustration Der Gotik und Frührennaissance*, Vol. I, Munich-Leipzig, 1884, Fig. 87, pp. 122–3.

51 Halm, p. 603.

52 Halm, p. 601. As for the trees, *cf.* the well-known scenes from the life of San Bernardino (1473, Galleria Nazionale del l'Umbria), attributed to Perugino and to other Umbrian masters. Similar trees appear in the predella of the *St Korbinian Altarpiece* by Friedrich Pacher.

53 Halm, pp. 602–3.

54 The chapel is dedicated to Sts Peter and Paul, whose images and stories of martyrdom appear in the frescos. These poorly preserved frescos, which cover the apse wall and the triumphal arch above, were discovered under the whitewash in 1956. Their subjects are a strange concoction of various unrelated iconographical themes and of typological details derived partly from other works by Fried-

rich Pacher. The date 1482 is claimed to be inscribed on the rainbow. See H. Schnell and J. Steiner, eds., *Schloss Taufers*, Munich and Zurich, 1971, p. 14.

55 Predellas with Veronica's veil: Conrad Laib, *Triptych of the Death of the Virgin*, *c.* 1460 (the predella repainted 1512 [Stange, p. 24 ff.] Prokrajinski Musei, Ptui, Yugoslavia); *The Altarpiece of the Trinity* attributed to Jan Polack (Blutenburg); Jörg Ratgeb, *The Altarpiece of the Passion of Christ* (Stuttgart Gallery); *The Altarpiece of Sts Peter and Paul* (Parish Church, Tiefenbronn). Sts Peter and Paul with Veronica's veil: a fresco in the Church of St Paul in the Lavant Valley by Thomas von Villach (1493); *see* K. Ginhart, ed., 'Die Kunstdenkmäler des Benediktinerstiftes St Paul im Lavanttal und seiner Filialkirche', *Österreichische Kunsttopographie*, Vol. XXXVII, Vienna, 1969, Pl. 152. Engravings: by Master E.S., 1464 (Lehrs, 190) and by Master L.C.Z., 1497 (Lehrs, VI, 9 [Fig. 25]). Woodcut by Albrecht Dürer, from the *Small Passion*, 1510 (*Bartsch*, 38). The same subject on a predella, *The Reichenhaller Altarpiece*, 1521 (Bayerische National Museum); St Veronica Between Sts Peter and Paul, *The Altarpiece of Sts Peter and Paul*, (Heiligenblut, Carinthia). See Shestack, *op. cit.*, n. 69; J. Braun, *Der Christliche Altar*, Vol. II, Munich, 1924, pp. 359, 455, Pls 267, 329.

56 The individual identities of the Jöchl brothers in their portraits on the predella have not yet been established. See Döring, 1913, p. 146.

57 A miniature in the *Grandes Heures de Rohan*, Bibliothèque Nationale, Paris, Ms. lat. 9471, f. 159 ('Office of the Dead'), contains the figure of the Dead Man before his Judge with a script-roll of the same verse.

58 During the fifteenth century, most German portraits continued to be appended to religious subjects as representations of the kneeling donors and their families in the lower part of the painting or on the shutters of an altarpiece. *Cf. The Mass of St Gregory*, a fresco ascribed to Friedrich Pacher in the Church of St Martin near St Lorenzen in the Puster Valley, and in Friedrich Pacher's *Hortus Conclusus* fresco in Bozen. The practice of relegating the portraits of the donors to the predella seems to

be peculiar to South German painting. The predella of the *Peter and Paul Altarpiece* is perhaps the earliest one of this kind known. *Cf.* an altarpiece of 1514 from Flitschl. See *Kärenten Kunst . . . , op. cit.*, no. 2, p. 103.

59 Döring, 1913, p. 145; Halm, p. 590; Allesch, p. 204.

60 Similar motifs appear in contemporary engravings intended as models for artists and craftsmen. *Cf.* a series of ornament leaves by the Master E. S. (Lehrs, 308, 310, 311, 312, 314) and by Schongauer in A. Shestack, *The Complete Engravings of Martin Schongauer*, New York, 1969, Figs. 109–15. Similar floral, decorations occasionally appeared on German predellas at the beginning of the sixteenth century. *Cf.* the predella of the *Perckhamer Altarpiece*, V. Oberhammer, 'Der Perck-hamer Altar des Marx Reichlich', *Pantheon*, Vol. 28, No. V, 1970, 9–10, Pl. 5.

61 This is another motif inspired by the North Italian 'Hard Style'. The foreshortening was condemned by Halm, p. 575, as *mehr gewollte als geglückte*. *Cf.* 'The Departure of St Augustine', from the *Altarpiece of St Augustine* by the Master of Utten-heim (Neustift Gallery [Fig. 27]).

62 *Cf.* the *Quo Vadis* scene in the 'Liberation of St Peter', and the 'Parting of the Apostles' (Pls 21, 25). Halm, p. 576; Picirillo, p. 200.

63 In the Gospels, as well as in art, the representation of the scene of Peter walking on the water can easily be confused with that of the calling of St Peter, the miraculous draught of fishes and even the storm on the Sea of Gennesaret (*cf.* Matthew 4:18 ff., 14:24 ff.; Mark 1:16, 6:47 ff.; Luke 5: 2 ff.; John 6: 18 ff., 21: 3 ff.). Döring, 1912, p. 305, maintains that the man in the boat is not Peter but another Apostle. The difference in the haloes supports his hypothesis. In a few other represen-tations of the same subject, only one Apostle appears in the boat, and he clearly differs from Peter in the water. *Cf.* the same subject in a painting in the Diozesan Museum, Brixen, ascribed to Leonhard Von Brixen.

64 E. Baum, *Katalog des Museum der Mittelalterliche Österreichischer Kunst.*, Vienna, 1971, p. 130. *Cf.* Rasmo, 1950 (1952), p. 19, n. 36. Although extolled by Rasmo as belonging to the apex of Friedrich's artistic achievement, the drawing in this work is cruder in a few places than in the Jerusalem panel.

65 Of course, no direct causal relation can be estab-lished between Leonardo's famous masterpiece and the painting under consideration, but the analogous display of virtuosity in foreshortening – one of the artistic goals of High Renaissance painting – may prove that Friedrich, at least in this case, was not unaware of certain aspects of this style. Significantly, the foreshortened hand of the Virgin, blessing the kneeling Francesco Gonzaga in Mantegna's *Madonna della Vittoria* (1496, Louvre) is nearly identical with that of Friedrich Pacher's Christ. This gesture is claimed by E. Tietze-Konrad (*Mantegna*, London, 1955, p. 194) to have been inspired by Leonardo's masterpiece and to have inspired Corregio's early Madonna of St Francis (1514–15) Gemälde Galerie, Dresden). *Cf.* A. C. Quintavalle and A. Bevilaqua, *L'Opera completa del Corregio*, Milan, 1970, pp. 90–91, fig. 14. *Cf.* also the right hand of Aristotle in the *School of Athens* by Raphael (*c.* 1510–11).

66 *The Adoration of the Magi* (St Aegidius Parish Church, Mitterolang [Fig. 41]), which was some-times ascribed to Reichlich; the central panel of the *St Katherine Altarpiece* (Neustift [Fig. 33]); 'The Flight into Egypt' (fragment from the *Altarpiece of the Virgin*. Ferdinandeum, Innsbruck [Fig. 34]), which even includes the same gallows in the middle distance.

67 *Cf.* the foreshortened figures of the ox and the ass in the 'Nativity', the cow and the sheep in 'Christ Driving the Merchants from the Temple', the sheep in the 'Feeding of the 5,000' (all in the *St Wolfgang Altarpiece*), and the lion of St Jerome in the *Altarpiece of the Fathers of the Church*, which directly inspired Friedrich Pacher in the *Triptych of the Trinity* (Vienna). See also the foreshortened beasts at the manger in the 'Nativity' (Kunst-museum, Basel).

68 *See* fn. 67 and Döring, 1912, pp. 307, 211; *cf.* the knight and his rearing white horse in the *Expulsion of Heliodoros* (Dominicans' Cloister, Bozen [Fig. 37]). Allesch, pp. 210–11, has rightly contrasted Friedrich Pacher's episodic use of perspective with the consistent logic of Michael's perspective system in the *St Wolfgang Altarpiece*.

69 Semper, 1911, p. 79 ff.; Rasmo, 1949, p. 52. A 'Conversion of Saul', thought to be one of the two surviving panels of the *St Peter and Paul Altarpiece* from the Monastery of Wilten near Innsbruck (now in the monastery's gallery), might also have derived its composition from Friedrich Pacher's work. *See* Pächt, *op. cit.*, p. 80. Pl. 82.

70 *Cf.* Halm, p. 584, Döring, 1912, p. 304.

71 *Cf.* the so-called *Baptism of St Katherine* by Friedrich Pacher (Bayerische National Museum, Munich). The origin of this particular type of pictorial frame is obviously the traditional design of the Gothic altarpiece. In late fourteenth-century paintings, the wooden Gothic frame was frequently made to appear as coinciding with the first bay of a vaulted Gothic interior represented in the painted scene. But even later, in the fifteenth century, when this wooden frame was frequently substituted by its painted imitation, it could never be interpreted as unequivocally belonging to the Gothic interior in the painting. The idea reached Germany mainly through the works of Rogier Van der Weyden and Dirck Bouts. The Master E. S., whose engravings did so much to propagate many ideas imported from the Netherlands, was probably Friedrich's source of inspiration this time as well (see Lehrs, 12, 13, 35, 73, 74, 191). As for the arch motif, its origin and history, *see* E. Panofsky, *Early Netherlandish Painting*, Vol. I, Princeton, 1956, pp. 58 ff., 103, 260, 279, 315, 349, n. 2 to p. 58. (Panofsky has coined the somewhat inexact term 'diaphragm arch' for this pictorial device); K. Birkmeyer, 'The Arch Motif in Netherlandish Painting of the Fifteenth Century', *Art Bulletin*, XLIII, 1961, 1–20, 99–112. There is a reference to the Master E. S. in Shestack, 1967, *op. cit.*, no. 61. As to the use of the arch motif by Michael Pacher, *see* Döring, 1913, p. 126; Rasmo, 1969, p. 138.

72 The only work by Friedrich Pacher which has a similarly conceived Gothic interior is his fresco *The Mass of St Gregory* (*c.* 1493).

73 Halm, p. 598, went so far as to note in the 'Marriage at Cana' (St Wolfgang) not only Friedrich's active participation, but his influence on its design. This thesis was justly contested by Hempel, pp. 21, 22 and Allesch, pp. 207–9, 216–17.

74 Halm, p. 602; Allesch, p. 209. The characteristic columns used by Friedrich Pacher recur in the following works by him: two scenes of the *St Katherine Altarpiece* (Figs 29, 31), the 'St Sebastian' of the *Triptych of the Trinity* (Vienna), the 'Presentation in the Temple' from the *Altarpiece of the Virgin* (Innsbruck), the 'Baptism of St Katherine' (Bayerische National Museum, Munich), and *Christ Among the Doctors* (Dominican's Cloister, Bozen). They also appear in a fresco of the same subject in the Cloister of Brixen, attributed to Leonhard Von Brixen. The probable source of inspiration is an engraving by the Master E. S. *Cf.* Lehrs, 12, 40, 191.

75 *Cf.* Halm, p. 603 and Reichlich's *Adoration of the Magi*, 1489 (Innsbruck).

76 The quoted passages are from *The Golden Legend, ed. cit.*, p. 336. The version of the story of the liberation of St Peter as told in the Apocryphal *Passion of Peter and Paul* by Pseudo Linus was apparently the principal literary source for this scene. *See* 'Martirium beati Petri apostoli (also entitled Passio sancti Petri . . .') a 'Lino episcopo conscriptum', in R. H. Lipsius, ed., *Acta Apostolorum Apocrypha* (reprint of the 1891 edition), Vol. I, Darmstadt, 1959, pp. 6–7. *Cf.* Halm, p. 580 ff.; Picirillo, pp. 200–1. There are two other Latin versions: *Passio Sanctorum Apostolorum Petri et Pauli*, p. 167 ff. and *Passio Apostolorum Petri et Pauli*, p. 232 ff. A rare example of the representation of the liberation of Peter from the Mamertine Prison (by one of his guards and not by an angel) is found in the so-called *Christgarten Altarpiece* by Hans L. Schäuffelein, 1516 (Alte Pinakothek, Munich), which follows even more closely than Friedrich Pacher the version given in the *Legenda Aurea*, since it shows the simultaneous liberation of the *two* Apostles (Fig. 40). (This fact apparently

escaped the attention of the compilers of the Alte Pinakothek Catalogue [II, 1963] p.180.) The two stories of the liberation of St Peter are confused in a panel by Alunno di Domenico (Bartolomeo di Giovanni?), (Lycett Green Collection, London). In this painting Peter is liberated by an angel, although the place is the Mamertine Prison, since in the same painting, the *Quo Vadis* scene follows immediately to the right. The inclusion of the liberation of St Peter and the *Quo Vadis* in a single painting, and the archaistic treatment of space, result in an ambiguous representation of the first episode, in which Peter's liberators seem to be leading him from the jail straight to the city gate, whereas Peter's flight from Rome should be part of the second episode, in which – according to all the literary sources–he passed through the gate unaccompanied. The church at the beginning of the Via Appia, where Peter is supposed to have encountered Christ, is now called *Domine Quo Vadis*.

77 The winding path strewn with pebbles is a common motif in Mantegna's works. *Cf.* his *St George* (Accademia, Venice). It spread quickly throughout Germany in the fifteenth century. *Cf.* the 'Ascension of the Magdalen' from the *Altarpiece of the Magdalen* by Friedrich Pacher (St Korbinian, Thal).

78 In the perspective vista of the street in 'The Warning for the Flight into Egypt' (Innsbruck) and in the surviving street scene on the right-hand side of the badly damaged fresco *The Rich Man and the Poor Lazarus* in the Cloister of Neustift, Friedrich moves nearer to Michael's rendering of pictorial space. As to the disputed attribution of the latter, *cf.* E. D. Theil-Salmoiraghi, *Michael Pacher in Neustift*, Milan, 1946, p. 35 ff.; M. Schrott, *Guida Storica descrittiva . . . di Novacella*, Florence, 1942, p. 61; Thieme–Becker, p. 121. The armed halberdier in the left corner and his relation to the analogous figure in the 'Conversion of the Queen' (Fig. 32) have already been noted by Allesch, pp. 217–18.

79 Halm, p. 603.

80 This device appears in the works of Piero della Francesca (*The Altarpiece of the Misericordia*), but it

may rather have been inspired by a work by Mantegna, such as the *St George* (Accademia, Venice, variously dated between 1450 and 1467).

81 *The Golden Legend, ed. cit.*, p. 337. The source used by Jacopo da Voragine and quoted both by him and in the script–rolls was probably the *Passio Sanctorum Apostolorum* (Lipsius, *ed. cit.*), Vol. I, p. 171: 'Petrus autem dum venisset ad crucem ait: "Quoniam *dominus meus* Jesus Christus *de caelo ad terram descendens* recta cruce sublimatus est, *me autem quem de terra ad caelum evocare dignatur*, crux mea caput meum in terra debet estendere, et pedes ad caelum dirigere."'

82 The crucifixion of St Peter is generally described in German painting in its preliminary phase, when Peter is still bound to the cross but not yet nailed to it. *Cf.* Friedrich's frescos in Schloss Taufers, a painting from an altarpiece attributed to Leonhard Von Brixen, (Diozesan Museum, Brixen), the *Peter and Paul Altarpiece* by Hans Süss Von Kulmbach (Uffizi, Florence), the *Christgarten Altarpiece* by Hans Schäuffelein (Alte Pinakothek, Munich [Fig. 43]), the *St Katherine Altarpiece* by Hans Holbein the Elder (Staatsgalerie, Augsburg).

83 *Cf. A Martyrdom of Two Saints* by Friedrich Pacher (Ferdinandeum, Innsbruck [Fig. 47]).

84 For references to Nero and Agrippa in relation to this scene, *see Acta Apostolorum, ed. cit.*, pp. 9 ff., 169 ff.

85 Döring, 1912, p. 304, maintains that the city represents Rome, while Halm, p. 582, n. 3, claims that it is Ostia.

86 *The Golden Legend, ed. cit.*, p. 421. The letter by Dionisius Areopagita is cited by Halm, p. 584, n. 2 from Boninus Mombritius, *Legendarium aut Sanctuarium*, Vol. II, Milan, *c.* 1476, p. 195. It may be more logical to suppose that the earlier and much more popular *Legenda Aurea* was used here, as elsewhere, as the chief literary source.

87 Picirillo, pp. 203–4, erroneously basing himself on a passage in the *Acts of Petrus and Paulus* by Pseudo Marcellus, gives this interpretation. The

meeting of the Apostles appears in the Byzantine Mosaics of Monreale Cathedral. The parting of the Apostles appears in the background of Fig. 43. *Cf.* the script-roll over St Peter (Pl. 1).

88   *The Golden Legend, ed. cit.*, p. 337; Döring, 1913, p. 144 wrongly reads *donator* instead of *dux*.

89   *Cf.* H. Holbein the Elder's *Basilica di San Paolo Fuori le Mura* (1504, Gemälde Galerie, Augsburg).

90   The scorpion was thought by Semper to have been the 'pictorial signature' of an anonymous artist active in the decoration of the cloister of the Cathedral of Brixen. He christened him the 'Meister mit dem Skorpion'. *See* Döring, 1913, p. 144; Thieme–Becker, Vol. XXXVII, p. 315; Semper, 1911, p. 3 ff. As for the iconographic significance of the scorpion, *see* M. Bulard, *Le Scorpion, symbole du Peuple Juif dans l'Art religieux des XIV, XV, XVI, siécles*, Paris, 1935, *passim*.

91   *The Golden Legend, ed. cit.*, p. 337. Jacopo da Voragine used the so-called *Passion of St Paul* by Pseudo Linus. *See Acta Apostolorum, ed. cit.*, Vol. I, p. 40.

92   One of the earliest pictorial representations of the miracle of the three fountains, appears in the thirteenth-century frescos of San Pietro a Grado, south of Pisa. *Cf. Basilica di S. Paolo Fuori le Mura* by Hans Holbein the Elder (Augsburg) and the *Peter and Paul Altarpiece* by Hans Kulmbach (Uffizi, Florence). The famous Abbey of the Three Fountains on the southern outskirts of Rome (east of the modern E.U.R. quarter) is said to have been erected on the spot of St Paul's martyrdom. The legend is referred to by all the earlier authors, but no ancient literary source is mentioned. For the topographical legend, *cf.* Christian Beutler and Günter Thiem, *Hans Holbein D.Ä., Die Spätgotische Altar – und Glassmalerei*, Augsburg, 1960, p. 66; E. Kitzinger, *The Mosaics of Monreale*, Palermo, 1960, p. 36, n. 48.

93   *See* n. 99.

94   An incorrect interpretation of this motif as 'a medieval "4"' was given by Döring, 1912, p. 306,

but he later (1913, p. 144) followed Halm, p. 586, suggesting the much more probable interpretation of the emblem as either a steel helmet or a 'Jews' hat' and noted its frequency in Tyrolese painting. Thus it alludes at the same time both to the Roman soldiers and to the Jews as enemies of Christ. The design is inspired by a particular type of a steel helmet which frequently appears in the fifteenth-century frescos on the vaults of the Cloister of Brixen, all belonging to the above-mentioned group, attributed to Leonhard Von Brixen (*The Resurrection, The Death of Absalom, The Death of Eleazar the Macabee*). Similar 'Jews' hats' frequently appear in fifteenth-century German pictorial representations of the Passion of Christ. In the Crucifixion scenes, they are often accompanied by other flags with signs and emblems referring either to the Romans or to the Jews – the scorpion (*see* n. 81), the SPQR, Hebrew or pseudo-Hebrew letters, dragons, etc. Here are a few examples: the *Flagellation of Christ* by Master Francke, Kunsthalle (Hamburg), where the 'Jews' hat' appears on the shield above the throne of Pilate (Fig. 48). *See Meister Francke und die Kunst um 1400* (Exhibition Catalogue), No. 3(e), Hamburg, 1969, p. 53. Crucifixion scenes with flags bearing 'Jews' hats': Jakov von Seckau (?), Klerikalseminar, Freising; by the same (?), fresco, Cloister of the Cathedral, Brixen; by anonymous masters, St Leonhard near Wasserburg; St Leonhard Im Buchat, Regensburg; private collection, Lenzburg. *See* Stange, Vol. X, Pls 106, 160, 250, 251, 304. An interesting variant appears in the *Crucifixion* by Hans Pleydenwurff (Alte Pinakothek, Munich). Professor B. Blumenkranz has kindly drawn my attention to the 'Jews' hats' on the flag of the *Synagogue*, by Konrad Witz (Kunstmuseum, Basel). The string of all these hats is twisted, forming a Greek γ.

95   This motif seems to have been inspired by the traditional representations of the capture of Christ in German painting.

96   Halm, p. 589, thought that this soldier might represent the 'pious Longinus' mentioned in one of the apocryphal legends. *Cf.* Döring, 1912, p. 306.

97   *Cf.* 'The Disputation with the Philosophers' from

the *Altarpiece of St Katherine* (Neustift [Fig. 30]).

98 *Cf.* 'Christ Driving the Merchants from the Temple', 'Christ and the Woman Taken in Adultery', 'The Stoning of Christ in the Temple', 'The Wedding at Cana', 'The Healing of a Possessed Woman by St Wolfgang' (all from the *St Wolfgang Altarpiece* [Fig. 51]) and 'The Martyrdom of St Katherine' (Neustift [Fig. 33]).

99 'The Martyrdom of St Katherine' (Neustift [Fig. 33]) and *A Martyrdom of Two Saints* (Ferdinandeum, Innsbruck [Fig. 47]). *Cf.* also 'The Martyrdom of Sts Justine and Cyprian' from the *Altarpiece of St Justine* (Lienz Parish Church); Semper, 1911, p. 258.

Bibliography

The following bibliographical list concentrates on books and articles which include particular references to Friedrich Pacher and to the *Peter and Paul Altarpiece*. The literature on Michael Pacher, of which only a fraction is mentioned here, is referred to in the notes. It is, of course, indispensable for the study of Friedrich Pacher.

While preparing the text for this book, I became fully aware of the difficulty it might present to the non – specialized reader. Even in Germany, the name of Friedrich Pacher is still little known. The English reader is primarily hampered by the complete absence of an adequate handbook which could introduce him to the history of German painting. As far as Michael Pacher is concerned, the situation has improved with the recent publication of an English translation (London, 1971) of Rasmo's monograph (1969), which is frequently referred to in the notes. An illustrated introduction to German painting in two volumes, which has also recently appeared in an English translation (Geneva 1964, 1968) – the first volume, *The Late Middle Ages* (1350–1500) by H.P. Landolt, and the second *From Dürer to Holbein* by O. Benesch – will provide a helpful guide to the beginner, as will Alfred Stange's *German Painting* (XIV – XVI Centuries, London, 1950). The numerous illustrations in Stange's very useful handbook *Deutsche Malerei der Gotik* (particularly Vol. X), which contains a special chapter on Friedrich Pacher, and the two excellent Exhibition Catalogues by Rasmo and Oberhammer will be of much help even to those who do not read German.

Allesch, Johann von, *Michael Pacher*, Leipzig, 1931, pp. 13 ff., 115 ff., 190, 200 ff.

Bagatti, P. Bellarmino, *Guida al Museo della Flagellazione in Gerusalemme*, Jerusalem, 1939, pp. 142–5.

Baum, Elfriede, *Katalog des Museum der Mittelalterlichen Österreichischen Kunst*, Vienna, 1971, pp. 129 ff.

Benesch, Otto, 'Der Meister von St Korbinian', *Zeitschrift für bild. Kunst.*, 61 (1928/9), 152 ff.

Böck W., 'Der Anteil Michael und Friedrich Pachers an den Gemälden des Altars in St Wolfgang', *Festschrift Luitpold Dussler*, Munich, 1972, p. 177 ff.

———, W. Buchowiecky *et al.*, *Gotik in Austria* (Exhibition Catalogue), 1967, p. 82.

Braun-Reichenbacher, M., *Das Ast und Laub Werk . . .*, Nürnberg, 1966, p. 39.

Dahlke, G., 'Michael Pacher', *Repertorium für Kunstwissenschaft*, VIII, 1885, p. 30 ff.

Döring, Oskar, 'Neues über ein Tiroler Altar Werk des XV Jahrunderts', *Christliche Kunst*, VIII, 1912, 301 ff.

———, *Michael Pacher und die Seinen*, München-Gladbach, 1913, pp. 9, 103 ff., 120 ff., 138, 156.

Dr. Johann Nepomuk Sepp (1816–1909), Ein Bild seines Lebens nach seinem eigenen Aufzeichnungen, Xenium zum Hundersten Geburtstag (published anonymously) I, Regensburg, 1916, pp. 80 ff., 164, n. 34.

Egg, Erich, *Tiroler Landesmuseum Ferdinandeum*, Innsbruck, s.d. (1964), p. 15.

Ginhart, Karl, 'Die Kunstdenkmäler des Benediktinerstiftes St Paul im Lavanttal und seiner Filialkirchen', *Österreichische Kunsttopographie*, Vol. XXXVII, Vienna, 1969, 109 ff.

Halm, Philip Maria, 'Der Ehmalige St Peter und Paulus Altar in Jöchlsthurn zu Strezing und Friedrich Pacher', *Kunst und Kunsthandwerk*, XV, Vienna 1912, 573 ff.

Hempel, Eberhard, *Michael Pacher*, Vienna, 1931, pp. 16 ff., 92 ff.

Huter, F., 'Archivalische Fünde zur Südtiroler Kunstgeschichte, Neues zur Geschichte der Brunecker Künstlerfamilie Pacher, *Der Schlern*, 20, 1946, 98 ff.

Mannowsky, Walter, *Die Gemälde Michael Pachers*, Munich and Leipzig, 1910, p. 46 ff.

Oberhammer, Vinzenz et al., *Gotik in Tirol* (Exhibition Catalogue), Innsbruck, 1950, p. 45 ff.

Pächt, Otto, *Österreichische Tafelmalerei der Gotik*, Augsburg and Vienna, 1929, pp 48 ff., 78 ff.

Picirillo, P. A., 'Le Storie dei Santi Pietro e Paolo, narrate nelle 7 tavole che si conservano nel museo della Flagellazione', *La Terra Santa*, XLII, 6–7 (Jerusalem), 1967, 197 ff.

Rasmo, Nicoló, 'In Margine all'Esposizione d'arte dell'Alto Adige', *Arte Veneta*, II, Bolzano, 1948, 162.

———, *Arte Medioevale dell'Alto Adige* (Exhibition Catalogue) Bolzano, 1949, p. 36 ff.

———, *Nuove Acquisizioni alla conoscenza dell'arte Medioevale dell'Alto Adige*, Bolzano, 1952 (Cultura Atesina, IV, 1950, 147 ff).

———, *Il Chiostro Monumentale di S. Domenico a Bolzano*, Bolzano, 1953.

———, 'L'Altare di S. Barbara a Novacella ricomposto', *Cultura Atesina*, VII, 1953, 159 ff.

———, *Michele Pacher*, Milan, 1969 (English translation, New York, 1970), pp. 13 ff., 98, 106 ff., 110 ff., 136, 138 ff., 140, 142, 170, 174 ff., 189, 192 ff., 198, 225, 228 ff., 232, 240.

Rihl, Berthold, *Die Kunst an der Brennerstrasse*, Leipzig, 1898, p. 100 ff.

Theil-Salmoiraghi, E. D., *Michael Pacher in Neustift*, Milan, 1946.

Salvini, Roberto, 'Una nuova opera di Federico Pacher e alcune conclusioni sulla cronologia del pittore', *Le Arti*, II, 1938/9, 187 ff.

———, *Sulla Posizione storica di Michele Pacher*, Bolzano, 1937, pp. 15 ff.

Scheffler, Gisella, 'Hans Pacher – ein Sohn Michael Pachers', *Der Schlern*, 40, 10, 1966, 451 ff.

Schegg, Peter, *Gedenkbuch einer Pilgerreise nach dem Heiligen Lande*, Munich, 1867, p. 275.

Schnell, H. and J. Steiner, eds., *Schloss Taufers* (Guidebook), Munich and Zurich, 1971, p. 13 ff.

Schrott, Maximilan, 'Michael Pachers Verwandschaft', *Cultura Atesina*, 1966, p. 13 ff.

———, *Guida Storica descrittiva . . . di Novacella*, Florence, 1942.

Schönherr, David, 'Urkunden und Regesten aus dem k.k. Statthaltereriarchiv', *Jahrbuch der Kunsthistorischen Sammlungen d. Allerh. Kaiserhäuser*, II (1884), XVI ff. (republished by the Kunstfreund, 1893.)

Semper, Hans, *Offizieller Bericht über die Verhandlungen des VII. Internationalen Kunsthistorischen Kongresses in Innsbruck*, Berlin, 1902, pp. 54 ff., 66.

———, *Alttirolische Kunstwerke des XV. und XVI. Jah.*, Innsbruck, 1902.

———, *Michael und Friedrich Pacher*, Eszlingen, 1911.

Sepp, Johann Nepomuk, *Neue Hochwichtige Entdeckungen auf der Zweiten Palästinafahrt*, Vol. I, Munich, 1896, p. 198.

———, *Jerusalem und das Heilige Land*, Schaffhausen, 1873, p. 202 ff.

———, 'Die Kirchenväter im Besitz des Prof. Sepp', *Repertorium für Kunstwissenschaft*, XI, 1888, 345 ff.

Sighart, J., 'Friedrich Pacher, Maler von Brunecken', *Mitteilungen der k.k. Zentral Kommission zur Erforschung und Erhaltung der Baudenkmäler*, IV, 7, 1859, 723 ff.

Stange, Alfred, *Deutsche Malerei der Gotik*, Vol. X, Munich and Berlin, 1960, p. 181 ff.

Stiassny, Robert, 'Ein Mitteldeutscher Alpenkunstler', *Deutsche Rundschau*, 1897, 422 ff.

———, 'Urkundliches über Friedrich Pacher', *Repertorium für Kunstwissenschaft*, XXIII, 1900, 238 ff.

————, 'Die Pacher Schule', *Repertorium für Kunstwissenschaft*, XXVI, Berlin, 1903, 20 ff.

————, *Michael Pachers St Wolfganger Altar*, Vienna, 1919.

Südtirol, Kunstwerke als Zeuge (Exhibition Catalogue), Innsbruck, 1946, p. 17 ff.

Thieme, U. and F. Becker, *Allgemeines Lexikon der Bildenden Künstler*, Leipzig, Vol. 26, 1932: 'Friedrich Pacher' by J. Clemens von Bayern, p. 120 ff.; 'Michael Pacher' by E. Hempel, p. 122 ff.; Vol. 37 (*s.d.*), 'Meister des Neustifter Barbaraaltares', p. 246.

Veröffentlichungen des Museum Ferdinandeum, Innsbruck, Vol. 31, 1958, p. 213.

Vischer, Robert. *Studien zur Kunstgeschichte*, Stuttgart, 1886, pp. 458, 464.

Weingartner, Joseph, *Gotische Wandmalerei in Südtirol*, Vienna, 1948.

————, *Die Kunstdenkmäler Osttirols*, Innsbruck, Vienna and Munich, 1958, p. 22.

Wolfsgruber, Karl, 'Beiträgezur Pacher-Forschung', *Der Schlern*, 43, 1969, p. 128 ff.

Photo Credits

Plates: Demanega, Innsbruck, 1–9, I; Hai, Tel Aviv, 10–32, II–VIII.

Text Figures: the author, 1, 16, 17, 18, 19, 24, 37, 41, 46, 50; Thaler, Vipiteno, 2, 3; after Lehrs, 4, 25; Ferdinandeum, Innsbruck, 5, 33, 34, 38, 42; Poss, Eisenärzt, 6, 29, 39; Hai, Tel Aviv, 7, 8, 13, 49; Staatsgemäldesammlungen, Munich, 9, 10, 40, 43, 45; Lala Aufsberg, Sonthofen, 11; The Warburg Institute, London, 12; Demanega, Innsbruck, 14, 20, 47; Gabinetto Fotografico Nazionale, Rome, 15, 30, 31, 32, 36; Ghedina, Cortina d'Ampezzo, 21; after Muther, 22, 23; after Schestack, 26; March, Brixen, 27; Österreichische Galerie, Vienna, 28; after Pomilio and Della Chiesa, 35; after Volponi and Berti, 44; Gundermann, Würzburg, 51; Kunsthalle, Hamburg, (Kleinhempel), 48.